Eugene Bullard, Black Expatriate In Jazz-Age Paris

Eugene Bullard

BLACK EXPATRIATE IN JAZZ-AGE PARIS

Craig Lloyd

University of Georgia Press

Athens & London

© 2000 by the University of Georgia Press
Athens, Georgia 30602

Designed by Erin Kirk New
Set in 10 on 14 Sabon by G & S Typesetters, Inc.
Printed and bound by Maple-Vail Book Manufacturing Group

The paper in this book meets the guidelines for
permanence and durability of the Committee on
Production Guidelines for Book Longevity of the
Council on Library Resources.

Printed in the United States of America

04 03 02 01 00 C 5 4 3 2 1

Library of Congress Cataloging-in-Publication Data

Lloyd, Craig, 1940–
    Eugene Bullard, Black expatriate in jazz-age Paris / Craig Lloyd.
      p. cm.
    Includes bibliographical references and index.
    ISBN 0-8203-2192-3 (alk. paper)
      1. Bullard, Eugene Jacques, 1894–1961.   2. Afro-American air pilots—France—
Biography.   3. Air pilots, Military—France—Biography.   4. Afro-American boxers—
Europe—Biography.   5. Music-halls (Variety-theaters, cabarets, etc.)—France.
6. Theatrical producers—France—Biography.   I. Title.
TL540.B7492 L96   2000
940.4'49'44—dc21   99-055336

British Library Cataloging-in-Publication Data available

For Alfonso Biggs and Judith Grant
In Memory of Roscoe Chester

Contents

Acknowledgments

Sometime in the mid-1980s, I became aware of the Eugene Bullard story while reading a survey of local African American history written by Liza Benham, then a reporter for the *Columbus (Georgia) Enquirer*. The poignancy of his life combined with the circumstance that I had lived in or near the neighborhoods he knew so well in Columbus, Paris, and New York compelled me to begin the research and writing of this book. I quickly became aware that there existed across the United States and in Europe an unofficial Eugene Bullard "fan club"—people who, like me, desired that his saga be more widely and accurately known. Many of these individuals have generously made available vital information and documentation on Bullard. One of the unexpected rewards in preparing this biography has been their friendship.

I am especially indebted to Wayne Fisk, who introduced me to Jacqueline O'Garro, Bullard's daughter, and her son Richard Reid, both of whom allowed me to read "All Blood Runs Red," Bullard's unpublished autobiography. Merryll Penson encouraged me to pursue the study, and through her I became acquainted with Alfonso Biggs, a fount of information on black history in the Columbus area. Mr. Biggs led me to the late K. C. Bullard of Richland, Georgia, who put me in touch with his great-aunt, Daisy Bullard Thomas, Eugene Bullard's first cousin and an indispensable source on the family genealogy. I am grateful as well to Jamie Cockfield, Nancy Fryer, Annie Canady, Caroline Corner, Betty Gubert, Ted Robinson, Jeff Jakeman, Callie McGinnis, and the late Roger Cestac.

Roger Harris, Hugh Rodgers, and John Lupold read sections of the manuscript and made useful suggestions. Fred Fussell, the late Roscoe Chester, Bin Ramke, Mark Strong, Bob Holcomb, Peter Barto, Frank Brown, Michel Fabre, and Barry Lefstad have lent me their support as have numerous archivists and librarians unknown to me by name in Atlanta, Norfolk, London, Oxford, Paris, Boston, and New York. I was able to visit these places with the assistance of Faculty Development Grants awarded me by Columbus State University. For technical help from the CSU staff, I thank Cynthia Fears, Shirley Hinckley, Darlene McClendon, Patty Chappel, Cheryl Hewitt, and Jon Haney.

My wife, Caryl L. Lloyd, shared her thoughts in innumerable conversations about Bullard and my manuscript and, as a professor of French, was an unfailing resource on French language and culture. To her I owe an appreciation of Paris and Parisians, an intangible but significant element in the making of this book. In 1969–70, while I finished my doctoral dissertation, she taught in Paris at the Lycée Jules Ferry in the 9th Arrondissement. We rented an apartment on rue Douai and became acquainted with the Montmartre streets that Bullard called home two generations earlier. In the late 1980s and early '90s, Caryl administered and taught in summer programs of study in Paris while I researched Bullard's quarter-century of life in the French capital. We were able to reacquaint ourselves with Montmartre and enjoyed meals and informative conversations with patrons at Haynes' Restaurant on rue Clauzel, the last vestige of the African American presence in the district. Though greatly changed demographically from Bullard's time, the streets and buildings of the neighborhood were little altered. In fact, Bullard's Gym at 15, rue Mansart was still a gym in 1987; and at 52, rue Pigalle, the site of Le Grand Duc, Bullard's nightclub, there still stood the tiny triangular structure of its entertainment heyday.

Finally, I thank my editor at the University of Georgia Press, David E. Des Jardines, for his suggestions improving my manuscript and for shepherding it to publication.

Introduction

The son of impoverished working-class parents in turn-of-the-century Columbus, Georgia, Eugene Bullard lived a life of adventure and achievement reminiscent of a hero in a Horatio Alger fiction. Destitute, possessed of only a third-grade education but eager to achieve, he left home and became a stowaway in 1912 on a merchant ship headed for Europe. Not long after landing in Scotland, he was performing with a vaudeville troupe and making himself into a successful prize fighter. He appeared on the stage and in the ring from Liverpool and London to Paris, Berlin, and Moscow. He could speak French and, with less ease, German. He was not yet nineteen years old. When the Great War broke out in 1914, he was a boxer living in Paris. Eager to defend his adopted land, he served and was wounded in the Foreign Legion, a French infantry regiment, and as a combat aviator in the nascent French air service. A Croix de Guerre recipient for bravery at the beginning of the Battle of Verdun, he became a hero for France. Between the wars, he owned nightclubs and a health spa in the Montmartre section of Paris, where his companions and patrons included Josephine Baker, Louis Armstrong, Charles Chaplin, Gloria Swanson, and the Prince of Wales. Wounded again opposing the German onslaught in 1940, he escaped to the United States and lived in New York City until his death in 1961.

Yet unlike a Horatio Alger hero, Bullard achieved neither fame nor fortune in his native land. He was an African American, and white America was hostile or indifferent to his conspicuous military and commercial successes in France. During his lifetime, American blacks might have learned about his exploits from occasional references to him in the African American press. In the 1950s, New Yorkers or Philadelphians might have noticed a few press items about new honors the government of France bestowed on him, and they might have seen his obituary in the papers.

Americans know of Bullard today largely through P. J. Carisella and James W. Ryan's *The Black Swallow of Death*, published in 1972.[1] With the breakthrough in civil rights of the previous decade and the heightened interest in black history that accompanied it, the time seemed propitious for the story of an amazing figure whose achievements had gone unappreciated for too long. Unfortunately, the book failed to do justice to the man. With the exception of their research into Bullard's French military records and their several useful interviews with his former associates, the authors rely almost exclusively upon Bullard's unpublished memoir, "All Blood Runs Red"; indeed, *The Black Swallow of Death* consists largely of lengthy quotations from the memoir. Seemingly unaware of the unreliability inherent in any memoir, especially one written hastily and incompletely as its author battled stomach cancer in the last two years of his life, Carisella and Ryan too often accept their primary source at face value. By not offering any historical perspective on the influential people and social settings in Bullard's life, nor on his varied careers, they failed to bring to his memoir, which they refer to inaccurately as a "journal," a much-needed biographical dimension.

In fairness to Carisella and Ryan, it should be noted that in purchasing the rights to use the memoir in July 1970, they were under a contractual obligation to produce within three months a work ready for publication; moreover, within nine months, they were expected to accept a binding agreement with a press to publish a work that would be released within a year.[2] These deadlines precluded the research necessary to correct the factual inconsistencies and misremembrances in the memoir. As a result, *The Black Swallow of Death,* though remarkable, lacked credibility and sold only a little over one thousand copies. Yet its errors have been transmitted to a broad readership by the many journalistic pieces based on the work.[3]

Problematic though it is, Bullard's memoir "All Blood Runs Red"—as he entitled it at the suggestion of his World War I comrade, Ted Parsons— remains the indispensable source on his life.[4] From a detailed reading of the typescript of the memoir, it is apparent that although not a literary man, Bullard wrote an account fully within the tradition of African American autobiography stretching from slavery times into the early twentieth century, a tradition that Darryl Pinckney has called the "from Can't to Can" genre: a "success story concentrat[ing] on humble beginnings transcended, on obstacles surmounted."[5] The opening sections contain some obvious and amusing anachronisms as the French–African American man tries to evoke the life of the Georgia black boy of a half-century earlier. For example, to enliven his narrative, he frequently uses dialogue. In a few instances, he has himself addressing humble black women as "Madame" or its French abbreviation "Mme." As if sensing the anachronism but too impatient to correct it, he wrote at one point:

> Thank you, "Madame," I said.
> Mrs. Mary—No "Madame" for me [she said]. I have to call that poor white I work for "Madame" and I don't want to hear it any more than I have to.[6]

In spite of these lapses, in which anachronism leads to gratuitous invention, there are other passages of dialogue that, given the dramatic circumstances and other evidence, seem reasonably close to what must have actually been said. Some readers of Bullard's manuscript, examining it for possible publication in the 1960s, complained not only about the contrived dialogue but also about the excessive and irrelevant detail. However, the latter quality has been useful in researching and documenting Bullard's life in the United States, England, and France.

The following pages critically examine "All Blood Runs Red" in light of the available documentation and other historical evidence, and in so doing, document important events in Bullard's life, especially in his youthful years, and provide information about the significant people, places, and events that shaped him. Fascinating in itself, Bullard's life in the United States and France, examined in historical and social context, offers a comparison of race relations in the two countries that starkly reveals the shackling effects of Jim Crow on African American aspiration in the twentieth century.

Since "All Blood Runs Red" covered only the years of Bullard's life through 1941, the final chapter takes up the last two decades of Bullard's life in New York City, years of obscurity, economic hardship, and racial affront. However, these were also years in which the former hero of France never lost his characteristic vivacity or his determination to attack racial injustice whenever he encountered it. This more accurate and extensive account of his life than is currently on record discloses an individual more complex but no less achieving and no less admirable than others have found. Finding new careers and identities as occasion demanded, able to withstand and transcend the shock of racism and twentieth-century warfare, Bullard emerges as a more remarkable man than the modest self-portrait he sketched in the pages of "All Blood Runs Red."

Eugene Bullard, Black Expatriate in Jazz-Age Paris

CHAPTER ONE

Columbus, Georgia, 1895–1906

Throughout his life, Eugene Bullard acknowledged Columbus, Georgia, as his hometown, and he began his memoir, "All Blood Runs Red," with a lengthy discussion of his upbringing there. Then, as now, the town was the county seat of Muscogee County. In 1900, the county was inhabited by some 30,000 residents, 15,600 African Americans and 14,230 whites.[1] Founded by the state of Georgia in 1828 as a trading center to the Old Southwest, Columbus was settled not only by planters but also by entrepreneurs who immediately used the water power at the falls of the Chattahoochee River to establish saw, grist, and textile mills. Located in west-central Georgia on the river border with Alabama, the Columbus area functioned as a major supplier of weapons, fabric, and foodstuffs to the Confederate armed forces. A week after General Robert E. Lee's surrender formally ended the Civil War, Columbus's waterfront industrial complex was burned to the ground by a large Union cavalry force—General James Wilson had not learned of the war's end because of disrupted telegraph and rail communications. Such knowledge spared Macon from the torch that, at Wilson's command, had been put not only to Columbus but also to Selma and Montgomery, Alabama.[2]

During Reconstruction, bitter Columbus whites chafed under the presence of federal military forces, some of them African American.[3] With the removal of these troops in 1868, local whites used force and threats of violence to "keep blacks in their place" and prevent them from exercising the civil and political rights granted by the federal government. By restoring the antebellum caste system of white over black, these "unreconstructed" whites reassured themselves that all had not been lost as a result of the destruction of the Confederacy. By the time Bullard was born in 1895, the white citizens of Columbus and the rest of the state had imposed de facto racial segregation and restricted black voting rights.[4]

The chronic poverty of many in Columbus, a condition exacerbated by the depression of the mid-1890s, added to the racial oppression experienced by local African Americans as young Bullard was growing up. Disadvantaged whites, economically anxious and insecure, often focused on blacks as the source of their troubles. This was especially true after the efforts by Georgia Populists such as Tom Watson to create a biracial political and economic alliance aborted with the disastrous collapse of their movement in the 1896 election year. Watson blamed the Populist failure on his ill-conceived, as he soon judged it, racial strategy. By 1905 an orator and editor-journalist in Georgia, his former resentment against rich and powerful whites was displaced by hostility toward the economic and political aspirations of blacks.[5] Watson's broadly based popularity worsened the plight of African Americans in Columbus and throughout Georgia.

By the late 1890s, Columbus was owned and governed, if often indirectly, by an economic oligarchy such as Watson had once hated. This elite consisted of men who owned mills, banks, merchant warehouses, and plantations. A number of these men had interests in all these concerns. Among them was W. C. Bradley, a figure who would play a major role in Bullard's early life. In paying low wages to whites but appeasing them by paying lower wages to blacks, Bradley and other members of the oligarchy benefited from the reestablishment of the racial caste system. On the other hand, men like Bradley were concerned that open campaigns of violence by whites against blacks—a concern that the frequency of lynching made all too palpable—could damage or even ruin their economic and political ascendancy. Thus the leaders of Columbus's ruling class were often moderates in Southern race relations, accepting segregation but opposing violence and disorders stemming from racism. This is not to say that a number of Southern whites, including some in the owning class, did not oppose racial violence on moral and religious grounds. Unfortunately for African Americans of this era, however, these leaders usually felt too insecure to give public expression to their views.

Sporadic antiblack violence and virulent racism marked Bullard's youth. The years of his life in Columbus and elsewhere in Georgia were framed by two local lynchings so flagrant that they could not be ignored by the local press and, in the second case, by the civil authorities. In 1896, a black man awaiting trial for rape—and another suspected of the crime—were dragged from jail and home and hanged from a large tree on Broad Street, the town's main thoroughfare.[6] Members of the lynch mob, surrounded by a crowd of onlookers, then fired their guns repeatedly into the bodies of the victims before everyone dispersed some hours later. In 1912, a black twelve-year-old accidently shot and killed a white playmate in rural north Muscogee County. Brought to trial, the youth was convicted of manslaughter instead of first-degree murder. After the verdict was read, outraged members of the white boy's family who were seated in the courtroom overpowered law enforcement officers and kidnapped the terrified youth. They then commandeered a trolley car, rode it out beyond the city limits to a location near the present site of the Bradley Memorial Library, and murdered the youngster with shotgun blasts. A courageous judge and grand jury indicted the ringleaders in the crime, but the jury hearing the case voted for an acquittal.[7]

As much as these lynchings, the reportage of the *Columbus Ledger* newspaper in these years offers sobering evidence of the unremitting pressure placed on local blacks to "keep in their place." News items repeatedly lament the passing of "another faithful darky," a person as loyal to the white family after slavery as he or she had been while in bondage. Younger blacks, "bravos," who refused to submit to the racial norms, are routinely disparaged as disobedient, delinquent, or criminal. A black customer is reported stabbed by a white butcher for protesting the amount of change returned to him after a purchase. A black man, a house painter, is found wandering stupifiedly on a street with a gunshot wound in the head; the reporter speculates he was mistaken for a burglar. A story runs for several days about a white man who shot a black driver of a timber wagon for failing to apologize after accidentally forcing his carriage off Glade Road (present-day Cusseta Road). Although the black man states he had fired back (without result) in self-defense, a local judge concludes that what the young white man did was a necessary "lesson to impudent and insolent Negroes" and the "best thing to have happened in Muscogee County in the past twenty years."[8]

Elsewhere in the *Ledger* of these years, a local Democratic Party leader defends lynching because the crime of rape is too heinous to permit the relatively painless death imposed by the judicial system. An editorial argues that those few black schools that train students for the professions are creating idle loafers, not good domestic employees. A local doctor, after considerable study, reports that nearby Tuskegee Institute in Alabama is turning out graduates who do not wish to be servants. He denounces the school's president, Booker T. Washington, for tolerating this state of affairs. Because of Theodore Roosevelt's public support of Washington and his appointment of blacks to federal government jobs, the local press frequently belittles the Republican president. In the March 3, 1903, *Ledger,* the editors entertain their readership with this item: "The last name registered at the Rankin [Hotel] last night was 'Teddy Roosevelt, Niggertown, N.S.A.' The name was written in pencil and afterwards someone added the letters 'N.L.' [nigger lover] to it."[9]

When African Americans are not being condemned for being "brutish" or "uppity," the local press offers their readers the reassuring and amusing spectacle of the black "sambo." Stories and editorial commentary poke fun at their shiftlessness, naïveté, drunkenness, and ignorance, their comical awkwardness in speech and behavior when brought before white authorities, and their aimless fighting among themselves in public places. The *Ledger*'s treatment of Columbus blacks affirms overwhelmingly the observation made a generation earlier by Frederick Douglass, the great antislavery activist and statesman, regarding what the recently freed people faced not only in the South, but virtually everywhere in America:

> Though the colored man is no longer subject to be bought and sold, he is still surrounded by an adverse sentiment which fetters all his movements. In his downward course he meets with no resistance, but his course upward is resented and resisted at every step of his progress. If he comes in ignorance,

rags, and wretchedness, he conforms to the popular belief of his character, and in that character he is welcome. But if he shall come as a gentleman, a scholar, and statesman, he is hailed as a contradiction to the national faith concerning his race, and his coming resented as impudence. In the one case he may provoke contempt and derision, but in the other he is an affront to pride, and provokes malice. Let him do what he will, there is at present, therefore, no escape for him.[10]

Such were the prevailing white attitudes and behaviors from which Bullard's parents tried to insulate him in his early years. He recalls in "All Blood Runs Red" that his parents would not allow him to play with white youngsters in his neighborhood, where black and white families lived in close proximity. About the time he entered school, probably in walking to and from school through white neighborhoods, Bullard became conscious of racial slurs. He was stunned when a friend explained, "you was borned [sic] brown and that makes white folks despise you." He was stunned, but not crushed. He credits his parents for giving him "the five years' head start [toward self-respect] without the single doubt that I was as nice as anybody and as smart."[11] As in the case of Jackie Robinson, a sharecropper's son also born in south Georgia (in 1919) and destined to be a pioneer in challenging Jim Crow in major-league baseball, the indignities and disabilities of racism remained for Eugene incomprehensible and inexcusable outrages throughout his life. Unlike Robinson, however, who so often would be compelled to hold his rage within himself, Bullard in France would be able to give vent to his anger with his fists and successful appeals to the law.

Bullard's father, William O. Bullard, was born into slavery on a "bottom land" Chattahoochee River plantation in Stewart County, Georgia, about forty miles south of Columbus. Historical sources do not sustain Eugene Bullard's contention that the family that owned his father's people, whose name he gives as "Strawmaker," had moved into Stewart County from Mississippi in the antebellum period and been broken up by the Civil War. Bullard wrote that his infant father was "lost" in the social upheaval of the last days of that momentous conflict. He was found, his account continued, by a French-speaking white Bullard family who took him "for good luck" and raised him lovingly on their land, which was adjacent to that of the Strawmakers;[12] and they bequeathed to him their Catholicism and love of France, a love that his father passed on to him "at a tender age." Bullard was likely indulging in a retrospective sense of historical destiny at this point. As he looked back at his extraordinary successes in France and his assimilation into all aspects of French culture, he generated in his memoir a creation myth, even noting that his father was found "like Moses hidden in the bulrushes."[13] What better way to organize his memoir than by a dramatic narrative structure in which the protagonist searched for, found, and finally lost the earthly paradise, France, made known to him in his earliest memories?

Bullard's father was indeed born into slavery on a Chattahoochee River plantation during the Civil War. His family's master was Wiley Bullard, a Primitive Baptist whose own parents had migrated into Georgia, like so many other families, from the Carolinas in the early nineteenth century. It is clear that William Bullard was living with his own parents when freedom came in 1865.[14] Daisy Bullard Thomas, whose father was an older brother of Eugene's father, confirmed these findings derived from census materials and an exceptionally informative history of Stewart County, sources which fail—as do Mississippi antebellum censuses—to disclose the existence of Strawmakers or any similar-sounding name.

Born in 1888, Thomas remembered her parents and uncles and aunts telling how they had come out of slavery on a plantation just south of the little Stewart County settlements of Louvale, Union, and Omaha (pronounced "Omahoy" by her and still today by older local African Americans), towns that sprang up along the Seaboard Airline Railroad after the Civil War.[15] Thomas recalled the exact location of the "ol' Massa's" place, "the old Bullard place." Once filled with cotton fields and the cabins of numerous sharecroppers and tenant farmers, the land is now a sparsely populated and uncultivated acreage inhabited by bobcats, herons, egrets, and, in the tributaries of the Chattahoochee, alligators. The Stewart County history reveals that this land was owned by a white planter, Wiley Bullard, from 1839 up until the Civil War. The land was located in the 22nd Census District in the northwest part of the county,[16] directly across the river from Cottonton, Alabama.

Thomas remembered well her "Uncle Billy," whose facial features she said closely resembled Eugene's, and her "Aunt Josie," whom she always heard came from near Omaha. She also had affectionate memories of a man who, she believed, was the "ol' massa's son." He became "the famous doctor in Columbus" whose home on 3rd Avenue she would visit when she worked in Columbus in the years just before World War I.[17] This man taught her father how to read and write, doing so secretly. Thomas believed Dr. Bullard also taught Eugene's father how to read and write. Later, when planning to attend school in Atlanta, the young Dr. Bullard talked about bringing her father to an educational institution there to further his education. Although these plans did not materialize, her father knew the importance of "giving [all his children] a learning, so you knew how to go through the world."[18] With the help of her father's preschool instruction, Daisy entered school as a fourth grader. She later became certified to teach and did so in Stewart and Chattahoochee County schools before moving to Columbus, Georgia, and ultimately to Cleveland, Ohio.[19]

The doctor was William Lewis Bullard, a nephew of Wiley Bullard, born in 1852.[20] He received his medical degree from Emory University in Atlanta and then undertook postgraduate education in Europe, interning in hospitals in Berlin, Vienna, and London, where he was present at the first successful use of a localized anesthetic for the eye.[21] Shortly after his marriage in 1881, Bullard set up a practice in Columbus as the first eye, ear, and throat specialist for the whole Southeast. He continued to practice out of his office on Broad Street (now Broadway) until just before his death in 1925. Remembered in his obituary as a "progressive practitioner" whose diagnoses and operations advanced medical knowledge in his field, he was also "generous, open hearted, and liberal. . . . To those of limited means he often booked no charge whatsoever."[22]

Eugene Bullard and Daisy Thomas agreed that their fathers were of mixed African American and Creek Indian heritage; Eugene believed that his was "one-quarter" Creek.[23] When Stewart County was surveyed and settled by whites in the late 1820s and early 1830s, there were still a number of Creek villages on sites along the Chattahoochee, especially in the 22nd District where Wiley Bullard bought land in 1839.[24] These were communities of "lower Creeks" who, according to scholars, were much more assimilated to white culture and society than the "upper Creeks" to the west and north in Alabama. These Indians held African Americans as slaves, and they also admitted free blacks into their communities. As within the expanding slave-based culture of the white South, there were inevitably children born of black and Indian parents.[25] A slaveowner such as Bullard could have come to possess them either as the result of a union between a Creek and one of his slaves or as the result of the theft (or purchase) of African Creeks at the time of the Creeks' removal from west-central Georgia and Alabama to the Oklahoma Territory in the 1830s. Creeks who had agreed to break with the tribe and submit to white authorities could purchase land and remain in west-central Georgia. This may have been the case with Eugene's maternal grandmother, who, he asserts, was predominantly Creek and who owned land near Fort Valley, Georgia, in Houston County (present-day Peach County).[26]

Eugene's parents, William and Josephine Thomas Bullard, were married on December 30, 1882, in Stewart County, and their marriage was certified a day later by Reverend Jerry Wynn.[27] If the 1900 U.S. Census data is correct, William was nineteen and Josephine seventeen years of age when they wed.[28] Deciding not to remain in farming in Stewart County with his brothers, William moved his family to Columbus in the early 1890s. There were then three children: Pauline, born in 1885, Hector in 1887, and Ben in 1889. Three other children had died as infants. The "lucky seventh" child, as his father impressed upon him, was Eugene, born on October 9, 1895, in the small three-room "shotgun" house that his parents rented at 2601 Talbotton Avenue.[29] In such a home, cooking was done on a wood stove in the rear room. The two front rooms, lit at night by oil lamps, served as living and sleeping rooms, heated in winter by a fireplace in the wall between them. The home was located in an African American enclave of similar dwellings between the white Rose Hill and Jordan City neighborhoods on the then-northern outskirts of Columbus. (The names for these districts continue to be used today.)

William Bullard worked as a drayman, warehouse man, steamboat stevedore, and general handyman for W. C. Bradley.[30] A rising entrepreneur, Bradley had inherited large bottom land plantations south of Columbus on both the Alabama and Georgia sides of the Chattahoochee. Moving to Columbus in 1882 and marrying there in 1887, he and his wife raised a daughter in a comfortable Victorian home on Fourth Avenue. His mercantile company on Front Avenue bought, shipped, and sold cotton and other agricultural produce up and down the Chattahoochee from Columbus to Apalachicola, Florida, on the Gulf Coast.[31] It is possible that Bradley knew of or was even acquainted with William Bullard in Stewart County before hiring him to work in Columbus. Bradley's friend, neighbor, and personal physician was William Lewis Bullard, whose uncle, "the ol' massa," owned river lands in Stewart County in close proximity to the Bradleys' Georgia river plantations in the 22nd District.

Josephine Bullard gave birth to two more sons, Joseph and McArthur, in 1897 and 1899.[32] The last child, Leona, was born in 1901. While raising her children, Mrs. Bullard supplemented the family's slender income by taking in clothing for washing and sewing repairs. This was rigorous work, involving walking often considerable distances to the customers' homes to pick up their bundles and then walking the washed and ironed clothes back to the owner.[33] Still, there was not enough income to cover the family's expenses. The Bullards somehow found space in their home to take in two boarders in the mid-1890s.[34]

As their parents toiled, Eugene and the other older Bullard children were able to acquire a rudimentary education in two of the colored schools in Columbus's segregated public school system. In the late 1890s, Pauline and Ben attended Claflin School, founded by the Freedmen's Bureau in 1868. From 1901 to 1906, Eugene attended the Twenty-Eighth Street School, founded in the late 1880s. About a twelve-block walk from the Bullard home, this school was a ramshackle frame building in which a handful of teachers taught reading, writing, and arithmetic to some eighty children through the fifth grade. In such schools, principals' and teachers' salaries were approximately one-half those earned by their counterparts in the white schools.[35] Moreover, in spite of the protests of Columbus's black bourgeoisie, basic skills and vocational training through the ninth grade were all the white Columbus school board would grant to African American students until 1929. Of education in the colored schools of the pre–senior high school era, Columbusite Roscoe Chester has recalled that "diplomas opened many doors—stable doors, back doors, barn doors, doors of chauffeur driven cars, and a whole lot of kitchen doors."[36]

In spite of poverty and the severe educational disabilities in this era, many large Southern black families like the Bullards functioned quite well. With both parents working, the older children, once they had completed their basic schooling, stayed at home to help out in the raising of their younger siblings. Overt racial oppression perhaps encouraged these disadvantaged families to band together and, in the spirit of Booker T. Washington, take pride in the successes, however meager, in "coming through" against adversity.

During summers, Eugene and his siblings could escape the insufferable heat of the late-spring schoolroom and their small home on Talbotton Avenue by living with relatives in rural Stewart and Houston Counties. Daisy Bullard Thomas remembered that her cousins Pauline and Eugene enjoyed spending summers with her family. Her father put Eugene to work on the farm that had been willed to him, she said, by the white Bullards.[37]

William and Josephine Bullard, however, could not escape the unrelenting burden of feeding, clothing, and sheltering their large family. For Josephine, the many childbirths, incessant cooking, and endless washing ultimately took its toll. On August 24, 1902, a sweltering Sunday, she died at home and was laid to rest the next day at Porterdale Cemetery, Columbus's black burial ground adjacent to the city's South Commons.[38] She was thirty-seven years of age. In the same column of the August 26 *Enquirer-Sun* that recorded, quite remarkably, her death, there was an item noting that "yesterday's maximum 89 degrees . . . shows a decided change in weather, being four or five points lower than it has been for sometime."[39] Curiously, Eugene wrote that the doctor who attended his mother in her last illness was "the family physician and close personal friend" of W. C. Bradley. That individual was William Lewis Bullard, but Eugene gave his name as "Cobb"[40]—perhaps because he did not want to disclose the non-French identity of his father's master, Wiley Bullard, and his father's benefactor, Dr. Bullard, Wiley's kinsman.

With his young wife's passing, it now fell to William Bullard and seventeen-year-old Pauline, whom Eugene recalled taking on the role of mother, to raise the family. His father, Eugene wrote in his memoir, rallied the children by telling them stories about the notable deeds of their ancestors dating back to when they had lived in Martinique.[41] When Eugene was about seven, his father informed the children of the disturbing news that the white foreman at the W. C. Bradley warehouse was abusing him and other black workers. Eugene related that Bradley "was especially fond of Father," calling him "Big Chief Ox because he was so strong and big, partly because he was one-quarter Creek Indian." William Bullard could and did complain about the foreman's behavior to Bradley in his office on Front Avenue. Bradley assured the big man that he would see to it that the maltreatment ended. Nonetheless, the abuse—both verbal and physical—continued. William told his children that he might have to retaliate: "Never did I forget father's next words: 'If I have to hit Stevens, I want you all to be good children. Always show respect to each and every one, white and black, and make them respect you. Go to school as long as you can. Never look for a fight. I mean never. But if you are attacked, or your honor is attacked unjust [sic], fight, fight, keep on fighting even if you die for your rights. It will be a glorious death.'"[42]

Shortly thereafter, the foreman, infuriated by the elder Bullard's refusal to discuss his conversation with Bradley, hit Bullard with a large iron hook used for loading bales of cotton. Withstanding the blow, the six-foot-four laborer seized his tormentor, lifted him over his head, and threw him through a hole in the warehouse floor into a deep storage cellar. He then walked to Bradley's office and explained what had happened. Returning to the scene together on the river side of the warehouse to avoid conveying the impression that something was amiss, they discovered that the supervisor, although badly injured, was still alive. Bradley instructed the witnesses—who happened to be African Americans—to testify that his foreman had tripped accidentally. He called in his family doctor, "Cobb," to care for the injured man. He then told Bullard that he would tell his supervisor to keep mum about the episode if he wanted to work in Columbus ever again.[43]

In spite of the attempted hush-up, white "crackers," as Eugene referred to them, learned what had happened. Late that evening a mob rode out on horseback to the Bullard home and tried to force the front and back doors. Inside, his father, training his loaded shotgun on the front door, told the terrified children to stay quiet. The members of the mob, drinking

heavily and unable to gain easy access into the house, convinced themselves that the elder Bullard had not come home after all and galloped
away into the night. This near-lynching of his father was the traumatic
event that led young Bullard to leave home sometime later.[44]

Before departing, however, Eugene was deeply impressed by the kindness of "Mr. Bradley." During the month or so that William stayed away
from home (Eugene believed that Bradley found work for him with a railroad company), his former boss saw to it that the Bullard children had
food and were comforted by his own house servants. Bradley himself visited the cabin, bringing with him food, clothing, and money; he compli-
mented the children for their good manners and dress. Most important of
all, he promised them that their father would return shortly.[45] When writing his memoir decades later, Bullard found occasion to praise Bradley as
a "good white person" whose example, along with that of other Cauca-
sians encountered during his life, kept him from becoming prejudiced toward all whites as a matter of principle.

In his Rose Hill neighborhood, young Eugene was a buoyant spirit—
"as friendly and as trusting as a chickadee"—playing happily with friends
and bustling about the streets intersecting Talbotton Avenue seated in his
little goat-drawn cart. The idyll ended with his mother's death and the
attempted assault on his father. Ironically, it was his mother's passing and
with her the enforcement of the ban on association with white youngsters
that led to his first bitter taste of racial scorn and contempt. Even before
the abortive attempt on his father's life, Eugene was dreaming of a place
where "colored and white folk were treated the same." Torn between love
of his father and his desire for respectful treatment, he made several failed
attempts to run away before succeeding. Cousin Daisy Thomas and two
former playmates concurred that Eugene finally left home when he was
close to or in his early teens. William Bullard knew the son whom he spoke
to as "Honey" had special qualities—if only, he agonized, Eugene would
allow them to develop under his tutelage. After foiling one attempt to
run away, the frustrated father placed his son in a pillory and whipped
him, an action that did nothing to dampen Eugene's ardor to escape
Columbus.[46]

   This harsh treatment sheds light on Eugene's youthful acquisition of the powerful sense of identity and strength of will that would carry him from the dusty streets of Columbus to the boulevards of Paris. He had acquired this determination not only from his father's teaching about the importance of dignity and self-respect but also through daring to stand up to the most feared and beloved individual in his life—the spiritually and physically imposing figure of William Bullard. (Late in life, Eugene would dedicate "All Blood Runs Red" to the memory of his father.) In defying his father, he became, perhaps as early as eleven years old, his own man, ready to confront the wide world beyond Columbus.

CHAPTER TWO

Youthful Vagabond, 1906–1912

The diminutive manchild who stole away from home in Columbus had $1.50 in his pocket, the proceeds from the sale of his goat to a white youngster whose father was instrumental in the construction of the Jordan City commercial district near Bullard's neighborhood. It is unlikely that Bullard was beginning a self-conscious journey in search of France, the land where, he said, his father had promised that all people were treated equally. What seems more likely is that he left home desiring to escape the stifling racism of his hometown and the restraints placed upon his restless spirit by his father. For all his love of his "Honey," his lucky seventh child, William Bullard could not abide, understandably enough, his son's penchant for leaving home. William doubtless also resented Eugene's abandonment of the role of an older child helping in the raising of younger siblings, especially five-year-old Leona. When Eugene did depart for good, perhaps as early as the autumn of 1906, he was searching simply for the freedom to find out for himself what new landscapes and human relationships might lie down the road beyond the next stretch of woods and fields of west-central Georgia.

On the road away from Columbus, Eugene interacted with a succession of families and surrogate parental figures: African Americans, a band of gypsies, and white families in the rural towns of Leesburg, Sasser, Dawson, and possibly other south Georgia communities as well.[1] As with Richard Wright's protagonist in his celebrated autobiographical novel *Black*

Boy, Eugene insisted that all these people regard him as a person instead of a creature expected to behave in racially stereotypical ways. He took great care to maintain his independence with all of them. Deeply grateful to the blacks who fed, lodged, and loved him, the young runaway continually felt compelled to bear the pain of tearful departures from them and the social constraints imposed upon them by white society.

After walking along a railroad track during the first day away from home, Eugene spent the night with a black sharecropping family, "Tom and Emma" and their thirteen children. It was cotton-picking time, and when the family rose at 4:00 A.M. to begin the day's work, Emma gave him a one-dollar bill, enabling him to take a train to Atlanta from a station a few miles up the tracks. On the train, a woman who made herself known to him as Mary Woods, a childless widow, was returning home to Atlanta. By the time the train had arrived at Terminal Station, he had tearfully confessed to her the story of his flight from home. Moved by the account, Mary held out the promise of motherly nurture and further education, including eventual enrollment at Morris Brown College. After spending the night and the next day at her home in downtown Atlanta, Eugene departed this "dear sweet lady who wanted to give me the love I had lost when my own beloved mother died." He joined a gypsy band he had met the day before at their camp near the stockyards at the end of Capitol Avenue.[2]

Although known in North America in the colonial era, the gypsies who roved the United States at the turn of this century had, for the most part, emigrated with the massive influx of peoples from southeastern Europe in the late nineteenth century. Interestingly enough, gypsies were often seen camping in the Columbus area in the years of Eugene's youth. An item in the *Columbus Ledger* of May 18, 1903, for instance, informed young lovers among its readers that they might have their fortunes told by a group encamped across the Chattahoochee in Phenix City.[3] Bullard himself had spent his first night as a runaway at a gypsy camp in an open field in the East Highland area of Columbus several blocks from home. After drawing water for the gypsies' horses in nearby Weracoba Creek, the youth had hid out from his anxious and angry father under one of the gypsy wagons.[4]

The particular band that Eugene joined in Atlanta was of the Stanley tribe, an English group sojourning in the States. An observer who encountered a family of Stanleys in New York in the 1920s described them as "one of the most remarkable Gypsy tribes of England." Well documented in Victorian England for their horse trading and racing, the Stanleys also valued horse power in pulling their brightly painted and decoratively carved wagons from campground to campground.[5] From an early age, Eugene had learned at relatives' farms to ride and care for horses, skills of value to these Romanies.

Living with these social outcasts, he learned the arts of the race jockey as well as how to "doctor" horses to make them appear younger.[6] More importantly, the acceptance of him into their community strengthened his sense that a social order tolerant of racial difference was possible—all other evidence to the contrary. From these exotic people, he learned of the possibility of a better life for an African American across the Atlantic. Moreover, his adaptation to gypsy life, even to using phrases from their ancient language, prepared "Jamesy," one of several names the nomads called him, for his encounter with other foreign cultures and languages a few years later.[7]

After a period of time, probably in 1907–8, the young adventurer decided to separate from the Stanleys, disappointed when he learned that they did not plan to return to England for several more years. He left the group at a campground just west of Bronwood, Georgia, a site uncultivated even today and still remembered as the "gypsy grounds" by people living in the locality.[8] Walking down the Dawson-Bronwood road toward Leesburg (present-day State Route 4), Bullard was soon induced to ride with a certain Travis William Moreland, who observed to him that bears and snakes came onto the road from the area's swamps at nightfall. Moreland was returning to his home one mile east of Leesburg. Seeing how well the youngster worked with his horses in unharnessing them and rubbing them down, he put him to work on his horse farm.[9]

Travis Moreland was the first of several white employers for whom Eugene worked in rural Georgia. Others were a Mr. Matthews of Sasser, a village a few miles south of Leesburg, and the John Zacharia Turner family of nearby Dawson, then and today the seat of Terrell County. For Matthews, a barber, and his wife, the industrious youth assisted in the shop and performed household chores. When Eugene fell seriously ill, Matthews rented him a private room and hired a doctor to care for him until he recovered. Fully recuperated, the restless youth longed to be on his way but wanted to work off his debt before leaving. The generous Matthews refused to hear of it. As they said their good-byes, Matthews told him that true democracy would one day be realized in the South. "It was God's will," he told Eugene.[10] His kindness helped nourish the sentiment kindled by W. C. Bradley: that some whites, at least, were to be trusted as decent and honorable. In spite of all the racial hatred and discrimination he would experience in the United States and later from Americans in France, Bullard never completely relinquished Matthews's conviction that the country would change its race relations for the better.

With Moreland and the Turners, Eugene's relations were more complex than with the altruistic Matthews family. Moreland, like Turner and Turner's oldest son, Doug, found in the vagabond a good-natured and hard-working youth whom they could not help liking. Nor could they refrain from habitually calling him "nigger" during the first days of their respective tenures together. They were astonished, each in their turn, by the teenager's sudden refusal one day to heed their commands. Barging into his quarters demanding an explanation, they found him, looking them straight in the eye, explaining firmly that he wanted to be called "Gene" or "Gypsy." After recovering their composure, the bosses, impressed by the youth's quiet sincerity, promised they would do so. Turner went so far as assembling his workforce in the yard in front of their living quarters in order to proclaim loudly with Bullard at his side: "This here is Gene; now he wants to be called Gene by everybody and that goes for all you niggers, too."[11]

With the Morelands and the Turners, the youngster was soon invited to eat and sleep inside the kitchens and attics of their homes, rather than in the workers' shacks out back. His willingness to confront their racism won him their respect. However, this same forthrightness also brought him the enmity of black laborers who resented his privileges. In fact, he was threatened by Moreland's workers and felt compelled for his own safety to report it to the boss.[12] Again, one is reminded of Wright's *Black*

Boy, whose hero, in defying the racial etiquette of the Southern caste system, finds himself in conflict with older blacks as well as whites.

The Turner family played a significant if unwitting role in fostering Eugene's independent spirit. Zack Turner was in the livery business, buying, selling, and renting horses in Parrot, Georgia, until 1909, when he moved his family to nearby Dawson, where Eugene worked for him. In an obituary notice, Turner is remembered as a man with a "genial disposition and popular with all classes."[13] Not long after moving to Dawson, he served as the town's chief of police and in 1914 was elected sheriff of Terrell County.[14] Bullard clearly remembered "old Zack" and his sons: Doug, twenty-one years old in 1910; John Angling, eighteen years old and known by contemporaries as "Ange"; and seven-year-old Raymond.[15]

After establishing himself as "Gene" rather than "little nigger," Bullard's months of residence with the Turner family were among his happiest in America.[16] Zack Turner and his wife, Clara, created a household whose warmth and liberality produced a brood of successful children. In addition to Doug and Robert Angling, who both became sheriffs, there were six daughters, all of whom had left home before Eugene's time with the family had begun. All of these women became teachers, one a professor of Latin at Agnes Scott College in Decatur, Georgia, who died just before receiving her doctorate.[17]

The prominence of the Turner family in Dawson and Terrell County and their broad-mindedness explain why they could sponsor, without repercussions, Eugene as their jockey in horse races down a stretch of Main Street in Dawson, one of the main events of the Terrell County Fair in 1911. In entering these races, Bullard, in effect, was able to break the "color line," something virtually unheard of in the Deep South in those years. The upcoming race was given much promotion through the grapevine, and several local families entered horses. The event acquired an added element of excitement when it became known that the Turners had wagered five hundred dollars that their horse would defeat their rival's steed. After secret trial runs with Doug along a lonely stretch of road, it was obvious that Eugene with his slighter build could run faster than the Turner boys on Happy Bob.[18]

Enhancing interest in the 1911 county fair horse races was the fact that such contests had not taken place in Dawson since the 1870s, and those were remembered by locals as legendary. For some reason, another fair did not occur until 1910.[19] In October and early November of 1911, the *Dawson News* celebrated numerous fair-related activities for which, the paper headlined, "Large Crowds Were Present and Much Interest and Excitement Prevailed." In addition to horse racing and trotting events, the paper reported automobile parades and races, a buggy parade, and a "flight by an aviator." The last day of the Terrell County Fair was reported as "NEGROE'S Day." No activities were listed.[20] (At this same time, in Macon, Georgia, much publicity was being given to the upcoming flights there at the Colored State Fair of Wesley Peters, billed as the world's first black aviator.[21]) Outfitted with a red and yellow silk jacket made for him by the wife of Pete Weston, the black supervisor of the Turner work force, Eugene raced before the excited crowd lining the course, which ran from the fairgrounds down Main Street to the finishing line at Lee Street in the center of town. After the race, which Eugene won, the Turners accepted a challenge for a rematch with a prize of five hundred dollars. Some weeks later, the slender youth competed for this sum before an even larger crowd that included the Stanley gypsies. In addition to the seventy he had earned as a stable boy, he was paid twenty-five dollars for his victories in both races.[22]

If the horse races highlighted the good times Eugene enjoyed with the Turners, an event that occurred the previous Easter season marked a demoralizing low point in his tenure with the family. Eugene received permission from Zack Turner to spend a week with his cousin James Bullard and his family at their farm in nearby Richland, Georgia, twenty miles northwest of Dawson. He arrived by the Macon train of the Central of Georgia Railroad on an Easter Sunday, telling his much older cousin Jimmy that he was en route back to Columbus "so he wouldn't guess I had left home and take me there himself." After a pleasant holiday with the family, the next day, with the parents at work and children in school, he walked into Richland to explore the town. As he was walking down Main Street, a white man named Dewitt Drew suddenly sprang out of a chair on the sidewalk, dragged him into a store, and screamed, "Where did you get dem clothes?" Eugene was still wearing his Sunday best. Locking the door, Drew started whipping him. Terrified, the teenager ran about the store and crawled under the counter in an unsuccessful effort to escape the lashes. Finally, he was able to kick out the glass of the front door and flee through a crowd that had been attracted by the commotion.[23]

Knowing that any attempt at retaliation could lead to lynching, Eugene told James at day's end that his lacerations had resulted from fighting with his sons. Aware that he was lying, the older man then administered to him his own whipping. The next day, Bullard returned by train to Dawson, where, still fearful of violent repercussions, he refused to tell the inquiring Turners what had happened to him.[24]

For Eugene, the whipping by Dewitt Drew chilled the happy period that he enjoyed with the Turner family. The incident was not only maddening in itself but also, like the episode involving his father, required a dishonest response rather than forthright action. The lashing firmed his "determination to get to a land where such things do not happen." Some months after the incident, he left the Turners and South Georgia. Although he had been treated even more kindly by the family after the Richland trauma, the young man had always felt their regard for him was somewhat like that for a favorite pet—one they did not want to lose. Bullard also recollected Doug Turner's worry that, after the second race, he might join the Stanley gypsies again.[25]

The opportunity to move on came when Eugene was dispatched by Zach Turner to deliver a horse to a turpentine prison farm near St. Andrews Bay on the Florida Panhandle coast. His route took him to Lumpkin, Georgia, where he spent the night in a stable, then on across the Chattahoochee to Eufaula, Alabama, and down through Montgomery to his destination. After receiving his fee from the "big boss," a Mr. Dan Sheppard, he stayed the weekend at the penal farm. Walking the shoreline of the Gulf, he fantasized about finding a ship that would carry him overseas. Instead of returning to the Turners, he took a train to Montgomery, where he lodged a few days at a Mrs. Palmer's Rooming House before boarding another train for Atlanta.[26]

In Atlanta, he declined to revisit Mary Woods, feeling that "it would have upset us both too much." Instead, he rented a room from a Butler family who resided on Decatur Street. Mr. Butler was a railroad worker, quite likely the man listed in the Atlanta city directories of 1911 and 1912 as Charles Butler. In the short period of time he was with the Butlers and their young boy, Sonny, the restless youth poured out his story to them and disclosed his plan to find his way overseas. Although dumbfounded, they gave him their encouragement.[27]

While with the Butlers, Bullard enjoyed the spectacle of his first motion picture, a western, from the gallery—the black section—of a movie house, probably the Bijou Theater on Marietta Street near Five Points in downtown Atlanta. A few days later, he took the Butlers, who had never seen a film before, to the theater. Mr. Butler was astonished when, after calmly approaching the white ticket seller, Eugene had the nerve to challenge the seller's overcharge on the price of admission. Although he ended up paying the quarter instead of a dime per ticket, Bullard was struck by Butler's poignant remark: "The way us colored folks is treated, I guess a lot of us hasn't got any respect for ourselves left."[28]

Several other racial incidents marred Eugene's second stay in Atlanta in early 1912. During his stays there, he occasionally bought a Sunday newspaper in order to read the "Buster Brown" comic strip. A few years earlier, he had even purchased the faddish Buster Brown suit for his Sunday best.[29] Having outgrown the knickerbocker pants, he went out in downtown Atlanta in search of a shop where he could purchase the ankle-length peg pants that were then the rage. He found a Jewish tailor shop,[30] where he picked out cloth and haggled over the price for the tailoring with a young man and his father, who spoke with a foreign accent. The older man grew impatient and said, "Say, little nigger, where do you come from?" Without saying a word, Bullard turned on his heel and walked out of the store and down the street, the son running after him, imploring him to return. As he walked away, Bullard heard bystanders muttering, "What have he stole? Come on, folks, leave the Jew and the little nigger together. That's where they belong anyhow."[31]

His feelings hurt, the Jewish youngster returned to the store, now followed by the black youth. Upon hearing of the slurs against his son, the father angrily observed that, having been born in America, "you have a right to be treated like any other American. . . . Don't let them insult you." Asked why he had returned to the store, Eugene replied, "Sir, I am an

American too and you called me a nigger." Apologizing, the father, after a discussion with his son "in some strange language," then agreed to make the pants at cost. Eugene had given his Buster Brown suit to Sonny Butler. One evening, the fun-loving teenager staged a fashion show for the older Butlers, Sonny modeling the Buster Brown suit and young Bullard his new peg pants. The occasion brought much merriment to the household. Several days later, his happiness, "I reckon pride," suddenly vanished on a street in Atlanta. Walking along a sidewalk, "a young white man passed me and I felt something on my right side. A few minutes later I noticed a good sized cut in my pants by my right pocket probably done by a razor carried by the man who was now out of sight." He returned home to the Butlers demoralized and outraged, "wondering how anybody could be so mean." Mrs. Butler mended the clothes as best she could while Mr. Butler gave vent to his frustration over the treatment colored folks had to endure and wondered "how long we can stand things like this." For his part, Eugene vowed that he would learn to box like Jack Johnson "so that when I meet anybody who acts mean . . . I [will be able to] show them that it don't pay." That same night he told the Butlers of his resolve to take a northbound train the next evening toward an Atlantic coast port town. After a night and day of fitful sleep, he said an emotional farewell to Mrs. Butler, Sonny having gone to bed and Mr. Butler not yet back from work. "Tears were rolling down her face. I went away fast so as not to cry too." [32]

Bullard had previously scouted out a night train leaving Atlanta on a regular schedule for Richmond, Virginia. The evening he departed Atlanta, he went to the station, and upon the arrival of his train at midnight, slipped onto a ladder held horizontally underneath the dining car. He rode the rods out of the city and into the piedmont of Georgia and the Carolinas, the steam engine whistling through the sleeping towns and hamlets scattered along the Seaboard Air Line route. By daylight the train had stopped on a trestle bridging a river. As the train began to move again, the vagabond dismounted. He followed the tracks to a town, where he found lodging with a black family named Hughes with whom he stayed for a week. Mr. Hughes was a brickmaker, and Eugene was able to work with his crew as a laborer to make some extra money for his voyage across the ocean. He told him that he was heading for the seaport at Norfolk;

Hughes told him that there was a nearer port at Newport News. After Eugene had told the family of his previous adventures, the Hughes family encouraged him and even feted him with a party at their home in his honor.[33]

Departing the next day, he walked into Richmond. There he found the depot complex and rode a freight elevator to a station platform well above street level. Once again, he was able to slide underneath one of the cars of a train about to depart. In actuality, he "had no idea where the train was bound for."[34] When the train stopped and he crawled out from under his car, he learned that he was at the end of the line in Newport News. A short walk brought him to the "beautiful wide water" of the Hampton Roads. After visiting a street fair, he slept that night in a coal bin and woke up tolerating the joke of a passerby that he was black enough as he was without the added coal dust.

Collis P. Huntington, president of the Chesapeake and Ohio Railway, had extended a branch of his line to Newport News in 1882 and then developed harbor facilities there at the confluence of the James River and the Hampton Roads. The port had prospered since the 1890s, selling the hundreds of thousands of tons of coal that the railroad delivered there annually from West Virginia mines. The relatively cheap coal was sold to the ocean-going steamships that began docking there to refuel after offloading and reloading cargo in the area. Thus in his first night in Newport News, Eugene had little trouble finding a coal bin in which to sleep; indeed, at the waterfront, there would have been little else on which to lay his head.[35]

Come morning, he searched for a ship outward bound for Europe. Finding a likely one, he recalled joining a line of men carrying cabbages on board in crates. A crate was placed on his back and up the gangplank he went. On deck, he hid between two cotton bales. Soon the ship left its moorings and after two or three hours docked again. Back on a pier, he asked a young colored man what city he was in. "Norfolk, Virginia, dumbhead," he answered.[36]

On the Norfolk docks, Bullard quickly located another big ship, the *Marta Russ,* and tried to talk to the sailors who were loading her. They were speaking in a foreign tongue but had enough English to explain to the young black man that they were from Germany, that their vessel's home port was Hamburg, and that they would be sailing on Monday. Since it was Saturday, he booked a room near the Norfolk waterfront for the night. The next day, he returned to the ship to run errands such as buying bread, cheese, and beer for the sailors. The gregarious wanderer became familiar with the crew. When night fell, he slipped on board undetected and hid under the canvas covering lifeboat number nine. The next day, Captain Westphal maneuvered his ship out of its berth and Eugene was on his way to the Old World and a new life.[37]

Eugene Bullard had left home in 1906 a precocious preadolescent. By the time he reached Europe, he had undoubtedly become a man at the age of sixteen. It is also clear that by this time he was fully imbued with the American success ethic. The encouragement he had received from African Americans such as his father, Mary Woods, the Butlers, and the Hugheses, as well as the learning experiences permitted him by whites such as the Turner family, had fostered the conviction that through hard work, a willingness to take risks, and a positive attitude he could get ahead. This ethic, taught in the schools, preached from the pulpit, and made the theme of fictional works such as those of Horatio Alger, also stressed the importance of careful attention to personal finance and the necessity of maintaining savings. Throughout his life, Bullard would take great pains, through weal and woe, to find the diverse employments that would always keep him out of debt.

In this context, it is useful to recall Bullard's interest in the "Buster Brown" comic strip, which he said he enjoyed whenever he could obtain a Sunday newspaper from Atlanta. The character of Buster Brown was conceived by Richard F. Outcault, who was already well known for his "Yellow Kid" strip of the 1890s that depicted the adventures of a youngster fighting to survive in the urban slums. The Yellow Kid was a creature of mixed ethnic heritage, vaguely oriental. In "Buster Brown," by contrast, Outcault created a white, Anglo-Saxon, Protestant youth, well dressed, somewhat prankish, yet always learning positive lessons from the varied experiences depicted each week. Perhaps Buster's lessons, recited at the end of each strip, were dutiful atonements to parental authority for his pranks, and mothers may have liked the character more than their sons—

many of whom resented having to wear the faddish suit. It is all the more interesting that young Bullard bought and wore the suit as his Sunday best and evidently took the character seriously as someone on whom to model his own progressive ambitions.[38]

After five years of travel and work in Georgia, the aspiring young man had learned that, excepting a few enclaves of tolerance, there was no escaping what for him had become a tormenting perversion of the American creed: for an African American, pluck and upward social mobility would be punished as impertinence.[39] By 1912, he was prepared to leave the United States and take his chances in the lands that lay across the Atlantic Ocean.

CHAPTER THREE

Vaudevillian and Boxer in Britain and France, 1912–1914

Three days after the *Marta Russ* left Norfolk, the sixteen-year-old Bullard, his food and water supply exhausted, presented himself to the startled crew and captain. After jocularly threatening to throw him overboard, Captain Westphal sent his young ward to work below decks in the ship's boiler room. Bullard thought the *Marta Russ* "an especially big ship." Though not among the largest cargo ships of that era, the ship did in fact have considerable size. It was a two-thousand-ton freighter, 279 feet in length, 40 feet wide, and 18 feet from bottom of the hold to the deck, the distance the slender youth hauled cinders and ashes in order to throw them overboard.[1]

During the three-week voyage, Hans, the cook, helped Bullard out on occasion with this wearying task. Through his interactions with Hans and other members of the crew, Bullard developed a rudimentary knowledge of German. When the *Marta Russ* reached Aberdeen, Captain Westphal paid him five English pounds and put him ashore in a rowboat, possibly to help the stowaway avoid penalties assessed by port authorities,[2] even though in these waning years of Western Europe's belle epoque—soon to be ended by the guns of August—travel across national frontiers required no passports.

Within a day of landing, Bullard traveled by train from Aberdeen to Glasgow. At first he had difficulty with the Scottish dialect and accent: "The language the natives spoke was sort of like English" but made him feel "hard of hearing." As with other African Americans newly arrived in Europe in these years, he was aware almost immediately of the absence of racial hostility on the part of people he encountered. The people were friendly, and when they addressed him as "darky" or "Jack Johnson," he could feel certain it was without malice. He found himself ceasing to tense up before strangers, as he had in the States, in expectation of a racial taunt or rebuke. "Within twenty-four hours," he recalled, "I was born into a new world." [3]

In Glasgow, where he spent about five months, Eugene made acquaintance with young Scotsmen who helped him find cheap but clean living quarters and inexpensive but nutritious foods in the local markets. Performers in the then-popular form of street theater in Scottish towns, several of his friends made their living as organ grinders, accompanied by pet monkeys who were trained to dance. Perhaps finding it too much like begging, young Bullard refused to work with them passing the hat before bystanders and pedestrians. Instead, he says that he earned some income from gamblers for whom he kept an eye out for the approach of the "Bobbies." During his Glasgow stay, he also received some additional formal education in night classes for working adults. [4]

Sometime late in 1912, Bullard "jumped" by train from Glasgow to Liverpool. Again the gregarious young man found companions, this time in a boarding house on Great Homer Street. After joining a union, he worked as a longshoreman, carrying huge sides of frozen mutton from ship to dock. Finding this work too arduous, he quit it for lighter employment as a helper on a fish wagon. Bullard's first Christmas overseas, in Liverpool, found him feeling "full of hope and happiness." About this time, he found a job at the Birkenhead amusement park near Liverpool. Noticing an attraction in which people paid to throw soft rubber balls at a person's head stuck through a hole in a sheet of canvas, he persuaded the proprietor that his black face would bring more business than white ones. This proved to be true. Soon he was earning more money in this employment than from any earlier job—and doing so by having to work only on weekends. [5]

As it turned out, this work was Bullard's entrée into show business. Some months later, he would wield a slapstick in a vaudeville variety act,

Belle Davis's Freedman's Pickaninnies. That he enjoyed facing audiences in what today seem demeaning roles is testimony to his secure sense of self and the pleasure he found in flaunting racial stereotypes in this delightfully tolerant (for an African American at least) European setting. With his weekdays free, he began to spend time at a gymnasium for prize fighters operated by a man named Chris Baldwin, who began giving him boxing lessons. The trainee progressed swiftly, developing agility and strength as he was taught the various punches and body movements of the trade. Soon he had built up his slender frame considerably. Three years later, American journalist Will Irwin would describe Bullard as "a young black Hercules, a monument of trained muscle." [6]

Baldwin arranged a ten-round match for him at Liverpool Stadium—a fight that Bullard won on points. On the same boxing bill that evening was Aaron Lester Brown, the famed "Dixie Kid," himself an African American and one who, in escaping Jim Crow, had also left, boxing authorities agree, the welterweight championship of the world back in the States. Brown was impressed by the youngster's debut in the ring. He and his entourage of African American pugilists were returning to London, where his manager, Charlie Galvin, had arranged matches. Brown promised he would continue to develop Bullard as a fighter and "take care of him" if he came with his group to London. Eugene was delighted with the idea and, after an arrangement had been made with Baldwin, was soon off by train to the cosmopolitan capital of Great Britain's world empire.[7]

In London, the Dixie Kid became a surrogate father for Bullard. A cover photo of Brown on a French boxing magazine of January 1914 reveals an affable family man, smiling engagingly with his two infant daughters on his knees.[8] As Eugene's trainer and manager, Brown arranged fights for him through matchmakers such as Dick Burge, the owner of the Blackfriars Ring. Bullard remembers fighting in and around London every week at a number of different boxing clubs. Through Brown, he met a number of other African American fighters in London, among them the legendary Jack Johnson. Eugene also met men less well known in the States but highly publicized and admired in England and France: Frank Creigs, Sam Langford, and Bob Scanlon.[9]

Among these African American boxers and entertainers, Bullard—despite all the idiosyncrasies of his own personal odyssey and the twists of fate that led him to Britain—was part of a substantial flow of American blacks to that land and to the Continent; indeed, it was a movement that had begun well before Bullard's arrival on European shores. Frank Creigs, whose trade name Bullard accurately recalled as the "Harlem Coffee Cooler," had fought a memorable fight in the Holborn district of London as early as the mid-1890s.[10] Born in Mobile, Alabama, in 1886, Scanlon had found his way to Scotland working on a steamer in 1903, and in 1905 he was boxing in Wales (in one of his fights there, as a last minute substitute for Creigs). Langford had been boxing in London at least since 1909.[11] According to a London correspondent, whose feature story appeared in a number of U.S. newspapers, among them the *Dawson (Ga.) News* of September 16, 1908, thousands of American Negroes had entered England "in the last year or two and thousands more are coming." The first arrivals, the story continued, were "artists and athletes who realizing that they suffered in England but few of the disabilities attached to their race in the United States" had written to friends to join them. Citing figures made available by the U.S. Embassy in London, the story reported that there were "five thousand American negroes in England and four thousand had come within the past year." The same source noted that a "Negro quarter" had developed in the Soho district of London, where two restaurants "were offering fried chicken, sweet corn and other delicacies dear to the negroe's heart."[12]

Fortuitously for the African American expatriates—whether they were boxers, vaudevillians, or other music hall entertainers—the last decades of the nineteenth century in Britain had seen a considerable rise in the standard of living of the working class. In the case of boxing, promoters found that they could build larger arenas in London, such as Blackfriars and the Wonderland, as well as in provincial towns, charge a sixpence per seat, and fill them to capacity, not only for the Saturday night fights but also for those scheduled at midweek. A historian of sports has observed that boxing in turn-of-the-century England was "not only a new spectator sport, it was the first popular, country-wide, working class sport until football [soccer] penetrated the inner cities. . . . At the Ring, in Blackfriars, matinees were well attended from 1912 [onward], presumably by market porters and others who finished work early." [13]

The rise in standard of living also swelled audiences for music hall entertainments in London and throughout Great Britain. Especially appreciated there from the 1880s into the early years of this century were minstrel shows that came to England from the States, where they had been the most popular form of entertainment since the 1840s in group or solo performance. In minstrelsy, whites blackened their faces and sang what were called in the trade, by whites and blacks alike, "coon" songs, sentimental ballads such as those written by Stephen Foster, James Bland, and others. Such entertainment also included banjo and tambourine playing, soft-shoe dancing, and comic dialogue or monologue using what was purported to be Southern black dialect. As performances and stock scenes within a minstrel show began to become more individualized and specialized, vaudeville and variety acts began to evolve out of the form. In the post–Civil War period in the States, African Americans began pleasing theatergoers as much as white minstrel players. At the turn of the century, audiences in Great Britain began demanding the "real thing" as well (real African Americans in performance), although the black comedians, in the States as in England, wore cork on their faces and whitened their lips and eyes in exaggerated fashion. One of the greatest of these entertainers, Bert Williams, enjoyed with his partner, George Walker, a great success in London in 1904 with their show "In Dahomey," which earned a command performance before King Edward VII at Buckingham Palace. [14]

So great was the demand for African American entertainment that the aforementioned London correspondent, reporting on the "Negro invasion" of 1908, observed that popular performers in the seaside resort towns of England—those catering to the weekend crowds of the "middle and working classes"—were no longer the native English "buskers," the blackface music hall comedians. These people were being "driven off the sands by the American negroes." White entertainers, moreover, were having to give up their "sentimental ditties of the London music hall" and take up "the coon songs of New York City, Chicago, and the nigger melodies of the plantation days." [15] For an American watching his English counterpart make this transition, the result could be amusing. One remembers an American lyric, "down in Atlanta, Ga.," being rendered "down in Atlanta gaaaa." [16]

For the African American entertainers in minstrelsy, performing in England meant a chance to make a decent living without the feeling that haunted some of their counterparts on American stages: that they were reinforcing stereotypes used to justify the American racial caste system.[17] Furthermore, outside the English theater, black entertainers were usually treated as respectfully as they had been onstage. In those few cases where such a performer was insulted in the street, he could literally strike back, as Charles Hart, principal comedian in "Come Over Here," did. Instead of the threat of the lynch mob, Hart, who had toured in Europe as early as 1904, and his wife had the law on their side in London.[18] The election of John R. Archer, of black West Indian ancestry, in 1914 as mayor of Battersea, one of London's boroughs, suggests the relative racial liberalism that existed in the British capital in these years.[19]

Having arrived at Number 2, Coram Street in the spring of 1913, Bullard found himself in the middle of the African American expatriate enclave in the heart of London. Located not far from Soho Square, Mrs. Carter's Boarding House was in the Holborn borough, a section in which performers such as the Harts and veteran American dancer Ida Forsyne, known on London billboards as "Topsy, the Famous Negro Dancer," had resided and entertained in nearby theaters such as the Palace, the Alhambra, and others.[20] While in London, Eugene was able to make a living in two professions: modest purses from his boxing matches and income as a slapstick performer in Belle Davis's Freedman's Pickaninnies.

Davis was one of a number of American female singers and dancers who hired black youngsters, their "Picks," to dance and frolic around them during their performances. A light-skinned woman, she had broken into show business in the mid-1890s with John W. Isham's Octoroons. In 1898, she was one of the star singers in the sensational New York opening of Will Marion Cook's "Clorindy, the Origins of the Cakewalk." The leading singer with the Octoroons when they disbanded in 1904, she formed her Picks and was entertaining with them in St. Petersburg and Moscow as early as 1907. One source identifies "Belle's 'Picks'" as one of the first American vaudeville acts to go to England. Interestingly, while Bullard was in Liverpool in 1912, Davis had danced with her Cracker-jacks at the Empire Theater in Liverpool in another routine called "Southern Pastimes."[21] In the tolerant atmosphere of Edwardian London, Bullard satisfied his yearning for a place in which he could be financially independent and freely express his extroverted nature.

Winning most of his professional fights, young Bullard was a good boxer but not a great one. His engaging personality and the compelling poignancy of his youthful adventures won him, however, the comradeship in London of some of the greatest fighters of all time. One of them was Jack Johnson, who whipped a series of "white hope" challengers, making him famed not only in the sport but also in the cultural history of the early twentieth century. Before Johnson's reign as world heavyweight champion, white boxing enthusiasts and the boxing press believed that the white heavyweight champion necessarily symbolized the superior strength, courage, intelligence, and conditioning of the white man over the black. Needless to say, Johnson's victories menaced these views, as did his open defiance of America's racial etiquette calling for black deference. He taunted opponents and flouted the taboo forbidding a black man from engaging in sex with a white woman. Wearing a stars and stripes belt and pausing occasionally between blows to suggest to telegraph operators at ringside what to wire to their newspapers, Johnson scored a July 4th victory in 1910 over Jim Jeffries for the heavyweight championship of the world. Heavily promoted in terms of its racial import, the bout resulted in nationwide disturbances as blacks publicly celebrated Johnson's victory.[22]

Too good to beat in the ring, Johnson was dealt with outside it. The showing of films of his famous victory over Jim Jeffries and other lesser "white jokes," as the black press referred to them, was banned by act of Congress in 1912 after two years of agitation by pressure groups concerned ostensibly with "morality."[23] For taking trips with his white lover, Belle Schreiber, he was selectively convicted in U.S. federal court for violations of the Mann Act, a law, purportedly in opposition to prostitution rings, preventing a man from taking a woman who was not his wife over state borders in order to engage in sex. Escaping his sentence of a year and a day in prison, Johnson joined the African American "invasion" of Europe, entertaining welcoming crowds in the ring in France and in a comic monologue act on the vaudeville stage in France and England in 1913 and 1914.[24]

Bullard's other African American boxing compatriots, not as controversial as Johnson, are remembered as among the best ever in their weight classes in boxing histories, especially those published in England and France, where they did most of their fighting. After an eight-month jail sentence for striking back after receiving a blow from a white man in Philadelphia, the Dixie Kid decided to fight in Europe, not only because there was more evenhanded justice, but also because of the greater opportunity to fight white opponents in his own weight class. In the States, for example, he had to fight the African American middleweight Sam Langford and was knocked out twice by the heavier man. Fighting in his own weight class, the Dixie Kid was the acknowledged welterweight champion of the world after his victory in San Francisco over defending champion Joe Walcott in 1904. Known for his grace and his tendency to shift from languid passivity into ferocious aggression, and also known as the first fighter to grab the rope with one hand in order to attack from another position, Brown routinely beat the best welterweights in England and France.[25]

The British Boxing Board of Control was racist in those years, refusing to recognize colored fighters as British champions in any weight class even when they defeated white champions. English racial politics also led to a ruling by Home Secretary Winston Churchill that cancelled a scheduled fight of Jack Johnson.[26] In spite of these disabilities, Bullard and his fraternity of expatriate boxers found England a hospitable place to live and work—a circumstance that testifies again to the oppressive racial situation existing in the United States at that time. The BBBC's policy of "white only" champions and the anti–Jack Johnson spirit reflected elite British opinion—Anglican Church and governmental leaders concerned about the impact of a black British champion on imperial politics—rather than the broadly based prejudice that obtained in America.

British boxing historians of this era were extremely appreciative of the African American pugilists. Fred Dartnell wrote that the Dixie Kid "was the finest entertainer one could wish to see. He combined the supreme artistry of his science with a grotesque diablerie that amused. . . . The Dixie Kid is the most extraordinary fighter I have ever seen, and in some respects the greatest. . . . He was a quaint personality and in his way as big an attraction for the boxing public as Charlie Chaplin is to the cinema patrons."[27]

British observer Maurice Golesworthy celebrated the greatness of Langford, a Nova Scotian who had initially settled in Boston, and was, like Bullard, a child runaway. Langford, Golesworthy notes, was a middleweight fighter who often fought and beat the best heavyweights in the world. Although he lost to Jack Johnson after fifteen rounds in 1906, the formidable strength and exceptionally long reach of the "Boston Tarbaby" were such that Johnson would not fight him again. Golesworthy wrote that Langford, toward the end of his career, should have been considered the heavyweight champion of the world. Dartnell, who credits Langford with coining the phrase, "the bigger they are, the harder they fall," states flatly that Langford was as great a fighter as Jack Johnson.[28]

As much as he had enjoyed Scotland and England, Bullard wanted to move on to France. He had the Dixie Kid arrange bouts in Paris, and the two of them boxed there on November 28, 1913, with Langford, Scanlon, and Johnson fighting a few days later.[29] The Dixie Kid and Langford had fought in Paris in 1911; but the fighters who had the greatest impact on popularizing the sport in the French capital were two others, Sam McVey and Joe Jeanette. As heavyweights, both men had fought respectably against Jack Johnson in the States—Jeanette met Johnson eight times during 1905–6, winning twice, losing twice, and drawing four times. Unchallenged in the States by white heavyweights who after being beaten by Johnson did not want the added disgrace of a loss to another black man, McVey and Jeanette also confronted in America hysterical racial hatred for their dominance—along with Johnson and Langford—of the symbolically potent heavyweight ranks.[30]

Welcoming a more appreciative, sports-oriented scene, McVey, a Californian by birth, arrived in Paris in late 1907. At the time of his arrival, the future of the Anglo-American mode of boxing was still uncertain. *La boxe française,* a traditional form of street fighting professionalized in the early 1900s and featuring kicking as well as punching with gloveless fists, still prevailed in French arenas. In 1903, its devotees had published its unique rules and called on all French boxing societies to adopt them in hopes of preventing what they saw as the graceless and brutal English sport from crossing the Channel.[31] Paying higher than usual prices for admission, the large crowd attracted to witness McVey's defeat of Englishman Harry Shearing in Paris in February 1908, however, sounded the death knell for *la boxe française*.[32] Within a year, French promoters had organized the Société de propagation de la boxe anglaise. Quickly, they constructed in Paris a boxing hall, the Wonderland Français, modeled on the famed boxing arena of the same name in London's East End, and arranged a match between McVey and Jeanette.[33]

Now being called the "Parisian Negro," McVey, the promoters noted, had proven himself in his two years of boxing in Paris to be invincible, but Jeanette, as the most serious rival to Jack Johnson, would make a worthy opponent.[34] McVey and Jeanette fought twice in Paris in 1909. On February 20, McVey won on points in "un combat magnifique de science sans être trop violent [a match of technical excellence without being too violent]."[35] A rematch even more highly publicized than the first took place on April 17 before a standing room only crowd. According to a French boxing historian, this fight created a sensation, going 49 rounds until McVey, his left wrist broken, withdrew. An anecdote attributed to Georges Carpentier, the legendary French fighter, attests to the fact that it was this second McVey-Jeanette fight that administered the coups de grâce for the French style. As a young boxing apprentice, Carpentier recalls, he was unable to enter the sold-out arena to witness the much-ballyhooed contest. The spectacle caused him to forsake *la boxe française* for English boxing; he dedicated himself to becoming so adept in it that in the future all stadium doors would be open to him, not only as a spectator but as a fighter himself.[36] With the future of English boxing secure, promoters of the Paris Wonderland began holding fights every Saturday and promising appearances by "the best American, English, and French boxers."[37] Other fight entrepreneurs quickly followed suit in the French capital.

When Bullard took the boat-train from London to Paris in November 1913, he arrived in a city that, according to its boxing press, prided itself on "increasingly attracting the most reputed boxers in the world," among whom were the Dixie Kid, Scanlon, Langford, Johnson, and Jeanette.[38] As noted above, because he had not yet built a reputation, Bullard's twenty-round decision victory over Georges Forrestal at the Elysées Montmartre was not covered in *La Boxe* as were the fights of Brown, Scanlon, Langford, and Blink McCluskey, a white American heavyweight.[39] For Eugene, it was less his match than his first glimpses of Paris that struck him. He walked all around the city, wild with excitement over its beautiful sweeping vistas of boulevards, parks, and architectural landmarks.[40]

When the Brown entourage had returned to London, Bullard asked the Dixie Kid to arrange more matches in the French capital. Brown informed him that he had scheduled a number of bouts for the next several months in London. Eugene felt that he "could never be happy for the rest of my life unless I could live in France." He got Brown's approval at this time, probably in December 1913, to let him tour on the Continent with the Freedman's Pickaninnies. Eugene and the group performed as far east as Moscow, appearing at the Winter Garden Theater in Berlin and at the Bal Taburin in Montmartre. Bullard decided to make this tour because he knew it would bring him to Paris. "When the troupe left Paris you may be sure I did not leave with them."[41]

Establishing himself in Paris, he earned income from prize fighting and by sparring with other fighters. Because he had no difficulty picking up languages and had learned a good deal of French and some German, he was also paid by other fighters to be an interpreter.[42] In leaving the Dixie Kid, he had, in effect, left another father, one whose generosity and kindness he would never forget.[43] In Paris, he resumed his comradeship with Langford, Scanlon, and Jack Johnson. Johnson, whose title as world champion was taken away from him in the United States and Britain, gained recognition by the French Boxing Federation in May 1914.[44] Bullard's boxing fraternity also included white American fighters such as McCluskey. Indeed, he fell in love with Paris not only because of its beauty and the friendliness of its inhabitants but also because "it seemed to me that French democracy influenced the minds of both black and white Americans there and helped us all act like brothers as near as possible."[45]

Bullard believed that from a tender age his father had told him that in

France he would find a place where all people were treated respectfully and equally regardless of skin color. He later considered his travels in the southeastern United States, as well as through Scotland, England, and on the Continent, as stages through which he passed in reaching this promised land. Recalling his brief stay in November 1913 and his return to Paris in 1914, he wrote as if his great quest had been realized.[46]

What is more likely, however, is that Bullard's incredible journey from Rose Hill in Columbus, Georgia, to Paris resulted from the restless wanderings of a youth in search of freedom. When the Stanley gypsies promised to take him to England,[47] he made the momentous decision to leave the United States entirely, rather than leave the South for the cities of the Northeast and Midwest as tens of thousands of his fellow African Americans were doing in these years. If his had been a mission to France, it is doubtful that it would have taken him so long to reach his destination; after landing in Scotland in the spring of 1912, he spent some sixteen months in Britain before seeing Paris.

In reality, he had been wandering alone, without knowing where he was going. His aimless wanderlust ended in Liverpool. In 1959, Bullard confided to interviewer Anthony Shannon that when he stowed away, "I wasn't quite sure where that boat was heading but it was going to a place I had never seen before and that was good enough for me."[48] In England, he found himself in the company of other African American boxers and entertainers who had been making a livelihood for a number of years in London and Paris. Paris had been welcoming black Americans of all walks of life from early in the nineteenth century. Bullard immediately enjoyed the warmth of this welcome in the cheerfully inflected musical greetings, "Bonjour, Eugène," "Bonjour, mon petit," that he heard on the streets of Paris.[49] Even more than in London, Paris allowed his African American and white American friends to behave normally and generously toward each other without the contorted poses they were forced to strike at home in deference to social conventions to which most whites remained deeply committed. In Paris, a place he had reached haphazardly, Bullard found a city in which he could get ahead and be admired for it. He would want to live there the rest of his life.

CHAPTER FOUR

A Hero in the Great War, 1914–1919

It is easy to see why Bullard would come to regard France in general and Paris in particular as the promised land. Among a people seemingly indifferent to racial or ethnic difference,[1] he could participate fully in the delights of *la vie Parisienne*—shopping in its bustling street markets, enjoying the sociability of its sidewalk cafés, relaxing in the peaceful splendor of its spacious parks, sitting in any seat in its many theaters, enjoying its famed art galleries and museums. James Weldon Johnson, the great American composer and intellectual, recalling his first visit to France in 1905, gave classic expression to similar sentiments recorded by so many African American visitors and residents newly arrived in that country:

> From the day I set foot in France, I became aware of the working of a miracle within me. I became aware of a quick readjustment to life and to environment. I recaptured for the first time since childhood the sense of being just a human being. I need not try to analyze this change for my colored readers; they will understand in a flash what took place. For my white readers . . . I am afraid that any analysis will be inadequate, perhaps futile . . . I was suddenly free; free from a sense of impending discomfort, insecurity, danger; free from the conflict within the Man-Negro dualism and the innumerable maneuvers in thought and behavior that it compels; free from the problem of the many obvious or subtle adjustments to a multitude of

bans and taboos; free from special scorn, special tolerance, special conde-
scension, special commiseration; free to be merely a man.[2]

Bullard's halcyon first months in this paradise suddenly ended when in
August, diplomacy having failed to resolve the crisis attending the assassination of Archduke Francis Ferdinand of Austria-Hungary, the major
nation states of Europe went to war, dragging their colonial peoples
around the world into the conflagration. Germany quickly conquered Belgium and invaded France. By September 5, 1914, elements of the German
army were in sight of Paris.

Responding to the desperate appeals of the French government for all
able men, French citizen and foreigner alike, to come to the assistance of
France, Bullard enlisted at the recruiting post in the boulevard des Invali-
des on October 9, 1914, his nineteenth birthday.[3] Accepted quickly into
the French Foreign Legion, he thus entered into a highly recorded history—the military history of the Great War. For the first eighteen months
of his participation in the war, Bullard experienced to the fullest the suf-
ferings of the foot soldier in French service. The setting for his and his
comrades' valor was along the Western Front, which, after a French coun-
terattack in the Battle of the Marne had taken the pressure off of Paris,
had stabilized by November 1914. With small variations, the front would
run for over three years from a point just east of Dunkirk on the English
Channel to lower Alsace-Lorraine. To the west of the front, French and
English soldiers with their colonials and foreign volunteers like Bullard
opposed the Germans and their allied troops ranged on the east.

All these combatants quickly came to know life in the trenches dug
for protection against artillery and machine gun fire. They would know
the often futile infantry charges across the no man's land between the
trenches—a terrain in which the soldier confronted not only shell and
shot but also land mines, poisonous gas, and barbed wire. In addition to
these novel terrors, the infantryman of the First World War had to endure
bombings and strafing from aircraft. Seemingly oblivious to the over-
whelming advantages held by a defensive force against one attacking
across no man's land, generals on both sides, desperate to pierce enemy
lines and break the stalemate, repeatedly called for infantry sweeps along

various sectors of the front. During several days of such offensives tens of thousands of men died; in the course of several months hundreds of thousands perished; and before the war ended, millions of men were dead on the Western Front alone.

By April 1915, the French Foreign Legion had enlisted over 32,000 volunteers of many nationalities, including six hundred white Americans and perhaps a dozen African Americans, one of them Bullard's boxing mate Bob Scanlon.[4] Well-conditioned as an athlete and further hardened by three months of rigorous training at the Tourelles Barracks on Gambetta Avenue in Paris, Bullard was as physically fit as any man for the ordeal that lay ahead. In the spring of 1915, he fought as a machine gunner in many engagements along the Somme at Frise, Dampierre, Harquest-en-Santerre, and Notre Dame de Lorette. After these battles, the loss of men was so great that it was necessary to consolidate three Legion regiments into one.

Bullard fought in the company of other *pauvres poilus,* the term the French citizenry bestowed on their heroic but lowly foot soldiers, infested with lice, too exhausted to shave, living, fighting, and dying in mud. Eugene braved lonely hours at night crawling into no man's land trying to avoid exposure by enemy flares while bringing back a dead comrade. Night work between the trenches also entailed the cutting of wire in preparation for an assault at dawn. He partook of the drink of better than 100 proof alcohol, "tafia," dispensed to the troops before being ordered over the top of their trenches toward the enemy's position. Sipping *un gout de rendre fou* [a drop of drive-crazy], as French officers called it, "made us more like madmen than soldiers."[5] On such assaults, Bullard saw many of his comrades grievously wounded or slain, sometimes cut in two by exploding artillery shells. He avenged them by cutting down many an enemy combatant with his machine gun as well as during *charges à la baionette* during hand-to-hand combats near the trenches.

Fighting in the Battle of Champagne at Ferme des Vacques, Vouzier, and Ferme de Navarin in late September 1915, Bullard and his fellow Legionnaires did succeed in pushing the Germans back several kilometers.[6] At Ferme de Navarin, he sustained his first hit under fire, "a little head wound," but "like all Legionnaires, if you could function you fought on." His ability to communicate in German became useful at this time in interrogating captured soldiers. When a German colonel refused to be questioned by a noncommissioned officer, Eugene took his helmet, ornate with its green cloth cover and gold-plated eagle, as a war trophy. French officers later good-naturedly ordered him to surrender his prize.[7]

A month before the French offensive in the Champagne, Bullard's father, now living on 6th Avenue in downtown Columbus (which William referred to as the "South Side") and ever anxious about his peripatetic son, had handwritten the U.S. Department of State this touching note: "To the Secretary of State. I has a boy in the war. He was there in Paris. When he enroll in war he was under age. He must have made a mistake when he enlist. He won't be 20 years old till Oct the 9 1915 and he enlisted Oct the 20, 1914." The distraught William, who identified himself as living at No. 812 6th Avenue in Columbus, Georgia, implored the authorities to "please have" Eugene "loose and sent home to his father. Please have him freed at once and sent home to his little sister." [8]

Even though Eugene had not communicated with his father since leaving home,[9] William somehow learned his son's military address in the Foreign Legion and forwarded it to the State Department. Acknowledging the note, an assistant at the Department replied but, as often happens, sent his message mistakenly to Columbus, Ohio.[10] Undaunted, William sought the assistance of a Columbus cotton commission merchant, Lucius Flowers Humber, who although not William's employer, was nonetheless well acquainted with him as well as with William's father. Their acquaintanceship derived from their common upbringing in Stewart County, for like W. C. Bradley, William's former boss, Humber had grown up there in the 22nd District, inheriting a large plantation that he sold to the Bradley family. Like Bradley, he moved to Columbus in the middle 1880s to copartner a cotton merchant company. On the banks of the Chattahoochee River near the steamboat wharf, his warehouse was adjacent to Bradley's on Front Avenue.[11]

Humber had local Columbus attorney W. H. McCrory type a letter undersigned by William in which he pleaded that the State Department "use all honorable means to get my son discharged from the French Army."

Enclosed was a document certifying Eugene's correct birth date, October 9, 1895, which had been recorded in the family Bible, and a photograph of Eugene. No less a personage than Robert Lansing, the U.S. secretary of state, forwarded William's request and documentation to William Sharp, the American ambassador in Paris.[12] If the Embassy did look into the matter, they would have found that even at age nineteen Eugene's enlistment into the Foreign Legion violated no French statute. And, evidently, the American government was no more inclined to take action on the grounds that he had violated American neutrality than in the cases of the hundreds of other American citizens who had volunteered to fight for France.

Perhaps William Bullard took some comfort in recalling that Eugene was his "lucky seventh" child. The young soldier continued to need every bit of that good fortune. Tens of thousands of Legionnaires had been killed or wounded in the offensives of 1915. After the fighting in the Champagne, survivors among under-strength Legion units were transferred to regular French army units. Paul Rockwell, an American invalided out of the Legion in 1915, noted that among the American Legionnaires now joining the 170th Infantry Regiment of the Moroccan Division was "a coal-black Negro, ex-boxer and musician, who gave his address as Columbus, Georgia, but was said to be of West Indian origin."[13] The ferocity of the soldiers of the 170th, according to Bullard, had led the Germans to refer to them as the swallows of death—which the French troops translated as *les hirondelles de la mort.*[14]

In the Foreign Legion, Eugene had survived murderous fighting. With the 170th in the opening phases of the Battle of Verdun in late February and early March 1916, he participated in combat that was inconceivably horrific in its butchery. In late 1915, the German high command began planning a campaign aimed at capturing the old fortress city of Verdun. The city was defended by French forces dug in around small villages and forts just to the north and east of the city. Their defenses had created a salient bulging out into the Western Front. Aware of the vulnerability of the forces in this sector, the German military planners saw an opportunity to capture the historic town, deal a mortal blow to French morale, and enable them to force a surrender of the French government. In preparing their attack in late 1915 and early 1916, they began stockpiling hundreds of artillery pieces—including the huge "Big Bertha" siege guns. Behind the artillery, they massed elite infantry units on the high terrain overlooking Verdun just east of the town. Responding to this buildup, the French strengthened their forces, sharing their view of the importance of the impending battle and determined to avoid a second humiliating defeat in less than a half-century by the hated *Boches*—an enemy now all the more despised for its ravaging of *la belle France* in territory taken in the invasion of August 1914.[15]

Bullard and the 170th Infantry were among the forces sent to the Verdun front in February 1916. Trucked toward Verdun, a rare luxury for the *poilus,* he and his comrades "didn't know if were we heading for heaven or hell." The congestion on the road caused by other troops and horse-drawn artillery compelled his unit to undertake a forced march for three days and nights into the battle zone. Hearing continuous artillery bombardment and seeing evidence of its destruction, they arrived at the ruins of what had been the village of Fleury on February 21. Bullard now knew "we were in hell for sure." [16]

"To bleed white" the French army—a phrase used since to convey the impact of the war on European civilization itself—such was the graphic description first used by German commander Erich von Falkenhayn to convey what he hoped to achieve at Verdun.[17] On a front a little more than six miles across, the Germans fired between two and two and a half million artillery shells on French forces in the twelve hours preceding a massive infantry assault. Among the troops on the outer perimeter of the defensive lines, Bullard and his fellow combatants were ordered by the French command to die rather than retreat. He survived this day and two nightmarish weeks more like it—a period in which "the whole front seemed to be moving like a saw backwards and forwards"; in which "thousand upon thousands died . . . [as] earth was plowed under, men and beasts [hung] from the branches of trees where they had been blown to pieces." [18]

Enduring days and nights with virtually no sleep, the survivors among the French fought on. Sustained by tafia and adrenaline, a feverish Bullard machine-gunned scores of Germans advancing through smoke and fog.

Once his machine gun jammed and he had to kill a German soldier who had slid into his shell crater, shooting him with his short-barreled carbine, a weapon issued to machine gun crews in the event they were overrun. On March 2, hiding in what was left of a farmhouse, he lost all but four of his teeth by a piece of exploded shell that killed four of his comrades, including his *tireur,* his partner in handling the machine gun. On March 5, in the ruins of Fleury, a setting resembling "a Chicago slaughter house," another incoming shell, screaming in his ear "Gene—eene—eene" blew him into a dugout and opened a hole in his thigh. This last wound, occurring as he exposed himself to enemy fire in carrying a message from one French officer to another, would lead to his award of the Croix de Guerre. The next day, he was picked up by the Red Cross and carried by a Ford ambulance out of the battle area. As was the case with Bob Scanlon—also transferred to the 170th and wounded at Verdun at this time—his ground war was over.[19]

In several months of fighting in the Verdun salient, an estimated three hundred thousand combatants were killed.[20] Bullard observed that among the dead, the lucky ones were those whose remains could be identified.[21] The thousands who were not are today commemorated at Verdun by a museum housing their bones and by white crosses dotting the landscape as far as the eye can see. Other reminders on the now-pastoral landscape of the horror that was Verdun are the historical markers noting that villages such as Vaux and Fleury, existing at that location, had disappeared in February 1916 along with the seemingly impregnable Fort Douaumont. The effort of the Germans did not bring about the capture of the prized city. Military historian S. L. A. Marshall has observed that the German military planners made a major conceptual error in thinking that an unprecedented massing of artillery fire could destroy an opposing force. "A man," he writes, "is but a tiny spot on a vast terrain."[22] Many such men like Bullard survived the barrage and used the resulting shell craters as fortresses to inflict terrible casualties on their swarming attackers.

By June 1916, the French military felt confident enough to vow to their countrymen that Verdun would not fall. An officer's pledge, *ils ne passeront pas* [they shall not pass], became a rallying cry for French patriots. Though bloody fighting would continue in the Verdun sector until November 1916, the French did hold, and their commander there, Marshal Henri-Phillipe Pétain, became a national hero. The survivors of the battle, *les pauvres poilus,* especially those wounded there, would acquire a kind of sanctification in the eyes of the French people.[23]

On the evening of March 7 at Bar-le-duc, a supply and evacuation point on what the French called the *voie sacrée* [sacred route] to the Verdun front, Bullard was placed on a Red Cross train with many other wounded. After a night of travel, the sounds of the artillery finally faded away. For three days the train moved south through verdant fields and forests unsavaged by the shell fire which had turned Verdun and other sectors of the front into a landscape of broken rock. En route, the train made frequent stops at villages in order to redress wounds of the living and remove the bodies of the dead. At each stop, women and children yelled "vivent nos poilus [hail to our soldiers]" and gave candies, cigarettes, and flowers to those able to receive them.[24]

At Lyon, the train's destination, Bullard was taken from the Gare des Brotteaux, the biggest station he had seen outside of Paris, to the hospital, the Hôtel Dieu.[25] In this mid-eighteenth-century neoclassical edifice on the Rhône[26] he would lay bedridden for three months in a spacious ward. As his thigh wound healed, doctors suppressed associated infections and performed extensive dental surgery to replace his lost teeth.

When he was no longer in need of close supervision but still required time to fully convalesce and undertake physical therapy, he was removed from the Hôtel Dieu to a privately owned care center. A Madame Nesmes, a member of a family of wealthy fabric makers in Lyon's silk industry, had rented rooms in a clinic for deaf and dumb children. Bullard was one of thirty-two recovering soldiers whose room and board were provided through her charity. The distance from the clinic to the Nesmes' fashionable home in the Croix Rousse section of Lyon was less than a mile.[27] Aided by crutches, the young man strengthened his leg by walking to their home, where, as with Mary Woods, the Turners, the Butlers, and the Smiths, he was treated like family.

It was during his convalescence in Lyon that he became the subject of reportage by American war correspondent Will Irwin, writing for *The Saturday Evening Post.* Irwin knew the American consul in Lyon, a white

Southerner, and had heard him telling about his surprise encounter with Bullard in the ward in the Hôtel Dieu. Later, after the soldier had become ambulatory, Irwin had sat in on conversations in the consul's office in which all three men discussed the war and the young black Georgian's experiences in it. The piece offers a rare contemporary glimpse of "Private Eugene so and so" (Irwin, evidently following French security procedures, does not use his last name) after two years of living, very perilously, in France. A Californian and a political progressive, Irwin rendered the initial exchange between Bullard and the consul, who had just awoken him in his hospital bed, in these terms:

> "Who dah?" exploded a voice from beneath the blankets. Off came the cover, revealing a comely black head and a row of teeth like new gravestones.
>
> "Why you ornery, no-account black hound!" exploded the consul affectionately. "What the blazes are you doing here?"
>
> "Fo' the lawd's sake, mars!" said the wounded American with pride and gratitude. "You'se from the souf, ain't you?"

Allowing for the distortion inherent in a white man's stock depiction of the Negro dialect as well as the inaccuracies in a secondhand account, Irwin's characterization of Bullard should not be rejected out of hand as simply a reflection of the reporter's genteel racism, his imposition of a white stereotype of Negro servility on a man who was anything but servile. Irwin recognized that Bullard wasn't at all the Negro they knew at home. War and heroism had given him that air of authority common to all soldiers of the line. He looked you in the eye and answered you straight with replies that carried the conviction of truth.[28]

Young Bullard had no qualms about offering his "black head" as a carnival target at Birkenhead or becoming a performer in Belle's Picks, an entertainment in which servile comedy and dialect were part of the act. He had earned his sense of self-respect years before in Dawson and Atlanta. On seeing and hearing the consul, he flashed back warmly to Zach, Doug, and "Ange" Turner, bosses he had defied and forced to respect him; individuals, moreover, who had not been able to "keep him down on the farm" even before he had "seen Paree." A man soon to be awarded the Croix de Guerre for bravery under fire, a circumstance that Irwin notes in his piece, could without any loss of face good-naturedly refer to a Southern white authority figure in France as "mars" or "boss," as when in ending the sketch, Irwin has him sum up Verdun: "'you wouldn't a'believed it, boss, if you'd seen it in a cinema show!'"[29]

Irwin noted Bullard's growing command of the French language and remarked how in retelling the horrors of Verdun, he would often suddenly shift from English into French, which he spoke very rapidly. But Irwin erred in attributing his gift for language to "his race [which] they say has a talent for spoken languages."[30] Language acquisition comes most readily to individuals who are confident, extroverted, and eager for new experiences. Bullard had these qualities in abundance.

Irwin's reporting of Bullard's attitude toward his own killing of German soldiers, including the one who had fallen into the shell crater with him at Verdun, is interesting because it bears out feelings Bullard would retain throughout his life[31]—that he had been sickened by what he had to do to save himself and his comrades:

> When you stopped to cool [the machine gun] and the other gun picked up the *feu* [fire], you could see 'em wriggling like worms in the bait box.
> Yassir, I was sick, awful sick! Every time the sargent [sic] yelled "feu!" I got sicker and sicker. They had wives and children hadn't they?[32]

In the late spring of 1916, Bullard learned that he would be decorated with the Croix de Guerre for his heroism at Verdun. Before the decorating ceremony, Lyon newspapers printed the names of those to be honored, and many people congratulated him in the clinic and on the streets of Lyon with shouts of "Bravo Bullard" and "Vive le cent soixante-dixieme!" His award of the Croix de Guerre with bronze star is listed in the June 27, 1916, edition of the *Lyon républicain* in a column next to one carrying the latest news of the continuing battle at Verdun, still raging in the vicinity of what had been Fleury. The ceremony occurred on June 22 in the Cours du Midi,[33] a location whose name would be changed to Cours de Verdun later in the year.[34]

At this point in the war, Lyon was charged with an emotional patriotism. The city's parks had become *jardins potagers-militaires* [victory gardens]. Women's organizations arranged entertainments for the wounded.

Young women, "Mariannes," were asked every day in the local newspapers to volunteer as personal correspondents to the *poilus* whose names
and military addresses at the front were given in the appeals.[35] On Bastille
Day (July 14), 1916, an immense crowd gathered in Lyon's Place Bellecour. The assemblage heard speeches and observed medal-awarding ceremonies and a long military parade that included French colonial troops,
wildly acclaimed, passing in review. Countless others witnessed the proceedings from all the windows of the spacious four-story buildings front-
ing the square. Speaking from a podium erected beneath the equestrian
statue of Louis XIV, politicians pledged themselves to maintain a sacred
unity in France's moment of crisis.[36]

As *Le Nouvelliste de Lyon* reported the following day, the parade had
brought forth "the soul of trembling patriotism," expressed in "the enthusiasm of the crowd . . . acclaiming both the combatants of yesterday and
those of tomorrow . . . brothers in arms of those who fight on heroically
at Verdun and on the Somme."[37] The *Lyon passe-partout* compared the
sacrifices of the soldiers decorated that day to those of the medieval cru-
saders.[38] Among those watching the ceremonies and parade from the front
rows of spectators were the "dear wounded," the *Républicain* reported,
men whose "bright multicolored dress uniforms contrasted with the brilliant whites of the nurses" attending them. Bullard sat proudly among
them. He could not have missed a "squadron of planes of the second
group of aviation which, pulled by their tractors, ended the procession in
superb fashion."[39]

Bullard's stay in Lyon lasted six months, three at the Hôtel Dieu and three
at the clinic provided by Madame Nesme in the company of her family
and the other *poilus* "adopted" by her. Among the many visitors and
French military officers sharing the Nesmes' hospitality was an air service
officer named Ferrolino, commandant of the airfield at Brun, five miles
from Lyon.[40] One evening, Ferrolino asked Bullard what he planned to
do after leaving the care of his doctors in Lyon. Now able to walk with
a cane, Eugene had recuperated from his leg wound far better than expected. However, it was clear that he was too handicapped to consider, or
be considered for, a return to the trenches. He did not want to wait out

the end of the war in Paris, forced to live off his meager military pay and perhaps appear as a slacker or an *embusqué,* a military man clinging to the safety of a desk job well away from the fighting front. He replied that he desired to be an aircraft gunner, a position in which he could utilize his experience as a machine gunner. Ferrolino promised that when the opportunity arose, he would ask to have him transferred to aviation. Bullard may already have been looking upon the aviation gunnery job as simply a step toward training as a pilot; Ferrolino's promise overwhelmed him with joy and excitement at the prospect of becoming the first Negro military pilot.[41]

Even before leaving the supervision of doctors in Lyon, Bullard had received permission to take leaves to Paris, staying with friends in the beleaguered French capital. After departing Lyon permanently he lived in Paris until early October 1916, when he began training as an aviation machine gunner at the military air station at Caz-au-lac. While awaiting the call to service, he fell in with a triumvirate of Parisian comrades: Gilbert White, an expatriate American painter; Moïse Kisling, a Polish expatriate painter; and Jeff Dickson, a young American from Natchez, Mississippi, who had ambitions of becoming a boxing promoter in Paris. Bullard had met Kisling in the Foreign Legion.[42] After surviving severe chest wounds at the battle of Carrency in May 1915, Kisling had returned to his spacious studio apartment at 3, rue Joseph Bara, a dwelling just west of the Luxembourg Gardens.[43] Kisling often welcomed friends such as Eugene to his home when they needed a place to stay. They would sleep in his studio loft overlooking the treetops of the Gardens.[44]

In his late thirties, White was considerably older than the others in this circle. He had come to Paris early in the century, studying art under James Whistler, and had exhibited his paintings since 1903 in the annual exposition of the Salon des artistes français.[45] The ruggedly handsome Jeff Dickson, whose buoyant, irrepressible personality was likened by a French friend to the spirit of a person of Provence in southern France, had only recently arrived in Paris. Like his fellow Southerner, Eugene, he fell in love with the city. Later he would serve as a noncommissioned officer in France with the American army and at war's end would realize his goal of becoming a successful boxing promoter and an owner of Paris's famed

Vélodrome d'Hiver as well, a venue for circuses and other spectacles. In the 1930s Dickson would bring to the "Vél' D'Hiv" attractions such as ice hockey and skating competitions starring Sonja Henie, with whom he had a brief romance. Returning to his home in Natchez, Mississippi, Dickson would join the U.S. Army Air Corps, train as a bomber pilot, and be shot down and killed in 1943 fighting to free his beloved France from another German occupation.[46]

During the Great War, the most famous of these three men was Bullard's "dear friend" Kisling. Known in Paris for his portraits even before the war, he is a key figure in Parisian cultural history. In establishing his studio at 3, rue Joseph Bara in 1912, Kisling helped spark the movement of avant-garde artistic and literary circles from Montmartre, where they had been located before the war, to Montparnasse, the Parisian Left Bank. Kisling was the best friend of the celebrated Amedeo Modigliani and counted among other close companions Pablo Picasso, Georges Braque, and many others of the postimpressionist Paris School.[47] Becoming prosperous through the sale of his portraits long before other painters of his generation, Kisling was well known for his generosity, not only to soldier friends such as Bullard but also to his fellow artists.[48] (Kisling was also the beneficiary of an inheritance gift of five thousand dollars from Victor Chapman, a mutual friend of his and Eugene's in the Foreign Legion and the first American aviator to die for France.[49]) As always, Bullard's joie de vivre and remarkable past captivated these buoyant spirits and kept him in interesting company.

In the fall of 1916, White, Kisling, and Dickson figured in a memorable episode of Bullard's war years. At that time, the many café terraces of Montparnasse were gathering places for artists and writers, many of them soldiers who, enjoying a break from the "stench of death not more than fifty miles away," luxuriated in an ambience of careless bravado.[50] Bullard and his three friends were drinking at one of these places, probably La Rotonde, where Kisling was a habitué and occasional bouncer during the war years.[51] The cocksure white Southerner, Dickson, asked the ebullient black Southerner about his plans now that he had been knocked out of the infantry. Bullard answered that he was going into French aviation, to which Dickson retorted, "You know there aren't any Negroes in aviation." Bullard shot back, "Sure I do. That's why I want to get into it." As the Mississippian continued to belittle the idea, Kisling rallied behind Eugene, arguing that he knew his character better than Dickson did and insisted that he would make good as a pilot: Eugene interjected that he was in France after all, not Mississippi. Dickson said he would wager two thousand dollars that Bullard would not become a pilot. Dickson then left the café.[52]

Saying that if Kisling believed Bullard could fly, so did he, White then proposed to loan Eugene the sum needed to call the challenge. White arranged a meeting of the four the next day at which Bullard deliberately provoked Dickson by pretending to doubt that he actually possessed the sum he was willing to bet. Dickson produced the money and Bullard, thanks to White and Kisling, coolly covered it.[53] In early May 1917, the successful young aviator, his oversized wings in full display on his uniform shoulder, accompanied his two artist friends to Henri's Bar in Paris, where they were to meet Dickson. After recovering from his shock at seeing the wings, Dickson paid off, saying good-naturedly that while "he didn't like to lose that kind of money to anyone," he "was glad that the first Negro military pilot came from Dixie."[54]

Bullard's progress through the French aviation schools to the status of pilot had taken a little more than seven months. Commandant Ferrolino had contacted Colonel Girod, inspector general of the French schools of aviation since 1915.[55] Girod sent Eugene a telegram ordering Corporal Eugene Jacques Bullard transferred to aviation as a machine gunner, with orders to report to training school at Caz-au-lac on October 6, 1916.[56]

At Caz-au-lac, located near the city of Bordeaux in southwestern France, Bullard became reacquainted with Edmund Genet, a descendant of "Citizen Genet," Revolutionary France's first minister to the United States. Eugene had known him in the Foreign Legion, where, with a number of other white American Legionnaires, Genet had also secured a transfer into the French air service. Genet would become a close friend in later months.[57] That he may not have been when Bullard arrived at the air station is indicated by Genet's last comment in his diary entry of October 5, 1916: "Bullard the American niger [sic] came here today to learn *mitrailleuse* [aviation machine gunning]."[58] It was from Genet that Bullard learned about the existence of the Lafayette Escadrille, a squadron of American pilots flying fighter planes in combat under French command. These men, he was informed, were being paid a sizeable sum per month out of a fund created by wealthy Americans living in Paris. Bullard now "knew damn well that he wanted to be a pilot rather than an aviation gunner." Accompanied by Genet, the young African American approached the commanding French officer at Caz-au-lac to file a request to change his status from student gunner to student pilot. Approval came from Colonel Girod, and on November 15, he was ordered to report to the aviation school at Tours in France's Loire Valley.[59]

In his 1917 book *Flying for France: With the American Escadrille at Verdun,* James McConnell depicts vividly and in some detail the training schedule he had completed about a year before Bullard underwent similar instruction. McConnell stresses how difficult the training was for the initiate learning to fly the *avion de chasse,* the fighter plane. To control these small, swift craft on the ground as well as in the air, students had to possess great dexterity of hand and foot. Moreover, fighter planes, unlike larger ones used for reconnaissance or bombing, were one-seaters, and the trainee had to have the courage to take off alone on his first flight. There was a great deal of weeding out among fighter pilots because "a man's aptitude for the work shows up, and unless he is by nature especially well fitted he is transferred to the division which teaches one to fly the larger and safer [and co-piloted] machines."[60] Some fifty-six Americans and an untold number of French student pilots failed to meet the demanding requirements and never served at the front.[61]

Bullard undertook his training through the late fall, winter, and spring of 1916–17. He would have begun in a "Penguin" or "roller," a low-powered, wingless Blériot machine in which the student learned the foot movements necessary to maintain a straight line on the ground. "The slightest mistake or delayed movement," would, McConnell observed, "send the machine skidding off to the right or left, and sometimes, if the motor is not stopped in time, over on its side or back." A successful student passed on to faster "Penquins," acquiring as he did deft control by foot of the rudder—movements that in the air had to be "so gentle . . . that they must come instinctively." The student pilot's first flights, breathtaking though they were for all, were never more than three feet off the ground and always in a straight line. When this phase was mastered, the apprentice was taught how to adjust to wind conditions and how to land properly, and allowed higher flights. Next came instructions on how to make turning movements of progressively greater precision. The student then had to fly at altitudes of two thousand feet, cut his engine, and land his craft on or near a designated spot on the airfield. When able to navigate with the aid of roller maps at seven thousand feet from one field to another an hour or so distant, the learner became a brevetted pilot-aviator, earning the right to wear "two little gold-woven wings on his collar and a winged propeller emblem on his arm." [62]

Ted Parsons was also trained to fly by the French in the months just preceding the pioneering African American's instruction. Like McConnell, Parsons emphasizes the skill and courage involved in mastering the Blériot and Caudron G-3 biplane on which both he and Bullard learned to fly: "After the Blériot and the Caudron G-3, nothing with wings could ever cause any misgivings in my heart. When a buzzard tamed those two ships, if he was still alive and not a nervous wreck, he could fly anything." [63]

During leaves from this rigorous flight training in the abnormally cold winter of 1916–17, Bullard continued to fraternize with Kisling, White, and Dickson in Paris. He also developed a comradeship with Jean Navarre, another dynamic personality who found in Eugene's adventurous risk-taking a kindred spirit. A sports enthusiast who counted many athletes among his close companions, Navarre had seen Bullard box at the Elysées Montmartre before the war. [64] Both men were nineteen when they enlisted. Navarre had scored his first "kill," the third for France overall, in April 1915. [65] By many accounts, he was among the most gifted, if not the most gifted, of the French pilots. *Un enfant terrible de la chasse,* he was also notorious for his reckless abandon in the air, his willingness to undertake maneuvers that placed his body and his machine under terrific stress. [66] Not surprisingly, he was frequently reprimanded and grounded for flying too many daily missions or failing to report them properly. In 1915, a much-told story has it, an enraged Navarre, infuriated at what he took to be a German dirigible bomber heading toward Paris, forced his aircraft into a long and dangerously steep ascent to intercept it. In his haste, he had forgotten to arm his aircraft. To the consternation of his spotter, he was preparing in a blind rage to bring the craft down with a butcher's knife before both men discovered that their target was a cigar-shaped cloud and collapsed in laughter.[67]

Navarre became a French national hero in the skies over Verdun at the beginning of the terrible combat Bullard had known from the ground. Among their other advantages at the outset of that battle, the Germans also controlled the air. Their means for doing so was their Fokker fighter plane which, first among fighters of any belligerent, was outfitted with a machine gun mounted just ahead of the cockpit and capable of firing by synchronization through the craft's propeller. With his machine gun automatically aligned along the line of flight, the German pilot could fire with deadly accuracy at his adversary for whom flying and firing were two separate actions. Although the French and the English would soon give their pilots a similar capability, when Navarre took to the skies over Verdun, he had no such advantage. He did not need it. Such was his virtuosity in climbing, diving, looping, and corkscrewing his plane that he quickly nullified the German technological advantage. As much as his kills, simply his flying prowess intimidated German pilots, negated their brief advantage, and earned him the sobriquet "The Sentinel of Verdun."[68]

Navarre had twelve kills by June 1916, when despite being shot through the body he was able to land safely at his home base. Except for a few weeks before the armistice, he would not fly in combat again.[69] Such was the man—although out of action a legendary figure for France—Bullard joined on occasion in Paris on leaves from his flight training at Tours. Once, he accompanied Navarre to a drinking spot, Chez le Père Lebas, on the rue Caumartin just off the Grands Boulevards. Here, in very close quarters, entertainers, military celebrities, their entourages, and the general public mingled nightly. It was always so packed that people used the toilet seats as bar stools until someone needed them for their intended purpose. The unusually cold weather and the weariness of a city still within shell shot of the front made the little bar a compelling place for those seeking intimacy and a respite from the terrors of combat.[70]

On his first visit with Navarre, the patrons, as they always did for war heroes, opened a passage to the bar, greeting the individual with patriotic shouts. Exposed in Navarre's wake, Eugene suddenly heard "Père" Lebas himself yell at Navarre, "Where did you get that? And what is it? Whatever it is, put it in the toilet and don't forget to pull the chain." Wild with rage at the obscene racial insult, the former boxer attempted to strike down his tormentor. Restrained by Navarre and others, he collected himself when told laughingly that they had set him up, that "le Père" initiated everyone to his establishment. Navarre convinced him that he never would have brought him there if any real insult had been intended. Bullard quickly laughed it off and returned on other occasions with "The Sentinel." "Being Navarre's companion and knocking around with him, whenever we met, was a real treat for me." He was convinced that because of the prank, he became known to influential Parisians who might never have known of him.[71]

Having successfully been initiated into the Parisian beau monde and passed all his flight tests, Bullard received his pilot's license on May 5, 1917, becoming military pilot number 6950 in the French air service.[72] He was granted a six-day leave in Paris. A few days later, wearing a blue pilot's uniform and "wings as large as a buzzard's wings . . . sewed on his collar," he collected his two thousand dollars from the startled Jeff Dickson at Henri's Bar, 3 rue Volney, Paris.[73] Henri's was a popular hangout for American Ambulance Corps drivers and aviators.[74] Dickson gasped, "how did you do it?" Bullard replied, "I guess because I am human, a soldier, and asked for the opportunity to see if I had the ability to become a pilot. . . . Because that opportunity was granted me, I am here."[75] Perhaps this unforgettable experience helped shape Dickson's decision as a much older man to fly for the liberation of France during the second war.

Having always had to carefully manage his slender earnings, Bullard luxuriated in the possession of the two thousand dollars. He was pleased to be able to treat White, Kisling, and Dickson to a four-star meal. That afternoon and evening the foursome made the rounds of Parisian bars and cafés, and Bullard's accomplishment was toasted in each. It seemed to Bullard that "by midnight every American in Paris knew that an American Negro by the name of Eugene Bullard, born in Georgia, had obtained a military pilot's license." The next day, he was interviewed by American correspondents Sparrow Robertson and Charles McCarthy of the Paris edition of the *New York Herald Tribune,* and also by his Lyon interviewer, Will Irwin.[76]

Bullard could be toasted by white American journalists in Paris but not in America. His achievement in aviation was never mentioned—not even commented on disparagingly—in American newspapers and magazines. In spite of the awkwardness for the neutral United States of having American nationals such as Genet, McConnell, and so many others flying for a belligerent, there was no attempt to keep their exploits from reaching the American and French print media before American entry into the war. The total media silence on Bullard, an *avis rara* if there ever was one, may have been a result of censorship, official or self-imposed, by the American press. Given the American establishment's conviction of black inferiority, a conviction shared by the American armed forces, numerous African American applications for service in the American air service were being routinely rejected. That a barely educated Southern black youth had successfully passed through flight training, and not to mention later flew in combat, could not be countenanced.

The only connection between Bullard and aviation published during the war appeared in the January 1918 issue of *The Crisis,* the journal of the National Association for the Advancement of Colored People. Eager to publish news of African American achievement, the best the magazine could do with Bullard was this item: "Eugene Bullard of Columbus, Ga., twenty-two years of age, volunteered in the French Foreign Legion in 1914. He was twice wounded at Verdun and has the Croix de Guerre, a much coveted decoration for bravery. After six months in the hospital he has enlisted in the Aviation-Corps."[77]

At the time of publication, Bullard had already fought in the air for several months and was now out of aviation completely. *The Crisis* was never able to note the complete story of his short career as a combat aviator. Although several brief references to him as a combat pilot appear in the African American press in the immediate postwar period, Robert Jakeman's statement is essentially correct: "The only black known to have publicly acknowledged Bullard's wartime flying record during the interwar years was George S. Schuyler."[78]

The acquisition of wings—becoming brevetted—did not itself qualify the pilot-aviator for combat duty over the Western Front. To attain such qualification, pilots needed further training in what the French called *écoles de perfectionnement*. Here pilots learned to fly the very latest fighting planes, both single- and double-engined. They were taught to fire the machine guns, now synchronized to fire through the propeller, and instructed in "fancy flying"—looping, corkscrewing, diving and recovery—maneuvers necessary for evasive actions. In the finishing school, they learned how to initiate combat both individually and in squadron formation.[79]

After his celebratory leave in Paris, Bullard acquired these skills at training schools first at Châteauroux (May and June), then at Avord, near Bourges (late June through early August), where he experienced the exhilaration of "acrobatic and stunt flying," and finally at Plessis Belleville, near Paris. Avord was a huge camp at that time whose many barracks were filled with pilots who kept "the air alive, night and day with humming *avions*."[80] In a letter home from Avord of June 22, 1917, James Hall described the camaraderie among his barrack mates in which their "black brother" was a prominent figure:

> There is a fine crew in this school, men from all colleges and men who don't know the name of a college. For instance, there are about half a dozen from Harvard, as many from Yale, some from Dartmouth, a few from Amherst, Williams, etc. We have a couple of ex-All-Americans, a Vanderbilt-cup racing driver, men sticky with money in the same barracks with others who worked their way over on ships. This democracy is a fine thing in the army and makes better men of all hands. For instance, the corporal of our room is an American, as black as the ace of spades, but a mighty white fellow at that. The next two bunks to his are occupied by Princeton men of old Southern families. They talk more like a darky than he does and are the best of friends with him. . . . This black brother has been in the Foreign Legion, wounded four times, covered with medals for his bravery in the trenches, and now uses his experiences and knowledge of French for the benefit of our room—Result: the inspecting lieutenant said we had the best-looking room in the barrack.[81]

At Avord, Bullard made many new friends among the Americans and "never had one word of misunderstanding with anyone during the entire time I was there." He enjoyed sparring with a number of the men. He was indeed "placed in charge" of his barrack, which held some twenty-two bunk beds. His good friend, American Reginald Sinclaire, had the bunk next to *le chef de chambre*. The lanky Sinclaire, almost a head taller than Bullard, accepted good-naturedly when Eugene designated him his *sous-chef de chambre*. In a photograph of the two men standing in front of their barrack, Bullard is wearing a woman's silk stocking on his head, something perhaps adopted from an affectation of his rakish friend Navarre that also served to keep dust and dirt out of his hair when cleaning. But the young African American did more than clean house. In his position of authority, Bullard was charged with calling roll night and day and reporting any absences. An American, a "Mr. R.," had the habit of taking a train to and from Bourges, the nearest large town, in order to enjoy the companionship of women of the night. "R." always returned in time to report at the morning roll call and did so even after the night he took the wrong train and was forced to pull the emergency stop lever as the train was passing the camp. He dashed off the train, slipped under the camp's fence, and sped into the barrack, where he shaved off his mustache. The angry train master appeared some minutes later demanding the identity of the reprobate whom he described as "ce cochon à une petite moustache [this pig with a little mustache]." Bullard covered for "R.," earning his abiding gratitude.[82]

At Plessis Belleville, Bullard received word that he would soon be sent into combat at the front and was lifted by his ground crew onto their shoulders in celebration.[83] On August 27, he reported to the front. With his pet monkey, Jimmy, recently purchased in Paris, tucked in his flight jacket for good luck, he flew his first combat mission with the French chasing squadron N-93 at the end of the first week in September. Occurring over the still-bloody Verdun sector, this pioneering first combat mission for a pilot of African descent was uneventful. Thankfully so, for he felt that "the eyes of the world were watching me. . . . I had to do or die and I didn't want to die." He had followed the orders of his squadron leader to stay in formation until he was judged capable of engaging in one-on-one combat. On their second mission of that same day, however, his squadron encountered four German bombers and sixteen fighters headed for Bar-le-duc, the supply center for the defenders of Verdun. During the ensuing battle, the warrior could not resist taking part in an action that concluded with the destruction of the German bombers and two Fokkers as well as the loss of two French pilots. He later learned that he had fired seventy-eight rounds of his machine gun and received seven in the tail of his plane. He had been "blooded." His commander told him, "You didn't wait this afternoon. Why wait tomorrow?"[84]

Bullard would fly at least twenty missions with squadron N-93 and squadron N-85 to which he was transferred on September 13. Although not a gifted flier like Navarre, he was a competent one with whom his fellow pilots liked teaming up. As with many other pilots, he reported several downings of enemy planes for which, however, there was no corroborating evidence and thus could not be scored officially as a kill. In one of the actions in which he believed he had shot down a Fokker, he himself was forced to land just behind Allied trenches, where for two hours his plane was a target for German machine gunners. After pulling him out under the cover of darkness, mechanics found ninety-six holes in his stricken craft.[85]

As a pilot, Bullard knew the relative comforts of the life of the aviator over that of the *poilus*. The infantryman ate when his rations reached him. At the air base, meals were served three times a day and coffee and snacks were always available. Unlike in the trenches, barracks provided clean dwellings, regular intervals for sleep, and the opportunities for diversions such as card games and reading. Instead of the foot soldier's fresh mud, bad weather afforded the flier more frequent leaves spent in Paris or hunting game in the vicinity of the base. However, in the air service, combat deaths, owing to the individuality of the combatant as well as greater esprit de corps in the squadron, took a greater emotional toll on the survivors back at the base. Mass death in no man's land produced a numbness, a death in air combat, grief. Such, at any rate, was Bullard's experience. Very few men could make such a comparison.[86]

As days passed into weeks, and as ever new deaths of comrades were absorbed, he and other pilots "just kept the daily routine of offering his own life [while] trying to take an enemy life." Suddenly, about a year before the war ended, Bullard's short career as a combat aviator came to an end. French military authorities ordered him out of aviation and into a noncombat position in the 170th Infantry.[87]

Evidence, albeit circumstantial, confirms Bullard's suspicion that it was the racial prejudice of Dr. Edmund C. Gros, an American, that led to the termination of his service as a pilot.[88] Born in San Francisco in 1867, educated at Stanford University, where he was a champion heavyweight wrestler, the doctor had long been resident at the American hospital in Neuilly, the fashionable suburb west of Paris. When the war broke out, Gros helped organize the American Ambulance Corps, created to transport wounded French soldiers to hospitals, such as Gros's, in the Paris area. He was also a key figure in the formation of the Lafayette Escadrille, the squadron of American aviators who began flying in combat under French command in April 1916.[89] The doctor was also vice-president of the Franco-American committee appointed to handle the affairs of American pilots flying in all the various French squadrons. It was in this capacity that he dealt with Bullard. After the United States entered the war in April 1917, Gros was commissioned as a major and later promoted to lieutenant colonel in the American Expeditionary Force, whose commander, General John J. Pershing, arrived in Paris in June 1917.[90]

According to Bullard, Gros, who personally paid the American fliers from funds donated by wealthy Americans in Paris out of his townhouse office at 23, avenue du Bois de Boulogne, revealed his racial intolerance by habitually making Bullard last to receive his check. After the United States entered the war and Eugene had received his wings, Gros pressured the French air service commanders to hold him out of combat. Unable to do so, Gros was able to use a small incident as a pretext to have him removed from French aviation entirely. The incident was an argument that Bullard had with a French officer who had insulted him. The episode occurred at an inn where Eugene was spending the night en route back to his base near the front. Other French officers intervened, finding fault with the behavior of his adversary, a racist officer commanding colonial troops, and assuring him that nothing would come of the episode. Four days later, a letter came to Bullard from Gros reprimanding him for "quarreling with an officer" and adding that "whatever punishment I might receive, I merited." Several weeks later came his mystifying severance from the French air corps. Bullard was told by his squadron's doctor that "he must be evacuated." When Eugene insistently questioned him for the reasons why, the doctor kept repeating, "I don't know what this is all about myself" and tried to console the flier by noting that "lots of other men in your spot would consider themselves lucky to get out of this mess."[91] In another insult in May 1918, Gros withheld from Eugene a scroll of gratitude from the French ministry of war that was sent via Gros to every other American pilot who had flown for France.[92]

On the issue of Bullard's attempted transfer, it is clear that American military authorities, having chosen privately not to accept American blacks in any capacity, even as ground crew in aviation units, were not going to accept Eugene into American service. In October 1917, the commander-in-chief of the American air service, Colonel Raynal C. Bolling, created a board to examine and approve the American fliers wishing to enter U.S. service. One of the four examiners was Gros. Bullard came to Paris with other Americans to take a physical exam, which, after some puzzling questions such as "how did you learn to fly" and observations that his feet and tonsils were too large, he passed. On October 21, 1917, Bolling sent a memorandum to the chief of the French air mission listing the Americans who had been graded and approved by the board for transfer "at such time as the French military authorities might be willing to release them." Of the twenty-nine men who first came under the board's review, twenty-eight were approved, one was "rejected physically." "E. Bullard" was the last name on the accepted list. The catch was that unlike the others approved he had not been given an officer's rank. To be "capable of being a pilot," one had to have at least the rank of a first lieutenant. Bullard was graded as a sergeant.[93] He received no further consideration. Perhaps deluded about the state of American race relations after five years of "normal life" in Europe and by his camaraderie with American whites in the Foreign Legion and the air corps, Bullard had sought the transfer in good faith:

> I was more and more puzzled until suddenly it came to me that all my fellow countrymen who were transferred were white. Later I learned that in World War I, Negroes were not accepted as fliers by the U.S. Army. This hurt me very much. Then as now my love for my own country was strong. I got

some comfort out of knowing that I was able to go on fighting on the same front and in the same cause as other citizens of the U.S. and so in a round-about way I was managing to do my duty and serve it.[94]

Bullard's rejection by the U.S. military was but one example—although an egregious one—of the racism disenabling blacks throughout American society in these years. The American racial caste system and its ideology of white supremacy crossed the Atlantic in late 1917 and early 1918 on the troop ships carrying the American Expeditionary Force into France.[95] Even before they had left their training camps in the States, white American officers were worried about diminished morale when black soldiers in their segregated units sought to assert their civil rights as citizens of the United States. In a March 1918 bulletin to all troops of the 92nd Division then stationed in Camp Funston, Kansas, General Staff Officer Lt. Colonel Allen Greer expressed his concern about a black soldier raising the color question by protesting discriminatory seating in a local theater. The "black sergeant [was] strictly within in his legal rights in this matter, and the theater manager is legally wrong. Nevertheless the Sergeant is guilty of the greater wrong in doing *anything,* no matter how *legally* correct, that will provoke race animosity." Believing that the success of the Division was dependent on maintaining "the good will of the nine-tenths white public," Greer warned his soldiers "to attend quietly and faithfully to your duties. . . . don't go where your presence is not desired."[96]

Once in France, the worries of white American army officers about their black soldiers shifted. Clearly, the problem now was not the loss of good-will of the general public, for the desperate French citizenry welcomed the American soldiers, white and black, who were arriving just in time to turn impending German victory in spring 1918 into retreat and eventual defeat during the summer and fall of that year. The problem now, such officers believed, was the morale of the white American soldiers, a morale sure to be lowered, they reasoned, if they saw black American troops enjoying freedom from segregation and discrimination, and especially the freedom to associate with white women—freedoms French law and custom were affording the first black troops to reach France in late 1917.

Among these early-arriving African American soldiers were those of the

15th New York Infantry. Ironically, these troops had been sent to France quickly—and placed under French commanders—because of the concerns of their white officers that racist provocations against them by white civilians in South Carolina, where the New York 15th was training, might lead to a retaliatory riot and a major racial disturbance. One of the soldiers who had been insulted was Noble Sissle, with whom Bullard would work in Montmartre entertainment circles after the war. Another soldier of the 15th New York was Willie Smith, later renowned as a jazz pianist under the nickname "The Lion." In Smith's memoir, there is a passage suggesting why the white American officer corps became so concerned in 1918 about the French maintaining strict racial segregation, especially between black American men and French women. As Smith recalled of the New York 15th's first weeks in France: "The French are an affectionate people. They move you. . . . I became very fond of the French girls with the red cheeks and bicycles. One of our big problems was sneaking away from camp at night and getting back in time in the morning. That was where those bikes came in handy—they would meet us with their bikes. In the dawn, there was always a weird parade of soldiers wheeling toward camp with chicks on their handle bars." The French officers, it would seem, were not unduly concerned about the late-night absences of their black troops if they did not interfere with their becoming good soldiers. Smith and his comrades proved to be good soldiers, winning many combat decorations in fighting against the Germans in the summer and fall of 1918.[97]

Bullard's rejection by the U.S. Army Air Corps in late 1917 was a foregone conclusion. But the desire of the white officers of the AEF to maintain Jim Crow made his continuing to fly for the French just as intolerable. Black American soldiers, soon to land in France by the tens of thousands, and their white counterparts by the hundreds of thousands, could not fail to know of Bullard's saga if only through rumor, especially if he began to accumulate victories in the air. Certainly, during his leaves in Paris, he would be noticed with his white friends, perhaps with a white woman at his side, for he "had gone dancing with lots of other French girls" before falling in love with the young woman he would marry in 1923, Marcelle Straumann. The romantic allure of aviators flying for France is suggested in Elizabeth de Graumont's recollection that in 1917 "pilots were greatly sought after; it was even *chic* to have an aviator lover."[98]

In an affectionate recollection of Bullard in a footnote to *The Black Swallow of Death,* Charles Kinsolving recalls that Eugene "wasn't a big guy, but well-built and wiry, pleasing women!"[99] Kinsolving and other American fliers remember him wearing a flamboyant self-styled dress uniform of red and black.[100] With two million American men in uniform in France, the heightened interest in the war might finally bring the flashy extrovert's heroism, air achievement, and attractiveness to white women to public attention back home. That these qualities were possessed by the largely self-educated son of a slave could not fail to weaken the myths and stereotypes that rationalized the sweeping racial discriminations in American life. To take but one small example, back in Bullard's hometown, blacks were being denied employment in textile mills because of their alleged inability to handle complex machinery. At this same time, the *Columbus Ledger* was editorializing that "drifting Negroes . . . should be rounded up . . . and those fit for service be sent to France and all others placed under guard and forced to get busy on the Southern farm."[101]

When American troops began pouring off their ships and marching through Paris and into the various sectors of the Western Front, Bullard was not only removed from the air service but ordered to report to a camp, the Fontaine du Berger, a mountainous rural post in the Puy de Dôme in the heart of France's Massif Central, three hundred miles south of Paris.[102] In this same period, American military authorities were making it very difficult for African American soldiers to spend leave time in Paris. If the intent of Bullard's posting in the Puy de Dôme was to keep him out of sight of Americans in Paris, it failed. He said he was granted leaves by the French authorities whenever he asked for them and remembered attending a boxing match between his friends Jack Johnson and Blink McCluskey in Spain, a fight that took place in April 1918.[103] Bullard implied that he was on leave in Paris when he learned of Navarre's death in an air stunt on July 10, 1919—a recollection at odds with his assertion that he had been demobilized shortly after the armistice on November 11, 1918.[104] If his demobilization date was October 24, 1919, as given by Carisella and Ryan,[105] he must have been on virtual permanent leave. In June 1919,

U.S. Army intelligence in Paris was reporting on him as a "habitual frequenter" of the Parisian boulevards and already "playing in a number of jazz bands."[106]

To understand fully the circumstances in which Bullard was pulled out of air combat, a notorious document needs to be cited here—a document written by a French-American liaison committee composed on the American side by men like Gros, if not by Gros himself. This remarkable memorandum was distributed to French military and civilian authorities throughout the war zone in August 1918. Although signed by a Frenchman named Linard, it has been demonstrated that it represented American opinion. When it surfaced in public, the document was denounced in the French general assembly, and the French ministry of war later ordered copies of it collected and burned.[107] Translated into English, the document reads as follows:

French Military Mission
Stationed with the American Army
August 7, 1918

SECRET INFORMATION CONCERNING BLACK AMERICAN TROOPS

1. It is important for French officers who have been called upon to exercise command over black troops, or to live in close contact with them, to have an exact idea of the position occupied by Negroes in the United States. The information set forth in the following communication ought to be given to these officers and it is to their interest to have these matters known and widely disseminated. It will devolve likewise on the French Military Authorities, through the medium of the Civil authorities, to give information on this subject to the French population residing in the cantonments occupied by American colored troops.

2. The American attitude upon the Negro question may seem a matter for discussion to many French minds. But we French are not in our province if we undertake to discuss what some call 'prejudice.' American opinion is unanimous on the 'color question' and does not admit of any discussion. The increasing number of Negroes in the United States (about 15,000,000) would create for the white race in the Republic a menace of degeneracy were it not that an impassable gulf has been made between them. As this danger does not exist for the French race, the French public has become accustomed to

treating the Negro with familiarity and indulgence. This indulgence and this familiarity are matters of grievous concern to the Americans. They consider them an affront to their national policy. They are afraid that contact with the French will inspire in black Americans aspirations which to them [the whites] appear intolerable. It is of the utmost importance that every effort be made to avoid profoundly estranging American opinion.

Although a citizen of the United States, the black man is regarded by the white American as an inferior being with whom relations of business or service only are possible. The black is constantly being censured for his want of intelligence and discretion, his lack of civic and professional conscience and for his tendency toward undue familiarity. The vices of the Negro are a constant menace to the American who has to repress them sternly. For instance, the black American troops in France have, by themselves, given rise to as many complaints for attempted rape as all the rest of the army. And yet the [black American] soldiers sent us have been the choicest with respect to physique and morals, for the number disqualified at the time of mobilization was enormous.

CONCLUSION

1. We must prevent the rise of any pronounced degree of intimacy between French officers and black officers. We may be courteous and amiable with these last, but we cannot deal with them on the same plane as with the white American officers without deeply wounding the latter. We must not eat with them, must not shake hands or seek to talk or meet with them outside of the requirements of military service.

2. We must not commend too highly the black American troops, particularly in the presence of [white] Americans. It is all right to recognize their good qualities and their services, but only in moderate terms, strictly in keeping with the truth.

3. Make a point of keeping the native cantonment population from "spoiling" the Negroes. [White] Americans become greatly incensed at any public expression of intimacy between white women and black men. They have recently uttered violent protests against a picture in the *Vie Parisienne* entitled "The Child of the Desert" which shows a [white] woman in a *cabinet particulier* with a Negro. Familiarity on the part of white women with black men is furthermore a source of profound regret to our experienced colonials who see in it an over-weening menace to the prestige of the white race. Mili-

tary authority cannot intervene directly in this question, but it can through the civil authorities exercise some influence on the population.

(Signed) LINARD [108]

White officers of black regiments, such as Allen Greer of the 92nd Division, went on record after the war accusing black troops, especially those led by black officers, of cowardice in battle and being predisposed to rape and general disorder when not at the front.[109] Hearing from black officers and soldiers of these falsehoods and many injustices suffered by African American soldiers at the hands of their white officers, W. E. B. Du Bois, editor of The Crisis, traveled to France in December 1918 to investigate the question of race relations within the AEF as well as to cover the peace negotiations at Versailles. Du Bois also took part in sessions of the Pan-African Congress convened in Paris in February 1919.[110]

Fluent in French, Du Bois traveled throughout France to gather information from black soldiers not yet demobilized and from French citizens in whose towns and villages they had been stationed. He wrote to "twenty-one mayors of towns and cities in all parts of France where Negro troops [had] been quartered asking them as to the conduct of black troops." The responses were uniformly commendatory: "no complaint, well-disciplined," "very excellent conduct," "fine character, exquisite courtesy," and the like. Du Bois found official statistics of the 92nd Division revealing that only "one soldier was convicted of rape" and none convicted of even "intent to rape." [111]

While a few white officers such as General Pershing did recognize the "discipline and morale" that had made the 92nd and other black regiments, in combat as well as supply, successful at the front, Du Bois found a systematic pattern of prejudicial speech and action on the part of many white American officers against their black troops. On the other hand, the editor of The Crisis knew from his own experience in France, and from his meetings with the officials of towns and their citizens, just why the black American soldier, in spite of the treatment of his officers, did not succumb to the German propaganda query, "how can you fight for a land in which you have less freedom than the country you are fighting against?" The reason was the "kindness and the utter lack of prejudice among the French." The African American soldiers

> gained friends everywhere. They saw the wretched suffering of the French and they toiled and fought mightily for them. French officers and civilians of high social position vied with each other in doing all they could to show consideration. A Negro officer entered a café. The American white officers resented his seat at the table and started to rise—the French officers at a neighboring table very quietly and courteously nodded . . . and the black officer found a seat with them.[112]

Over and over at meals with French people in their homes, Du Bois found them "baffled"—as baffled as Bullard's squadron doctor in trying to explain his demotion—"by the thing in America we call 'Nigger-hatred.'" Not only was it not there with the French, they simply could not comprehend it: "It was a curious monstrosity at which civilized folk laughed at or looked puzzled. There was no elegant and elaborate conde-scension of—'we once had a colored servant'—'my father was an Aboli-tionist'—'I've always been interested in your people'—there was the com-munity of kindred souls . . . the quick deference to the guests you left in quiet regret, knowing they were not discussing you behind your back with lies and nonsense. God! It was simply human decency." [113]

At an inn at Domfront in Normandy, Du Bois wrote unforgettably of black American officers awaiting shipment back to the States in the spring of 1919. "Bitter and disillusioned at the bottomless depths of American race hatred—so uplifted at the vision of the real democracy dawning on them in France," they sang the opening stanza of the French national an-them with local officials at the top of their lungs:

> Allons enfants de la patrie!
> Le jour de gloire est arrivé!
> Contre nous de la tyrannie,
> L'étendard sanglant est levé [114]

These words were hurled defiantly up a hill toward, as Du Bois put it, Domfront's "Jim Crowed" hotel billeting white American officers.

As much as these African American officers, Bullard knew the difference between the American and French practice of the ideals both nations professed. When he returned to Paris in the spring of 1919, this difference would be painfully driven home once again. According to various French newspapers of late May 1919, a young American Negro of *belle stature,* later identified as Bullard, was drinking on the terrace of the Café de Paris, located where the rue Scribe meets the Grands Boulevards. When he stood up unsteadily under the influence of alcohol, he accidentally bumped into ("heurter," "bousculer") a white American officer who was seated behind him. When this man realized he had been jarred by a black, he became furious and remonstrated with him. The "bumper" then excused himself with a joke ("une plaisanterie") by one account, or, according to another, responded with a dismissive laugh ("ricanement").[115] All accounts agree that the white man then struck the "unfortunate black" with a punch to the head that sent him reeling into the arms of a newspaper vendor at a nearby kiosk.[116] No sooner had the man been steadied on his feet than came another blow that sent him crashing unconscious to the pavement. He was taken to the Beaujon hospital where, having been examined and found with no major injury, he was released the next day.[117]

For some reason, the first French press accounts of the episode reported that the black assault victim was the Dixie Kid and that he had been killed. Follow-up stories said that Bullard, not the Dixie Kid, had died. *La Presse,* which on May 30 finally established that Bullard had not been killed, editorialized against the racist violence as indignantly as it could given the outpouring of French goodwill toward the American military and the increasingly anti-German stance being taken by President Wilson in the peace negotiations then nearing their conclusion at Versailles: "A Negro has the right to take a beer with everyone else in a café. It can happen that one bumps another without meaning to do so. We don't make anything out of the difference between white and black. . . . When jostled by Americans on the sidewalks of Paris, we wouldn't dream of striking at the passerby be they white or black."[118]

Evidently unaware of *La Presse*'s final accurate account of the incident, on June 2, 1919, the publisher of the African American *New York Age,* Fred R. Moore, inquired of Emmett J. Scott, the U.S. War Department's special assistant on race relations, into the circumstances of the death of Eugene Bullard. He enclosed clippings from the black press that reported that "the Chicagoan" who had flown for France had received a mortal blow to the head outside a Paris café. The editor noted that "if the young man was unfairly dealt with, it would seem proper that it have the attention of the department." [119] Receiving no word of Bullard's fate, the *Age* on June 14 repeated the story of his death at the hands of a white officer and printed a photograph of Bullard, with his pet monkey Jimmy on his arm, standing before his airplane. On the same date, the *Chicago Defender* announced the death of "Dixie Kid (Eugene Bullard)" on its sports page and published a photograph of alleged French comrades decorating his grave—one marked by the propeller of his aircraft. The *Washington Eagle* reported his death on the same date. [120]

Meanwhile, the War Department cabled the military attaché at the American Embassy in Paris to investigate and report back on the episode, which it believed had occurred on May 25. [121] American military intelligence in Paris reported back to Washington on June 18:

> The American negro named Bullard . . . served in the French Foreign Legion and came to Paris following his discharge. He played in a number of jazz bands, and was an habitual frequenter of the boulevards and an insulter of American women. This latter characteristic of Bullard's one evening attracted the attention of Pvt. Breaux, who knocked Bullard down after having an argument with him. Bullard got up again, but Breaux knocked him out, and he had to be taken to a hospital, which he left 24 hours afterwards on his own initiative, his injuries being very slight. The report in the French newspapers was that Bullard, simply because he was a colored man, was killed in a fight with an officer of the American army, both statements being utterly without foundation. A representation has been made to the French authorities by the Provost Marshal here that Bullard is an undesirable citizen and ought to be deported, but as yet this recommendation has not been acted upon. [122]

While the French press uniformly reported that it had been an unintended bump that led to the white American's aggression—and *La Presse* took pains to follow up on the initial story—the military intelligence report alleges Bullard's "habitual insulting of American women" as the cause. If not a complete fabrication to whitewash Breaux's assault on an incapacitated man, it is likely that Bullard's "insult" lay in nothing more than having been frequently seen with white women conspicuously in his company in cafés along the Grands Boulevards.[123] After all, white Americans became "extremely incensed at any public expression of intimacy between white women and black men." The reference in the report to having Bullard "deported" indicates that the American authorities were aware that under French law his wounds entitled him to French citizenship. The suggestion of deportation can only be interpreted as the expression of a desire to terminate African American men's fraternization with white women, perfectly natural in France but not to be tolerated in the United States.

The deportation request would not be acted upon, for Bullard was a war hero to the French nation. In spite of continuing confrontations with white American visitors to Paris, his "golden years" as an impresario in Parisian nightclub life were about to begin.

CHAPTER FIVE

Man of Montmartre, 1919–1940

In the postwar era, pleasure seekers, most notably Americans but also moneyed citizens of many other nations, swarmed through the streets and alleys of the 9th Arrondissement in Paris en route to drinking, dancing, and entertainment in the district's many cabarets. The boundaries of Paris describe a circle divided in the middle by the Seine flowing from west to east. The 9th was, and is today, located in a north-central sector of the city on what Parisians refer to as the Seine's right bank.

Until World War I, the name "Montmartre" connoted a section of Paris outside the 9th, north of boulevard Clichy, a terrain that rises steeply to a summit, "La Butte," the location of two Parisian landmarks: the white turreted basilica, Sacré Coeur, and nearby, the picturesque Place du Tertre. This Montmartre had been a village independent of Paris as recently as 1860. In the belle epoque, the small buildings, windmills, and narrow twisting streets of the quarter became home to avant-garde painters and writers who patronized cabarets and music halls such as the Moulin Rouge, made famous in the lithographs of Henri Toulouse-Lautrec.

By 1919, this bohemian Montmartre was already a fading memory. Along with Bullard's friend Moïse Kisling, artists, writers, and patrons such as Gertrude Stein had moved to Montparnasse, a section of Paris south of the Seine on the left bank. Moreover, Montmartre had now expanded territorially south of the boulevard Clichy. As a 1925 guide to the cabarets of Montmartre observed, "what one now called Montmartre" began in the vicinity of the two churches St. Trinité and Notre Dame de Lorette in the southern reaches of the 9th Arrondissement.[1] Like Zelli's, a nightclub in the "new" Montmartre in which Bullard worked in the early '20s, the cabarets and music halls of the "old" would henceforth be patronized by tourists, rarely the local residents.

The many clubs that opened in this "new" Montmartre were situated on crisscrossing streets: rues Blanche, Pigalle, Notre Dame de Lorette, de la Rochefoucauld, and Fontaine as well as the narrower connecting passageways, rues Mansart, Douai, Victor Massé, de la Bruyère, and des Martyrs. Some Parisian writers, such as Francis Carco, Pierre Macorlan, and André Warnod, lamented the passing of the "village spirit of our fathers" farther up the hill; they remembered the stimulating all-night conversations in the cabaret Lapin Agile with young artists like Picasso which, for them, characterized the real Montmartre.[2] They deplored the emphatic commerciality of the district that was making it indistinguishable from the rest of Paris. In a 1924 essay, "From a Roof Top," Albert Flamond commented that the garrets under the sloping orange-tiled and slate roofs, broken by innumerable gables and chimney pots, still reminded him of Mimi Pinson, the sickly seamstress of Henri Murger's *Scènes de la vie de Bohème* and Giacomo Puccini's opera. Down on the streets and on the first floors, on the other hand, "all is changing. . . . The sounds of raucous jazz music made [him] feel under the influence of laughing gas."[3] These nostalgic sentiments, however, would find little favor with most Parisians. Desiring to put the war behind them, they welcomed the influx of wealthy foreigners and the African Americans who would entertain them.

After his return to Paris in the spring of 1919, Bullard settled into an apartment in a pleasant building constructed around an interior courtyard on the rue Navarin,[4] a location just around the corner from the Bal Taberin, where he had performed with Belle Davis's Picks in early 1914. While training for a return to boxing, he needed income, not only for his own living expenses, he said, but also to reciprocate the dinners and parties to which he was frequently invited by his many Parisian friends. He quickly became acquainted with black American drummer Louis Mitchell and members of his Seven Spades Band. Soon he was learning to play drums from Seth Jones, the group's percussionist, and from Mitchell himself.[5] His decision to do so was opportune, for Parisians and the French in general were already enthusiastic for this novel African American music.

American musicians, including Mitchell and another drummer, Buddy Gilmore, had been among the first jazz musicians to appear in Paris just before the war with dancers Vernon and Irene Castle.[6] During the war, in 1917, an African American jazz band had appeared in Paris playing for Gaby Deslys, a French music hall performer who had discovered jazz on an immensely successful tour in the United States. In Paris, her singing and dancing routines were backed by one hundred female dancers, brilliantly plumed like herself in egret feathers, pulsating frenetically to the rhythms of jazz. These performances created a sensation in crowds of civilians and Allied soldiers, finding in their vitality a release from the scourge of war. On one occasion, American military police, anxiously surveying the racially mixed audience erupting into spontaneous dance, were observed drawing their revolvers and pointing them at the ceiling in a feckless effort to restore order. Deslys and her American dancing partner, Harry Pilcer, continued to perform in Paris into 1919 when Mitchell, styled the "King of Noise" by French writer Jean Cocteau, and his band moved from London to accompany their act.[7] Mitchell and his group would remain in Paris for much of the interwar period.

Jazz became popular all over unoccupied France during the war thanks to the performances of the African American band of the 15th New York Infantry led by James Reese Europe. Sergeant Noble Sissle, regimental drum major, remarked to a correspondent of the *St. Louis Post-Dispatch* in June 1918 that in the band's first appearance before a French provincial audience, American marches such as "The Stars and Stripes Forever" were greeted with ringing applause. However, it was their final piece on the program, a syncopated rendition of "The Memphis Blues," that brought pandemonium. After the "jazz spasm" of the trombone players, "the audience could stand it no longer, the 'jazz germ' hit them and it seemed to find the vital spot, loosening all the muscles. . . . When the band had finished and the people were roaring with laughter, their faces wreathed in smiles, I was forced to say that this is just what France needs at this critical moment. . . . All through France the same thing happened." This band enjoyed a similar triumph in Paris in August 1918, playing in the Tuileries Gardens, in Europe's words, "before such a crowd as I never saw anywhere else in the world."[8]

In the postwar years, a number of African American jazz musicians would follow Mitchell to Paris, especially to the many nightclubs that would welcome them in Montmartre. The word had spread quickly among them that in these clubs wages were supplemented liberally by tipping, unlike in England and the States, where gratuities were not customary.[9] Bullard knew these clubs and would earn a living in them both as a performer and, utilizing his fluency in French, as a hiring agent for other American musicians.[10] The "new" Montmartre would become a mecca for African Americans in the interwar period, and Eugene would become a central figure in their expatriate community. The popularity of black Americans in France and the willingness of French authorities to support them overtly—attitudes and behavior so markedly different from those in the United States—were deeply rooted in French history and culture.

Where the leading exponents of American revolutionary and democratic doctrine, many of them slaveholders such as Thomas Jefferson, were overtly racist, the French revolutionary movement produced an abolitionist society embraced by leaders as diverse as Lafayette, Robespierre, and Henri Gregoire, a theorist and Jesuit scholar whose treatise on race comprised an extended refutation of Jefferson's self-interested views on the subject. In the United States, 250 years of slavery and 60 more of racial segregation were rationalized by the white majority's assumption of African inferiority. Metropolitan France, by contrast, had never known slavery, had guaranteed "liberty, equality, and fraternity" to all its citizens in its great revolution, and abolished servitude in its colonies in 1848. Accordingly, Parisians and French provincials had been welcoming American black writers and artists since the middle of the nineteenth century.[11] This relative absence of racism had attracted not only intellectuals but prize fighters and entertainers whose graceful beauty were appreciated early in the twentieth century. Well before the "jazz virus" had gripped the French, as early as 1904, the old habitués of the Moulin Rouge had appreciated the dancing of Douglas and Jones and a group called the Colored Girls.[12]

Where law and custom in the States sanctified the caste system of white over black, French national leaders believed that their colonial peoples in Africa, the Antilles, and Indo-China should assimilate to metropolitan France's forms of politics, law, and culture. Undeniably, there was cruel exploitation of colonial peoples by French administrators and businessmen. However, a native youngster excelling in a French colonial school could attend France's elite schools, graduate with honors from the University of Paris, and enjoy success in a career in business, law, or politics in France itself. Unlike the United States, where blacks were not allowed to practice the "success ethic," France honored achieving people of color.[13] The French could not comprehend why white American officers treated their black soldiers so unjustly. French officers had given the heroic African American 369th Regiment (into which the New York 15th Infantry had been incorporated) the signal honor of being the advance guard of Allied troops in the triumphal march to the Rhine on November 17, 1918; their American counterparts had refused to allow any black American soldiers to march with other Allied soldiers, including colored colonial troops, in the victory parade through the Arc de Triomphe and down the Champs-Elysées on Bastille Day in 1919.[14] Because of racism and ignorance of African American history, white Americans would view the American Expeditionary Force for decades as an all-white army. For the French, the "Sammies" would always be honored regardless of the color of their skins.

Of course, the Americans who had volunteered to fight for France at the outset of the war, two and a half years before the United States entered the conflict, were especially revered. Among these men was Bullard, a decorated hero of the battles of Champagne and Verdun, and a man with the added luster of having been a combat aviator. Although he maintained his American citizenship, his wounds had brought him French citizenship as well. Now seeking a livelihood in Paris, he would find powerful French patriots coming to his assistance. One of these men was Robert Henri, whom Eugene had come to know during the war.[15]

In 1919, Robert Henri had just completed a six-year term as the president of the French equivalent of the American Bar Association. He had been admired in France as a brilliant defense attorney in a series of sensational murder cases tried in Paris between 1891 and 1908. Well-publicized in the French press, Robert Henri's emotionally stirring pleas became legendary and won acquittals or commuted sentences for individuals whom he convincingly presented as victimized by the high status or wealth of their accusers.

Robert Henri was legal counsel for associations of actors and writers, for the city of Paris, and for the Legion of Honor, in which he held membership as a commander. The lawyer's stature was such that in 1915 his life and work were presented in a popular film that also featured the achievements of other great contemporary French citizens: Auguste Rodin, Claude Monet, Pierre Renoir, Camille Saint-Saëns, Anatole France, and Sarah Bernhardt. During the war, he joined French president Raymond Poincaré and other dignitaries at patriotic war rallies in Paris. His "patriotic impulse" made him a key figure in the concerted French effort to assign a French family to each newly arrived American soldier in late 1917. In 1919, he published a biography of Marshal Ferdinand Foch, commander of the Allied forces in France during the late war. In short, he was "very well known in high Parisian society with friendly ties to all people of standing in politics, letters, and the arts." [16]

In 1919, when he first assisted Bullard, Robert Henri had just switched from the practice of criminal to civil law. In addition to Eugene's war record, the prestigious lawyer may have been impressed with the twenty-four-year-old's youthful struggle to overcome poverty and racism. Born in 1863, he had been abandoned by his parents in infancy and raised by a godfather, an assistant mayor of the 9th Arrondissement.[17] He knew well the section of Paris Eugene now called home. After becoming proficient enough as a drummer (he admits several times he was never more than that), Bullard found work with a band employed in a nightclub owned by Joe Zelli on the rue Caumartin. An entrepreneur who had owned clubs in New York and London, Zelli realized that if he could secure a license permitting him to remain open past midnight, something then forbidden by Parisian law, he could steal a march on his competitors in the cabaret business.[18] This was a sector of the Parisian economy about to thrive through the patronage of wealthy tourists, especially Americans anxious to escape prohibition and eager to exploit the lower cost of living afforded by the marked devaluation of the franc against the dollar. The competition among club owners promised to be especially sharp since the beautiful city on the Seine had been closed to foreign pleasure-seekers since August 1914. Bullard contacted Robert Henri "and told him that I would have an interest as artistic director for Zelli if he got a [all night] club license. I explained that this was a question of my livelihood. Maître Robert promised he would see that I worked. Fifteen days later Joe Zelli and I were instructed to meet the lawyer at the License Bureau. There we received the club license." [19]

As Bullard noted and many others have confirmed, Zelli's quickly became the most celebrated night spot in Montmartre. Not long after receiving the license, the club moved to an even more lucrative location on rue Fontaine. For a considerable period of time, other cabarets continued to close at midnight. At that hour Zelli's opened, selling champagne by the bottle to its clientele and providing them with female drinking and dancing partners. The club closed after serving breakfast in the early daylight hours.[20] At Zelli's, Bullard earned a comfortable income as a drummer and manager of the club's musicians. As *directeur artistique,* he was also paid to book entertainers: singers and dancers, small animal and comedic acts, and acrobats, tumblers really, who worked on the ground performing a dazzling array of flips, somersaults, and spins.[21] These performers were often personally known to Eugene from his days of touring with Belle Davis's Picks.

Attracting a cosmopolitan crowd of Americans, Italians, Spanish, Mexicans, Chileans, and British, among other visitors, Zelli's popularity was such that some said the owner earned a half a million dollars in his first five years on the rue Fontaine.[22] In its mirrored interior, Zelli's consisted of a large rectangular hall lined with tables, with space enough for a bandstand, stage, and dance floors. From what Zelli called "Royal Boxes" set out along a balcony, patrons could look down upon the festivities taking place on the floor as well as talk to other parties on telephones in each "loge." Also installed on the balcony was a modern American-style bar that created an atmosphere of agreeable luxury and pleasure. The young women hostesses hired by Zelli earned their pay by taking a percentage of the price of each bottle of champagne purchased by a customer—champagne was *obligatoire,* and one could not order a simple glass.[23] Thus many bottles were sold—after one of them most patrons stopped counting—and Zelli's was invariably a very merry place.

Joe Zelli's warm personality and skill in running his club were the chief reasons for its success. He greeted everyone who entered, whether regular or newcomer, with the warm handshake of an especially favored friend. For all his business acumen, he was a generous individual, possessing "a large collection of uncashable checks whose givers were never pressed." Charlie McCarthy and Sparrow Robertson, reporters at the *Paris Herald,* whom Bullard recalled toasting him in 1917, were habitual ramblers up and down rues Pigalle and Fontaine in the 1920s. For both, Zelli's was a favorite hangout. "Saint Joe" gave them free drinks and entertainment on occasion, and, after McCarthy's sudden death in 1925, Zelli paid for the funeral service down the hill at Trinité Church, saw to it that "his girls" attended, and bought McCarthy's funeral plot at St. Ouen cemetery in Paris.[24] Bullard learned much about the business of nightclub management by observing Zelli during the four years he worked for him.

Realizing he could always return to Zelli's, Bullard in December 1921 departed Paris for Alexandria, Egypt, where he had contracted with the Hotel Claridge to perform with a jazz ensemble. The contract ran for six months. While in Egypt, he fought his last two prize fights, the first on December 21, 1921, the second on April 28, 1922. Both contests ended in draws. In Egypt, Eugene became reacquainted with Blink McCluskey, his prewar boxing buddy who in several years would become his doorman at his Paris nightclub.[25] Bullard badly injured his hand in the second fight, his last in the ring.[26] The sore hand notwithstanding, he would fight on many more occasions in the streets and night spots of Paris.

Some of Bullard's associates in Paris, such as Jocelyn "Frisco" Bingham and Ada Louise Smith, better known as "Bricktop," have suggested that Bullard's "trigger temper" was a character flaw made more volatile when he was under the influence of alcohol.[27] Others, such as Opal Cooper, a distinguished African American actor, AEF veteran, and Bullard's trainer in his second Egyptian fight, and Maud Rumford, a black American student at the Sorbonne who worked as a domestic for Eugene, observed that Bullard's fights in Paris were always a response to racial insults.[28] As Bullard himself put it:

> Defending my self respect and that of others who were unjustly abused or insulted is the reason I had so many fights outside the prize ring. Any contempt shown to a fellow human being because of his race, creed, or color I consider a sickness. . . . I have no respect for a man who is too cowardly to stand up for himself. Everybody admires a man who defends his honor. . . . By demanding that people treat me with as much respect as I treat them I have made many friends.[29]

Most of his street fights in Paris appear to have occurred in the early 1920s when he was working at Zelli's. There were usually two dance bands each night at Zelli's, "our Negro jazz band and an Argentine tango band." One band would play a twenty-minute set while the other relaxed across the street at Mario's Bistro. Occasionally, someone who had been put out of Zelli's for a racial insult to Eugene or a member of his band would be encountered again at Mario's, hurl another insult, and "the fight would be on."[30]

Some of these fracases were spectacular. Cooper, who had settled in Paris as a club singer and banjo player in 1920, remembered a man, much bigger than Bullard, who approached him at a bar, demanding, "Are you Gene Bullard?" When Bullard acknowledged that he was indeed, the man threw an unprovoked punch that the ex-boxer easily slipped, causing the man to smash his fist into the bar. Bullard then "beat him every kind of way you could think of." Cooper recalls another instance in which Bullard had his "old London pal," the Dixie Kid, at his side. A dispute with a group of sailors had boiled over into shoving at the Olympia, a spacious dance hall in Montmartre. Bullard and the Dixie Kid raced up the broad central stairway in the establishment, their antagonists in hot pursuit. Bullard suddenly turned, seized the lead sailor, and flung him down onto his mates. He and the former welterweight champion then "cleaned out the whole bunch." The affair was the talk of Paris for weeks.[31]

Bullard believed most of his adversaries were white Americans "who could not conceal prejudice of a kind which is not tolerated in France." [32] One of his fights hit the front pages of the *Chicago Tribune*'s European edition, and the incident itself and the newspaper's coverage of it revealed the astonishing extent to which, as within the AEF, elements of the white American civilian establishment in Paris expected Jim Crow to be observed in France as it was at home. Episodes of American racism in France embarrassed Eugene. When his French friends would bring up the subject in his presence, he would attempt to downplay the problem. It is not surprising then that, like the incident on the rue Scribe in 1919, this affair involving the *Tribune* is not mentioned in his memoir.

On January 2, 1923, the *Tribune*, founded in 1917 to cover American participation in the war and sold at newsstands all over Paris and other European cities, providing American residents and visitors with news at home and abroad, ran on its front page a story with the headline, "American Felled by Negro Armed with Brass Slug." Beneath this was a smaller heading, "Hit As He And British Officer Escort a Woman." The aggrieved white men involved in this encounter were Harry McClellan and Ronald Reuter. At the time, both were residing at a palatial townhouse on avenue d'Iena belonging to Baroness de Reuter, widow of the late James Gordon Bennett,[33] who had expatriated to Paris and bought the property years before.[34] Until his death in May 1918, Bennett was a major figure in American newspaper publishing as owner of the New York and Paris *Heralds*. These newspaper properties were sold out of his estate in 1920.[35] However, as a relative of Bennett's widow, Reuter had the necessary influence and connections to have his and McClellan's side of the story and more printed in the *Tribune*'s European edition.

According to the account given in the six-paragraph column, McClellan, of Stockton, California, and Lt. Reuter "were jostled by the Negroes as they were leaving a restaurant in the rue Daunou." When McClellan "remonstrated, Dick Bullard, formerly a drummer in a jazz band," seized him "by the lapel and threatened him." When McClellan "pushed the Negroes away with some force," Bullard "struck him with brass knuckles," knocking him down. Bullard then "attacked Reuter" as the other Negro began pummeling McClellan. Police soon intervened, the story continued, moving the "entire party" to a nearby station house. Bullard showed papers stating that he had been in French aviation during the war and accused McClellan and Reuter of attacking him. "As a result, Bullard was not held by the police nor was he searched for the brass knuckles." The final two paragraphs observed:

> Dozens of Negroes are now said to be infesting Montmartre. It was pointed out by Americans yesterday that American authorities here, cooperating with the police, could see to it that many of these men, nearly all of whom have prison records, were deported.
>
> Bullard was in the Foreign Legion for a time during the war but obtained a transfer to aviation rather than go in the trenches. He was shifted out of aviation on the grounds that he declined to fly. Since the armistice he has frequented Montmartre occasionally playing in jazz bands.[36]

In the column next to this piece, the *Tribune* ran a story implicitly condemning "murders" and other "outrages" of the Ku Klux Klan in Louisiana. However, this did not deter the newspaper's editors from publishing on January 5 a reader's letter recommending that Klansmen be brought to Paris "to roundup and tar-and-feather . . . those parasites who call themselves 'guides' and make themselves annoying to the Americans and others who appear in the Boulevards."[37]

Albert Curtis, an African American soldier who decided to remain in France, became a foreign correspondent for the *Chicago Defender*. He wired home Bullard's side of the incident, which was published on January 6. Eugene was dining in Ciro's restaurant when a French woman at a nearby table in McClellan's party spoke to him. When Bullard responded, McClellan objected, telling him that he "didn't want any 'damn nigger' talking to women in his company." "Bullard," Curtis continued, "resented the white man's abuse." The ensuing argument was carried out into the street where fisticuffs concluded the dispute. No brass knuckles were involved, and McClellan and Reuter were detained by police when Bullard was released. Curtis's story summarized Bullard's war record accurately except for the statement, "as a sergeant in the French army he refused a lieutenancy in the American flying corps after having passed the examination." The article ended by stating that "during the last year [Bullard] has been interested in starting an aviation school in France for Americans of his Race. He has permission for the project from the French government and has invited Americans to correspond with him. He is acquainted with Miss Bessie Coleman, aviatrix." [38]

Curtis's story is the only evidence suggesting that Eugene and Coleman, a Chicagoan, may have met. She came to France after learning from her brother, an AEF veteran, that women there were able to receive flight training. In early 1921, she enrolled at a school at Le Cretoy in the Somme. Learning to fly in a Nieuport plane, she was awarded her flight certificate on June 15, 1921. She left France in September 1921, returning in February 1922 for a stay that lasted until May of that year. Neither she nor Bullard mentioned meeting one another in their memoirs, nor does Doris Rich, Coleman's recent biographer. [39] The aviation school mentioned by Curtis was never established.

As for the *Tribune*'s libel, Bullard was too proud a man and too well connected to influential Frenchmen to let it go unchallenged. He could do nothing about the defamation appearing in the Chicago edition and in other American newspapers. In Paris, however, he had on his side French law and undoubtedly the assistance of Robert Henri, now practicing exclusively in civil law. Taking his case to court, he won the right to rebut the story. His rebuttal appeared on the front page of the *Tribune*'s European edition on May 24, 1923, in a column located, according to the court's decree, in the same position, second column from the left margin, as the libelous one of January 2.

Under a headline, "A Letter from Mr. Bullard," Eugene began by noting that the incident of the night of "December 30–31 last between [him] and [his] countrymen, M. Fernando Jones, on the one hand, and on the other Messrs. Harry McClellan and Donald Reuter was nothing of great importance." Having been struck first, he and Jones had defended themselves legitimately. "But the paper had thought it necessary to write an article ... which he judged defamatory from a threefold point of view: namely, military, professional, and private." In his rebuttal, he pointed out that his citation for his wound at Verdun and his flying certificate had been sent to the judge presiding over the case and "are at the disposal of anyone who would like to see them." His military dossier would also disclose that he had "served at the Front as an aviator pilot in the chasing squadron N [Nieuport]-93, C.G. [Groupe de Command] 15."

Bullard then inserted a statement from Colonel Girod, the French officer who had personally approved his request to enter flight training as well as his later appeal to be sent into air combat. Girod certified that he "had the soldier BULLARD working under his orders as Aviation Pilot. Aviator BULLARD gave an example of the best conduct, discipline and courage, and showed such qualities that the Americans present, who were somewhat dubious of him on account of his color, testified to an enthusiaste {sic} admiration for him." The Colonel concluded by saying that as "his former chief" he offered his testimony very willingly.

In the second place, Bullard continued, the story was libelous by insinuating that he was unemployed. On the contrary, he was "a musician and have always worked regularly and earn my living very well." As to the charge that he had fought with brass knuckles, he noted that the police report of the incident, filed at the station in the rue de Choiseul, would show otherwise as well as "who were kept and who were released" from there. He concluded his letter, which was considerably longer than the libelous piece, with a moving if awkwardly expressed peroration:

> To finish with, let me add that I do not know to whom you refer when you speak of deported negroes who infest Montmartre but be sure that you may tell your readers that the pilot aviator, a black man and French, Eugene BULLARD, wounded during the war, cited, who has spilt his blood for his country, and for Justice. {sic} Alas! Justice is so often denied to his race, is not among those negroes. It is time to finish with these ridiculous prejudices of colors of People who forget too soon the German danger of yesterday and the German threat of tomorrow.[40]

The *Chicago Defender* of June 16, 1923, gleefully reprinted Bullard's reply in full beneath Albert Curtis's introductory paragraphs stating that "countered by the even-handed justice of French law, the Paris edition of the *Chicago Tribune* and the *New York Daily News* [the two papers had just merged] has been forced to eat up sensational untruths published in connection with . . . Eugene Bullard." A full-length photograph of Bullard accompanying the story discloses a determined young man staring defiantly at the camera, a cigarette in his right hand. He wears a fedora, a sports suit, and a high starched collar and tie. In spite of the civilian clothes, he has the demeanor of a man still at war.[41]

In his letter to the *Tribune,* Bullard identified himself as a French citizen, stating that his wounds at Verdun, under "article 8, paragraph 2 of the French civil code," had granted him that status. In passing, he mentioned that he was born in America and that his mother was American, but he claimed falsely that his father was from Martinique. Bitter over the repeated rejections, insults, and slanders from white American military and civilian officialdom in France, the proud twenty-seven-year-old found it easy to embrace France and renounce his native land in these years. This renunciation led him to make false statements, as when he said to Curtis that he had spurned a lieutenant's commission in the U.S. air service, and when in his letter of rebuttal he stated that he served at the front as a pilot "until August, 1918, on which date the wound I had received at VERDUN got worse" and he was sent to the camp in the Puy de Dôme. However, even in this bitter period, his rejection of the States was not total, as evidenced in his reference to Fernando Jones, a black Chicagoan, come to Europe as a dancer with Belle Davis's Picks, as a "friend and countryman."[42]

In truth, Bullard's fights with white Americans were episodes in a much larger setting of white American ugliness toward people of color in the French capital, whether they were African Americans or people from France's African and Caribbean colonies. Frequent assaults by white American servicemen on blacks—such as Private Breaux's on Bullard—dated back to 1919. When the soldiers went home, the assailants became white American civilians. On the same day of the *Tribune*'s libel of Eugene, January 2, 1923, an "expatriate spokesman" had a letter published in the *Los Angeles Times* calling for "a deportation of the Negroes who infest the Montmartre section of Paris." An African American theater manager in Paris, Bob Davis, wrote the *Cleveland Gazette* in August 1922 that white American tourists, in not "checking the color line at the three mile limit," were creating a furor in France. Davis cited a number of instances in which white American tourists created commotions in their open expressions of hostility at seeing black French colonials not only dancing with white women but also having equal access to public accommodations.[43] In a description of the Moulin Rouge, a French writer observed that the "good conduct of the Negro patrons could well serve as an example to representatives of races said to be civilized."[44] A French newspaper reported that a black French surgeon had been forced off a tour bus a few miles outside of Paris by outraged white Americans who were the only other passengers. The Americans were unmoved by the doctor's argument that having served during the war, he had as much right as they to visit sites of the battlefields, the tour's object.[45]

As in the case of this bus company, some Paris café, cabaret, restaurant, and hotel owners were compliant with their free-spending white American patrons' demand for a "whites only" policy. The evictions of colored people from such establishments, not only in Paris but other French towns as well, led Gratien Candace, a member of the French Chamber of Deputies from Guadeloupe, to persuade the French foreign ministry to order all French newspapers to publish on August 1, 1923, a stern note to foreign "guests" admonishing them to obey French law and custom with respect to people of color or else face sanctions from French authorities.[46] Two days later, Prince Kojo Touvalou of Dahomey, a decorated war veteran, possessor of a doctorate in jurisprudence from the Sorbonne, and a lawyer at the court of appeals in Paris, was literally thrown out of a Montmartre cabaret, breaking his glasses on the sidewalk of the rue Fontaine not far from Zelli's. Several months earlier, he had been chased out of the American-patronized Jockey-Bar in Montparnasse.[47]

The roughing up of the prince sparked a number of editorials in the French and Parisian press condemning American racism and the presumption of the unruly Americans that they could violate French law with impunity. Several commentators observed, perhaps hollowly, that while prohibition seemed odd to the French visitor in the States, the law was nonetheless observed. One columnist wrote that:

> since the Americans are savages, it won't do to send them diplomatic notes they won't understand. We must train them. . . . We must put them under Negro custom officials. . . .
>
> In Paris, we must form a brigade of Negro cops, specially detailed to look out for Americans.

As for the establishments in Montmartre, instead of repressing Siki [a Senegalese heavyweight boxer, briefly, a year earlier, champion of the world], don't you think it would be more politic to use him bringing back Americans to courtesy and good manners? [48]

Bullard was trying to be "politic" in just this very way.

In his August 11, 1923, essay in *L'Homme libre,* Candace called Paris "a moral and intellectual capital superior to those of all other nations" and argued that no merchant or foreigner should be allowed "to destroy the historic originality of our great and beautiful land. . . . France must not abandon even a parcel of its ideal of justice." No American should forget, he concluded, "that [France] throughout history has contributed more than any other [nation] to the liberation of oppressed people and lands." [49]

The explosive Parisian racial atmosphere of 1923 began to be defused when the French government suspended the licenses or shortened the hours of cabarets in which black clientele were denied entry or maltreated. Prince Touvalou had his day in court and received satisfaction. Because French law permitted censorship of expressions of foreign media deemed destabilizing to the French social order, authorities had forced Parisian cinema owners for several years to cut scenes deemed offensive to people of color from the film *Birth of a Nation.* The furor over the recent "race war" in Paris led French officials to completely ban the film on August 19, 1923. [50]

Given these actions by the French government enforcing the law of its land—a situation contrasting so sharply with American practice in which the law was rarely on the side of blacks—it is little wonder that the allure of France and Paris for African Americans grew even stronger. When Prince Touvalou, visiting the States in 1924, spoke before members of Marcus Garvey's Universal Negro Improvement Association, he spoke of Paris as "the promised land" of the black race. In his Parisian journal, *Les Continents,* he published, a few weeks later, an article entitled "Paris, Heart of the Black Race," in which he proclaimed France "as the only country which, not only has no race prejudice, but struggles against it." [51] Bullard could easily subscribe to these views and, indeed, began to conceive of his life as a struggle to attain just such a promised land.

Bullard's battles in the American race conflict in Paris in the early 1920s were for him but incidents in a period in which he was, as he told the *Tribune,* "earning his living very well." Indeed, he was becoming financially comfortable for the first time in his life. He supplemented his considerable income from Zelli's by hiring musicians and other attractions to entertain at private parties hosted by members of the Parisian social elite, including Edmund Blanc, who owned a stable of racehorses and the St. Cloud racetrack east of Paris, and Princesse de Polignac, American-born heiress to the Singer Sewing Machine fortune, whose enthusiasms ranged from boxing matches to avant-garde composers. His familiarity with elite society was such that in 1926, his friend Paul Chapotin, owner of the famed Café de la Paix, asked him to furnish the music and entertainment for his wedding reception.[52]

Bullard also earned income as a masseur and exercise trainer for Chapotin and other prominent Parisians, including Jack Dean, the husband of Fanny Ward, an American actress turned Parisian society hostess; Horace Dodge, millionaire heir to his family's automobile fortune;[53] and Noel Coward, the English dramatist, composer, and actor, who made Parisian cabaret society his playground in the interwar period.[54] Others Bullard coached were Wellington Koo, Chinese delegate to the Versailles peace conference in 1919 and a frequent visitor to Paris in the '20s,[55] and Craney Gartz, an eccentric Californian who had inherited millions of dollars yet was a vociferous social radical well read in Marxist literature. Gartz had fled the States in 1919 because of the "red scare" that had resulted in vigilante activities against leftists as well as imprisonment by the federal government.[56] Because of his connections with these people, Bullard was familiar not only with the boisterous Montmartre scene but also the more sedate, socially exclusive domains of Paris' Faubourg St. Germain and fashionable suburbs such as St. Cloud and Neuilly. The ease with which he functioned in high society may have owed something to the fact that during the war his two painter friends, Gilbert White and Moïse Kisling, had introduced him to the wealthy Straumann family: Monsieur Louis Albert, his wife, Hélène Héloïse Charlotte Pochinot, and their daughter, Marcelle Eugénie Henriette. After his demobilization, Bullard was "invited many times to Mons. de Straumann's home. He made no objection when I asked to take the charming Marcelle out dancing. This I often did." [57]

Bullard had "gone dancing with lots of other French girls," but he noticed that when apart from Marcelle, still in her late teens when he first met her, he found himself lonely and unhappy. In love for the first time, he discovered, to his great joy, that Marcelle had become deeply attached to him. On July 4, 1922, the African American man who had slept as a youth on a pad on the rough plank floor of his parents' cabin, confessed, with great trepidation, his love for Marcelle to her parents. The Straumanns laughingly assured him that he was not crazy, as he feared; they knew how much Marcelle, their only child, reciprocated his love. A little over a year after receiving this parental blessing, Eugene and Marcelle, at age twenty-two six years his junior, were married on July 17, 1923, in a late-morning civil ceremony at the Mairie (city hall) of the 10th Arrondissement. Bullard remembered that their marriage caused somewhat of a sensation among their acquaintances, not owing to race, but because of the great gulf between their class backgrounds. [58]

After the ceremony, M. Straumann hosted a large party for the newlyweds. Marcelle's aristocratic relatives mixed with friends from Bullard's various military units as well as from the worlds of sports and entertainment. After a multicourse dinner at the Brassierie Universelle, located at the intersection of the avenue de l'Opéra and the rue Daunou—a meal lasting, in the French fashion, long into the afternoon—Straumann hired ten taxicabs and moved his invitees up the hill to Montmartre where the party lasted into the wee hours of the next morning. Eugene and Marcelle departed Paris that day for a two-week honeymoon at the fashionable resort town of Biarritz on the Bay of Biscay near the frontier between France and Spain. [59] The couple returned to Paris to occupy a luxurious apartment at 15, rue Franklin, [60] a location affording a magnificent view of the Eiffel Tower across the Seine.

While Bullard continued working as drummer and artistic director at Zelli's as well as for private clients, Marcelle prepared their apartment for the children that both of them desired. A daughter, Jacqueline, was born to the couple on June 6, 1924, followed by Eugene Jr. in October 1926. Baby Eugene died at six months of double pneumonia. Lolita Josephine, their last child, was born in December 1927. The christening party for Jacqueline was as notable a social affair as their wedding reception had been. Each of Zelli's many champagne suppliers sent a case of their finest for the affair. Eddie South, a well-known jazz violinist, and his band volunteered to entertain, although the Bullards' sixth-floor walkup was too crowded to permit dancing. Guests included Marcelle's parents and her aunt, the Countess de Lucy, Joe Zelli and his wife, and Bullard's pals, many of them "musicians, aviators, cyclists and boxers." Marcelle served soft drinks to children of the guests in a room away from the main party, where "champagne flowed so freely that the guests were more thoroughly baptized than baby Jacqueline." Bullard spent a good deal of the afternoon and evening helping people down the six flights of stairs. He got three hours of sleep before taking his position on the bandstand at Zelli's at midnight. While playing, he was amazed to see several of his guests still partying at the bar upstairs.[61]

Bullard estimated that "three months after Jacqueline's christening party, I left Zelli's and bought a club on my own, Le Grand Duc."[62] The establishment had been opened by Georges Jamerson, a Frenchman with reputed underground connections; the club's name derived most likely from the facetious phrase *la tournée des grands ducs* concocted several generations earlier to describe the dissipated nocturnal wanderings in Montmartre by aristocrats. Located a few steps down the hill from Zelli's at 52, rue Pigalle in the V formed by the intersection of Pigalle and rue de la Rochefoucauld, the club would blossom into one of Montmartre's most prominent cabarets. Within his first few months on the premises, Bullard hired aspiring poet Langston Hughes as a dishwasher and part-time cook.[63] Then twenty-two years of age, Hughes had crossed the Atlantic working on a tramp steamer, which he had deserted in Rotterdam in order to come to Paris. After visiting the Louvre and other Seine landmarks, he had taken the long walk up rue Notre Dame de Lorette to Montmartre, where he had been told the American colored people worked and lived. After sharing a room (platonically) with a Russian dancer employed at Zelli's and finding that a job as a bouncer at a club was not to his liking, he learned from Rayford Logan, Eugene's friend, of the position at Le Grand Duc.[64] Logan, who had never felt more racial humiliation than when he served as an officer in the AEF under white commanders,[65] had stayed on in France to postpone the return to life as a second-class citizen in the States. Eventually he did return to become a distinguished professor at Howard University.

Several months after employing Hughes, Bullard hired the redheaded Ada Louise Smith, already well known in entertainment circles in the States as "Bricktop," as the establishment's singer.[66] Hughes' and Bricktop's recollections supplement, and sometimes contradict, Bullard's comparatively spare memories of his experience at the club. Both Hughes and Bricktop remembered Bullard as the man who hired them not in the late summer of 1924 ("three months after Jacqueline's christening party"), but much earlier in the year, Hughes in February, Bricktop in May.[67] Moreover, they recalled him hiring them acting as the club's manager, not its owner. Indeed, Bricktop identified the owner as Jamerson, who, she said, sold Le Grand Duc to her in late 1927; she held it for a year before moving across the street to open a new club, Bricktop's,[68] which would come to rival Zelli's as Montmartre's most celebrated cabaret.

Bricktop recollected that "Gene didn't take too well to my being the boss, but he stuck it out, and I stuck it out and after a while we became friends."[69] Although she did not say so, presumably Bullard did buy Le Grand Duc from her sometime in 1928, owning it into the 1930s. Bullard said he sold the club after he had purchased L'Escadrille, a bar a stone's throw away at 5, rue Fontaine.[70] Bullard's proud acknowledgment of his brief mention by Hughes in his autobiography, *The Big Sea,* suggested that his exact status—whether owner or manager of the club—was not of great significance to him when he was writing "All Blood Runs Red." As a matter of fact, just before his death Bullard hoped that Hughes would proofread and find a publisher for the work.[71]

Whatever his situation at Le Grand Duc, Bullard was undoubtedly a central figure in the dazzling panorama of late-night and early-morning Montmartre. Evidence of this is glimpsed in Florence Gilliam's 1945 *France: A Tribute by an American Woman,* which included a chapter on the interwar American expatriate community of which she was a member from 1919 to 1941. Recalling "the heyday of the American Negro entertainer in Paris," she wrote that the period "was essentially the epoch of the entertainers who did not come and go but remained abroad." "How," she reminisced, "their names come rolling back for they were so much a part of that fabulous span between Versailles and Munich." First in her recollections stood "Gene Bullard, left over from a military career in the Lafayette Escadrille, beating the drum and shouting 'It ain' gonna rain no mo,' or receiving guests in black tied urbanity." Bullard was prominent enough for Ernest Hemingway to base a minor character on him in *The Sun Also Rises,* his celebrated novel depicting lost generation white expatriates in Europe in the early '20s. At Zelli's, a black, southern-accented drummer sings and exchanges pleasantries with Lady Brett Ashley, who acknowledges to Jake Barnes, the novel's protagonist, "He's a great friend of mine." [72]

Bullard's Montmartre was a social setting in which cabaret personnel, entertainers, and patrons all wore formal dress: the men, tuxedos, the women, the latest gowns of Parisian designers such as Paul Poirot and Eddy Molyneux, who outfitted Bricktop. [73] With his political connections, Bullard had helped establish Zelli's, where he would continue to beat the drums at least until 1928. In introducing all-night entertainment and early-daylight breakfasts of pancakes and sausages, but, most of all, in hiring Bricktop, he would also bring success to Le Grand Duc, which had languished since opening its doors in 1921. In his dual role as a black Frenchman and an African American, he was the vital link between his club and the black American jazz talent then so much in vogue.

When first at Le Grand Duc, "struggling to make a name" for himself, he had "more free than paid entertainment . . . from good professionals . . . who remembered how I had helped them as hard-up entertainers in the years before I was married." [74] One of these professionals was jazz drummer Buddy Gilmore, who had played in Paris before the war with dancers Vernon and Irene Castle. Irene Castle would later credit Gilmore and James Reese Europe as the inspiration for the upbeat, syncopated dances such as the foxtrot that the Castles popularized among American whites in the prewar years. [75] Also associated with Gilmore and Europe and performing for Bullard without compensation was his friend Arthur "Dooley" Wilson. Born in 1894 in Tyler, Texas, Wilson left an impoverished home to work in minstrel shows, circuses, and vaudeville.

In 1910 he signed on with Europe's Clef Club in New York and during the war came to France with Europe's African American band of the 15th New York Infantry. Wilson would soon form his own band, which entertained audiences throughout Europe and North Africa. He would later achieve international celebrity status as the character "Sam" singing "As Time Goes By" in the 1942 film *Casablanca*—a role that his work in Le Grand Duc and other Parisian clubs ideally prepared him for. In the 1930s, Wilson returned to the States to become a theatrical and motion picture performer. He did not have to endure, as Bullard and so many others did, the flight from Nazi aggression—the great exodus dramatized in *Casablanca*.[76]

Among artists whom Bullard paid to perform were Palmer Jones, a pianist, and his wife, Florence Embry, a singer. It was her talent, Hughes believed, that attracted patrons such as Jack Dean and Fannie Ward,[77] although Bullard in catering to the socially influential couple at their residence may have already brought them into the club. Other patrons Hughes remembered from the pre-Bricktop period were Nancy Cunard, the English shipping heiress who would champion the African American cause in the States and take several black American lovers in Paris, most notably, in 1928, pianist Henry Crowder; Anita Loos, the silent film dialogue writer whose satirical 1925 novel *Gentlemen Prefer Blondes* has a "bimbo" character recalling "devine" Paris and her visit to "Momart"; the Dolly Sisters, the celebrated Hungarian American dancing team who resided in separate châteaus just outside Paris in the 1920s; Sparrow Robertson, the sports reporter for the *Paris Tribune;* Louis Aragon, French surrealist poet and political activist; and Prince Touvalou of Dahomey,[78] presumably now secure in his pleasure-taking under the watchful eye of Bullard and his bouncer, Blink McCluskey.

In addition to these celebrities, a number of others spent their early-morning hours at Le Grand Duc in the 1920s: Harry Pilcer, an American dancer who had come to Paris in 1917 with the Gaby Deslys review; noted singers Mabel Mercer, a light-skinned Negro woman from England, and Sophie Tucker, a veteran American music hall star who had supported black entertainers in the States for years; and movie stars Charles Chaplin, Edward G. Robinson, and Gloria Swanson. The stylish Swanson, the acknowledged diva of the silent film era and extremely popular in Paris in the middle '20s because of her starring roles in a series of films based on French themes, was a regular at Le Grand Duc.[79]

In April 1928, there were memorable celebrity appearances—perhaps especially so for Bullard because of his knowledge of the French language and culture. American comic actor Roscoe "Fatty" Arbuckle entered Le Grand Duc in the company of wrestler Ed "Strangler" Lewis. Performing a comic monologue at the Empire Theater in Paris, Arbuckle's career and reputation had disintegrated in Hollywood following the alleged rape and murder of a young woman there in September 1921, a circumstance of which Eugene was unaware. French music hall star Mistinguett, whom Bullard "had known for years and had always found . . . a gracious and charming lady," happened to be among the clientele that night. Upon recognizing Arbuckle, she began directing a torrent of cutting remarks toward him in French as well as criticizing Bullard for letting him on the premises. Bullard was "on the spot," for "la Miss" was then an idol whom, in the words of a French music hall historian, "Paris venerated . . . as one of its monuments and believed . . . to be as eternal." Nonetheless, he felt he must insist that she leave, "pretending not to hear her protests" as he escorted her to the door. When Arbuckle asked him what "Miss Stinkey" had said, Eugene could only reply "not much."[80]

The Prince of Wales, Edward Windsor, heir to the throne and briefly king of Great Britain in 1936, also patronized Le Grand Duc on visits to Paris in the 1920s and '30s.[81] The prince had won the affection of British troops during the war for defying protocol by coming to their trenches under artillery fire, where he once saw his driver killed by a direct hit. In his mid-twenties at the armistice, he, like so many men of his generation who had known the horrors of the front, found in the jazz music played in cabarets in London and Paris a soothing counterpoint to the dirge of the war.[82] A competent jazz drummer, the prince learned to dance the "black bottom" from Bricktop in 1926 and was a familiar figure at Frisco's, a club near Le Grand Duc owned by Bullard's friend Jocelyn Bingham, a black Jamaican. At Frisco's club, Bingham photographed the prince, his fiancée Wallis Simpson, and other notables including Mistinguett, the Marquis de Polignac, Salvador Dalí, Bricktop, and Bullard himself.[83]

Florence Embry left Le Grand Duc in the spring of 1924 to open another club in the neighborhood, Chez Florence, at 61, rue Blanche—a place she would own with Louis Mitchell, Bullard's drum instructor.[84] The task of finding her replacement fell naturally to the man who had been hiring attractions at Zelli's for years. Bricktop related the circumstances of her hiring, as Bullard had told it to her. Palmer Jones had recommended her to him, saying "she don't have no great big voice or anything like that, but she has got the damnedest personality, and she can dance. She'll be a big success over here." Bullard had inquired, "But won't she be competition for your wife?" Palmer replied that Florence "needed competition. Her head's gotten so big that nobody can get along with her." Bullard had cabled a Montmartre friend, Sammy Richardson, an African American dancer then in New York, to make her the offer. Bricktop was working at Connie's Inn in Harlem. Although perfectly happy there, she accepted on "the spur of the moment," embarking on the "new adventure just for the sake of adventure." On May 11, 1924, she arrived dreadfully seasick at Le Havre. Waiting for her at the dock was "Gene Bullard . . . a tall handsome American Negro." They were both then twenty-nine years old.[85]

After the two had arrived by train in Paris, Bullard took Bricktop into Le Grand Duc to show the singer her new "room." Accustomed to performing in the spacious clubs of Chicago and New York, she burst into tears at the tiny size of the triangular cabaret. After spending several nights with Bullard touring the other clubs in the area, she realized that its size by Montmartre standards was not unusual.[86] Since much of Le Grand Duc's clientele had departed with Florence Embry, Bricktop entertained few customers for the balance of 1924 and into the spring of 1925. In this slow period she settled into Parisian life, furnished an apartment, and bought the gowns that were de rigueur in the cabaret night scene. Hughes and Bricktop found great enjoyment at the club when black musicians, their work at other nightspots completed, would gather there in the predawn hours to gossip, eat soul food prepared by a black cook, and enter into impromptu jam sessions, a term which, as Hughes noted, had not yet come into existence. These same sessions were the inspiration for his bringing jazz rhythms into his poetry.[87] Neither he nor Bricktop seem to have realized that without Bullard's presence at Le Grand Duc, the musicians, who were his personal friends and sometime playing partners, would never have congregated there.

In the late spring of 1925, Bricktop's incomparable charm as a hostess, the intimacy with each listener she established as a singer, and her considerable dancing skills—traits that in a few years would make her internationally known—began to draw customers away from Florence Embry and back to Le Grand Duc. The 1925 guide to Montmartre observed that the clientele arrived at the club between 2:00 and 3:00 A.M. "Buddie Gilmore, the King of Jazz," and "Bricktop, the creole singer . . . created such excitement that the customers were left with an irresistible urge to dance the dance of St. Guy on the sidewalk."[88] Fannie Ward and Jack Dean, put off by Florence's aloofness, led the way back. In their tow were show people such as Fred and Adele Astaire, Clifton Webb, and New York's party-going mayor, Jimmy Walker.[89]

In the fall of 1925, a large contingent of patrons began arriving from Montparnasse. Most prominent among these was F. Scott Fitzgerald, whose novel *The Great Gatsby* had just appeared. In spite of Fitzgerald's frequent drunken sprees at Le Grand Duc, episodes he would later rue in his 1931 short story "Babylon Revisited,"[90] Bricktop developed a maternal affection for him, frequently accompanying him by taxi to his and his wife, Zelda's, home in Neuilly. Invariably, Zelda would have returned much earlier.[91] Other American writers at the club were Ernest Hemingway, Robert McAlmon, and Louis Bromfield. She also played host at this time to artists such as Picasso, Man Ray, and Kikki, a famous Montparnasse café personality[92] and nude model for a number of artists, among them Eugene's wartime friend Kisling.[93]

More than any other patron, it was American songwriter Cole Porter who "made" Bricktop's career at Le Grand Duc and later at her own place. Unrecognized by her sitting among the clientele at the club, he had admired her treatment of one of his songs, "I'm in Love Again"; but what kept him coming back was his delight in her "talking feet and legs" as she danced the Charleston. Soon "Bricky," as friends and regulars at the club called her, was giving Charleston lessons at parties in the Porters' fauviste-decorated apartment on rue Monsieur in St. Germain. Her pupils there were wealthy Americans and European aristocrats such as Elsie de Wolfe, a former Broadway stage star who had become Lady Mendl in Paris upon her marriage to Sir Charles Mendl, the press attaché at the British embassy in the French capital. Soon these people were hiring her to do Charleston and Black Bottom parties at their princely residences. And, of course, these same people would bring their chic to Le Grand Duc.[94]

It is possible that Bullard played a role in the Bricktop-Porter connection, because he had been instrumental in drawing Elsa Maxwell to the club after entertaining with a jazz band at one of her parties.[95] An American who had made a fortune in hotel ownership along the French Riviera, Maxwell was an archrival of Fannie Ward as hostess to the Parisian-American beau monde in the 1920s. A member of Maxwell's entourage, Porter had been introduced to Le Grand Duc through her. A prankster who enjoyed wearing a variety of military uniforms in Paris during the war and who married and settled there afterwards, Porter had been befriended by Maxwell in New York in 1916 when he was struggling to get his music accepted.[96]

Bricktop's regard for Bullard was ambivalent. While acknowledging his many kindnesses in helping her get established in Paris, she disliked his "trigger temper" and his persistent use of "bad language" in her presence. She was so angry with him at one point she might have shot him.[97] If they sometimes rubbed each other the wrong way, their radically different routes to Montmartre may have been the reason. A dark-skinned Southerner, Eugene had spent much of his life confronting Jim Crow and had done so even in Paris in the years before she arrived. His had been the rough company of gypsies, sailors, boxers, soldiers, and jazzmen.

Light-skinned Ada Louise Smith had grown up in a southside Chicago neighborhood not yet Balkanized into ethnically exclusive enclaves. She had attended integrated public schools with integrated teaching staffs and had been raised by a loving but firm mother who had insisted that her children speak decorously. Unlike the case with her other children, Ada's mother, recognizing her talent, had not opposed her desire to leave school at age sixteen for the stage. As a result, her red-haired daughter loved her, stayed in constant contact with her, and retained much of her gentility: "I always had good manners thanks to Moma."

Ada's singing and dancing career with various Negro reviews had taken her through Northern metropolises where, in and out of African American theaters and hotels, she had rarely personally felt the sting of racial discrimination.[98] In meeting Bullard, so assimilated to French life and involved with his Parisian family, she may have failed to grasp how embittering his experience had often been. For his part, Eugene's occasional provocations with "bad language" may have masked a bit of envy over the ease with which the pretty little songbird was rising to stardom in a city whose recognition he had earned much more dearly.

Perhaps because of Bullard's marked "foreignness," Hughes and Bricktop saw nothing remarkable about his past in their memoirs. In Hughes' lengthy recollection of Le Grand Duc, Bullard played a small role amid characters described in much greater detail. His only references to him by name were in two sentences, "Gene Bullard, the colored manager, told me to be at work at eleven o'clock" and "the evening Bricktop arrived, Gene Bullard, the manager, went to meet her at Le Havre." "The manager" was mentioned in several other comic anecdotes in which the brawny black cook, Bruce, and a waitress, Annette, protest violently against their firings. In both instances, the manager, interestingly, stayed out of the frays and, in Bruce's case, facing a butcher's knife, completely backed down.[99] As a poet recently published in *The Crisis* and drawn to black writers and intellectuals such as Logan and Alain Locke, whom he met in Paris at this time, Hughes may simply not have been interested in Eugene's story even had he known it. What Bricktop said of his earlier life was brief and inaccurate: "he'd come to France in 1914 because he couldn't get aviation training in the U.S. After serving in the Foreign Legion, he'd gone on to become a pilot with the Lafayette Escadrille."[100]

Although these two notables failed to take up the Bullard story, there is evidence that for other black Americans in Paris, his life, perhaps because only partially known through rumor, was the stuff of legend in the 1920s. Writer Gwendolyn Bennett, who spent a year in Paris after arriving in June 1925, knew well the Montmartre cabaret scene and Le Grand Duc.[101] Although she did not mention Bullard in her private journal of this period, one of her Paris stories, "Wedding Day," published in 1926, seems to have been fashioned loosely from various aspects of his life in France. Her protagonist, Paul Watson, knows the "somber," "otherworldly" beauty of the gray Paris dawn as he saunters down rue Pigalle to the Flea Pit on the rue de la Bruyère. About to be married to a white woman, his racial hatred has turned to compassion. He had come to Paris in 1910 and made his living giving boxing lessons. He played banjo with the first colored American jazz musicians to arrive in Paris. The narrator of the story has "heard almost every Negro in Montmartre tell about the night" that Paul beat up white-compatriot patrons in a bar after being called "nigger" by a Kentuckian. "Every tale I have heard . . . was different and yet there was something of truth in each of them." Widely reputed a "black terror," he had done time in prison for shooting and wounding two white soldiers. When pardoned, he becomes "free and a French soldier. . . . Because he was strong and had innate daring in his heart, he was placed in the aerial squad and cited many times for bravery." [102]

Like Bennett's Paul Watson at the end of her story, Bullard was, at the time she wrote, a much more settled person than the flamboyant individual in the French air service who had worn outsized wings on his customized dress uniform of scarlet and black. While he would never completely renounce fighting for his honor, photographs of him in his nightclub tuxedos at Le Grand Duc and Zelli's from the mid-1920s reveal a sober, contemplative, even shy family man. Instead of the hard glint of his stare in the *Defender* photo, a softness has crept into his eyes. [103] For Bullard, his marriage into a loving white family had swung him back once and for all to a perspective from which he perceived people as "good" or "bad" regardless of skin color. As he prospered in this period, he was compelled to help out struggling individuals as he had so often been aided in the past. [104]

Bricktop herself recalled how solicitous Eugene was in bringing her into Paris and setting her up there. She might not have survived without his resourcefulness. One evening, within a week of her arrival, she doubled over in pain. Bullard rushed her in a taxi to a pharmacist, who advised that she see a doctor. He stopped another taxi and directed the driver to a surgeon, who diagnosed acute appendicitis but said he could not operate for several days. "Gene lost his temper," according to Bricktop. "He raised the roof," forcing the doctor to schedule surgery for the next day. When she asked Eugene what he had said, he replied that he had made known to the surgeon that as a flier he had offered his life for France and now he wanted him to do something for his "countrywoman" and "he would kill him if he didn't do the operation real quick."[105] Bricktop observed that after the friction between the two when she bought out Jamerson, she and Eugene "became friends" and "grew to respect each other." With all her new responsibilities, "I was glad to have a big tough man like Gene around to take care of any problems." In December 1929, after she had sold Le Grand Duc (presumably to him), Bullard was the best man when she married jazz saxophonist Peter Duconge. At a Mairie, quite likely of the 10th Arrondissement where he and Marcelle had exchanged vows, Eugene "guided us through the intricacies of a French marriage ceremony and prompted us when to say 'oui.'"[106]

Bricktop and Alberta Hunter recalled that black entertainers enjoyed "a strong pro-Negro prejudice" in the Paris of the 1920s.[107] It was difficult for French jazz musicians to find work in the Montmartre clubs without "blackening up." Without acting ability or skill, Bob Scanlon, Bullard's old boxing and soldiering friend, was given an important role in a French motion picture. That this pro-Negro bias especially favored African Americans is indicated in the observation of a French music critic who reported the case of an old acquaintance, a Senegalese jazz band leader, who admitted changing his name to "William's" [sic], an appellation which "coming from America" was more appealing to the French than his native name.[108]

The wave of appreciation for African American music and dance in Paris swelled to new heights in the fall of 1925. On October 2, a troupe of twenty-five black American musicians, singers, and dancers opened "La Revue Nègre" at the Théâtre Champs-Elysées. A week before opening night, the owners of the theater, Rolf de Mare and Andre Daven, had invited French performing artists, painters, and writers to a preview of two of the revue's nine tableaux. The ecstatic reaction of people like Mistinguett, who revealed her beautiful legs in shimmying with the troupe's dancers on tabletops at an after-preview party, ensured that the troupe would perform before a packed house on opening night. Nineteen-year-old Josephine Baker, although hardly unknown in black American entertainment circles, would emerge as the star of the show. Persuaded to perform bare-breasted—a mode lately fashionable for female dancers in French music hall spectaculars—she had stunned the crowd with her solo performance in the second tableau, a frenetic dance in which she was a blur of bending knees and arms and forward and backward movements of her derriere. She skittered off the stage on all fours, her rear end in the air, her legs straightened. During this set, her metamorphosis from a grotesque, cross-eyed, animal-like creature at one moment into a beautiful woman of beguiling, sensual charm an instant later was transfixing.[109]

In the concluding tableau, clad in a feathered satin bikini, Baker was borne on stage upside down, her legs in a split position, on the back of muscular Joe Alex. After slowly dismounting, she again transfixed the audience with a *danse sauvage,* pulsing to the syncopated beat of the jazz orchestra. As the curtain fell on a crescendo of movement and sound, the audience knew it had witnessed something special, an avant-garde Parisian cultural moment akin to the first performance of Stravinsky's *The Rite of Spring* in 1913 and the openings of exhibitions of postimpressionist artists earlier in the century. French critics would discuss for months the reasons for the shattering impact and appeal of the revue and of Baker herself.[110]

Baker's performances in "La Revue Nègre" and in "La Folie du Jour" in 1926 at the Folies-Bergère, in which she danced in the banana belt—which quickly became a Parisian cultural icon—made her a star rivaling Mistinguett as a music hall attraction. Bricktop had introduced the Charleston in Paris, but when Baker danced it on stage it became the rage of the town. Her appearances in Paris touched off a craze for all things "Bakair"—from staining the skin with walnut oil to suntanning to hairstyling, complete with a product called "Bakair-fix" to attach the signature "Bakair curl" to the forehead. There were also "Bakair" perfumes, dolls, and a Poirot-designed pink gown, "la robe Joséphine."[111] The publicist for "La Revue Nègre," Paul Colin, would publish the lithographs of his posters for the show under the title *Le Tumulte Noir,*[112] the term quickly adopted by the Parisian media to describe the enthusiasm for black entertainers in Paris in the '20s—an enthusiasm also recognized by French historians.[113]

As Bullard had guided Bricktop through the mundane realities of getting around in Paris, finding an apartment, and shopping, so Bricktop now helped Baker, who, as a semiliterate late teenager, "brought out the mother instinct in me, just as Scott Fitzgerald had. . . . She'd come into the Grand Duc and ask me about everything. She'd say, 'Bricky, tell me what to do.' She wouldn't go around the corner without asking my advice." However, within a year, Josephine met a new mentor, her lover, Giuseppe "Pepito" Albatino, a dance instructor at Zelli's and habitué at Le Grand Duc. Under his tutelage, according to Bricktop, Josephine learned how to "read, write, and speak proper French," observe "the social graces," and appreciate classical traditions in music and art.[114] By December 1926, when she opened her dance salon well up the hill from Zelli's and Le Grand Duc at 39, rue Fontaine,[115] Baker had, in Bricktop's judgment, begun to distance herself from the African American expatriate enclave in Montmartre.[116] She was on her way to a lifetime of expatriation in France, spent mostly in the company of Europeans.

Although Bullard was acquainted with Baker, both as a drop-in at Le Grand Duc and as a babysitter for his daughter Jacqueline,[117] neither mentioned the other in their memoirs. However, one of the other stars of "La Revue Nègre," clarinetist Sidney Bechet, became a close friend. Bechet's recollection of him revealed Bullard's generosity and how he sought to bring his familiarity with French law and officialdom to the assistance of his fellow countrymen in Paris. Bechet had come to know the Montmartre jazz clubs in the early-morning hours after finishing his performances with the revue in the fall and winter of 1925–26. When Baker left the troupe to perform in her own show at the Folies-Bergère in the spring of 1926, Bechet had spent the rest of that year and most of 1927 working with jazz bands all across Europe. In 1928, he was back in Paris, playing in Noble Sissle's orchestra at Les Ambassadeurs on the Champs-Elysées and then, when Sissle returned to the States, at Chez Florence on the rue Blanche.[118] When not at work, Bechet enjoyed joking, gossiping, playing cards, shooting pool, and drinking with other jazzmen at the Flea Pit, an institution that also sold the sterno stoves used by patrons for cooking and heating in their nearby apartments.

John Zacharia Turner Jr. employed Bullard as a stable boy in Dawson, Georgia, in the years 1910–1911. "Zach" and his sons Doug and Ange trained Eugene to ride their horse in races held during the 1911 Terrell County Fair. (Courtesy of Sally Turner Loska.)

DIXIE KID
l'ex-champion du monde poids welters et ses deux jeunes espoirs.

Aaron Lester Brown, the Dixie Kid, trained and managed Bullard as a prize fighter in England and, in 1913, arranged for the first bouts Bullard fought in Paris. Brown is acknowledged as one of boxing's greatest welterweights. (From *La Boxe & Les Boxeurs*, January 21, 1914.)

Colonel Girod, Inspector General of the French Schools of Aviation,
initially admitted Bullard to flight school as a machine gunner and then
later approved his request to be trained as a combat pilot. Girod also
testified on Bullard's behalf against the libelous attack on Eugene's war
record that appeared in the January 2, 1923, Paris edition of the *Chicago
Tribune*. (From James Norman Hall and Charles Bernard Nordhoff,
The Lafayette Flying Corps, vol. 1 [Houghton-Mifflin Company:
Boston, 1920].)

Jeff Dickson, Bullard's friendly antagonist, who lost a $2,000 wager with Bullard that Eugene would never learn to fly. Between the wars, Dickson promoted prize fights and other spectacles in Paris. A Natchez, Mississippi, native, Dickson served as an American Army Air Corps pilot in World War II until he was shot down and killed in 1943. (Courtesy of Andy Dickson.)

Bullard on a French Air Service identification record created early in his flight training. Over his heart he wears the Croix de Guerre awarded for his valor at Verdun. The pin beneath his right shoulder is an insignia of the French Air Service. (Courtesy of Richard Reid and Jacqueline O'Garro.)

Jean Navarre, the talented, unconventional French aviator, was sometimes Bullard's drinking pal when they went on leave to Paris in 1917 and 1918. (Bibliothéque nationale de France photographic plate. By permission.)

Ted Parsons, an American pilot in French service, told Bullard about discriminatory actions taken against Eugene by American officials in Paris in 1917. A lifelong friend, Parsons urged Bullard to write his memoir and suggested its title *All Blood Runs Red*. (From James Norman Hall and Charles Bernard Nordhoff, *The Lafayette Flying Corps*, vol. 1 [Houghton-Mifflin Company: Boston, 1920].)

Bullard stands with the band at Zelli's, just to the left of the reveler with the conical hat. Nearest to the camera, champagne glass in his right hand, is proprietor Joe Zelli, Eugene's mentor in the nightclub business. (From Frank Driggs and Harris Lewine, *Black Beauty, White Heat: A Pictorial History of Classic Jazz* [William Morrow and Company: New York, 1982]. Courtesy of Frank Driggs.)

Bullard at the bar of Le Grand Duc. In the center is Blink McCluskey, a fellow boxer from pre–World War I years who became a bouncer at the club. At the far left is Fernando Jones. Like Bullard, Jones was a "graduate" of Belle Davis's Picks who lived and worked as an entertainer in Paris in the 1920s. (Courtesy of Richard Reid and Jacqueline O'Garro.)

Bullard used this 1929 photograph when he applied
to the Aéro-Club de France for a reissue of his flight
certificate. During World War I, he had sent the
original certificate to his father in Columbus, Georgia.
(By permission of Musée de L'Air et de L'Espace/
Paris–Le Bourget.)

Bullard attacked by law officers while attempting to enter the grounds of the Paul Robeson concert in Peekskill, New York, September 4, 1949. (Courtesy of *People's Weekly World*.)

Bullard, in his Rockefeller Center elevator operator's uniform, listens to Dave Garroway comment on his many medals from three services and the two world wars, during his interview on the National Broadcasting Company's Today Show, December 22, 1959. (Courtesy of Richard Reid and Jacqueline O'Garro.)

Bechet has these evocative memories of Montmartre at this time: "Any-time you walked down the street you'd run into four or five people you knew—performers, entertainers, all kinds of people who had a real talent to them. . . . Everybody had a kind of excitement about him. Everyone, they was in a craze to be doing. Well, you'd start to go home, and you'd never get there. There was always some singer to hear or someone who was playing. . . . It seemed like you just couldn't get home before ten or eleven in the morning." [119] Sometime in this heady period, Bechet and Bullard became friends.

In December 1928, at one of the musicians' gatherings, Bechet became involved in a violent argument with two other African Americans, Mike McKendrick, a banjo player, and Glover Compton, a veteran ragtime pianist who led the house band at Zelli's. [120] Exactly what was at issue— a dispute over music, a woman, or simply personal animosity—is not clear. Bechet believed that Glover, a Chicagoan, enjoyed baiting Southern blacks, drawing attention to their relative lack of education and sophistication, and was encouraging the younger McKendrick, also from Chicago, to belittle Bechet, who had grown up in New Orleans, on this score. Whatever the reason, the result was a shootout between Bechet and McKendrick on the rue Fontaine. Neither of the shooters was wounded, but Glover was hit in a leg, a twenty-two year old Australian dancer in a lung, and a French pedestrian in the neck. A witness, jazzman Charlie Lewis, said it was like the "scene of a fight straight out of a cowboy movie. It provided a talking point for years for the Montmartre musicians." [121]

Police arrested Bechet and McKendrick, each of whom claimed to have fired in self-defense. Both men were brought to trial and needed legal assistance. Nancy Cunard, who may have had a love interest, paid for McKendrick's expenses. [122] Although playing with Compton in the Zelli's band, Bullard came to the aid of Bechet. [123] What we know about his role comes from the clarinetist:

> Gene Boulard [sic] was a real man about Paris; he had a way. He was a man—well, the only way I can say it, he was what Glover Compton would have liked to have been in regards to making a name for himself. Except Gene had no meanness in him. If someone needed help, he did more than any Salvation Army could with a whole army; and what he wanted to do for himself, he could do in a smooth, smart way. He'd made himself the kind of man

people around Paris had a need for. The cabarets, the clubs, the musician-
ers—when there was some trouble they couldn't straighten out by themselves, they called on Gene. He was a man you could count on.[124]

No doubt Bullard sought the assistance of Robert Henri on Bechet's
behalf, but because of the injury to the French woman, he was found
guilty along with McKendrick and served an eleven-month jail sentence.
If it were not for the woman, "Gene could almost have fixed this."[125] Still,
Bullard had attended the court proceedings. When he saw the verdict taking shape, "he jumped up right there . . . where he was with the spectators
[and] came hurrying up before the court and told them no, that wasn't
the way it happened. . . . Well, like he had gone crazy. It was like the
whole court went crazy. . . . Lawyers [were] shouting, court officials [were]
pounding . . . and before anyone understood what was going on, the court
got recessed."[126]

When Bechet got out of jail, Bullard did him one final favor. Glover
Compton, feeling that Bechet had gotten off too lightly, was working with
a lawyer to devise arguments justifying his reimprisonment. "Getting
God-almighty sick of it all," Bechet warned Compton "to watch out for
his other leg. . . . But this Gene Boulard, he could see there was . . . trouble
coming. He took Glover aside. 'You stay away,' he told him, 'you really
better stay away.' And he made him do it. I never had any bother from
Glover after that."[127]

Bullard intervened on behalf of whites in racial disputes in Chez Florence, a club near his own in which gamblers played into the daylight
hours. Once he saw that Tommy Bowen had been falsely accused of speaking a racial slur and told piano player Bobby Jones that if he fought the
reluctant Bowen, Jones would have to fight Bullard too. On another occasion, he forced Bob de Rhodes to give back to Courtney Burr two thousand dollars de Rhodes had won using loaded dice. Burr, who would later
become a successful Broadway producer, sent Christmas cards to Bullard
in Paris and New York for the rest of his life. Eugene's willingness to help
others did not go unnoticed. Once, when having a drink at the Capital,
yet another cabaret in the vicinity of Le Grand Duc, he recalled being
called to the table of a white American who identified himself as "Good
Time Charlie" Chanler from Opelika, Alabama, a small town only thirty

miles west of Bullard's hometown, Columbus, Georgia. Chanler said he had heard a lot about him. "Good or bad," Eugene inquired. "I don't know. Some say you fight at the drop of a hat; others say you'll do anyone a favor." When Eugene acknowledged that "both descriptions fit," Chanler said, "I know all about you and am proud of your record." He knew Eugene "had given and given and yet was not rich." Since he was financially able, Chanler wanted to give him one thousand dollars. Bullard demurred but after being persuaded that "he meant it in the kindest way," he accepted his check.[128]

Bullard's close relations with American musicians enabled him to organize free concerts on behalf of various groups in Paris in the interwar years. On such occasions, he would borrow drums from Jocelyn Bingham and play with the likes of Bechet, Buddy Gilmore, Noble Sissle, Palmer Jones, Florence Embry—whoever was available at the time. Bullard's delight in assembling "his band" for other organizations was diminished somewhat since sometimes it brought reminders of American racial discrimination. In the late 1920s, he began bringing musicians out to Neuilly to play at the annual graduations of nurses at the American hospital. Eugene viewed these appearances as repayment for the health services offered to the musicians and other entertainers living in the city. All the nurses and doctors were appreciative except Dr. Gros, who continued to slight him. Gros's latest affront was his refusal to invite Bullard to the July 1928 dedication ceremony for the monument constructed in Garches, a Paris suburb, commemorating the American pilots who had died flying for France. Bullard's steadfast friend Ted Parsons had apprised him of the event and accompanied him to it.[129]

Bullard also brought out musicians to greet American Gold Star Mothers, women whose sons had died on the Western Front, as they descended from their trains in the rail stations of Paris. In 1931, he and a group traveled to Le Havre to welcome such a delegation as they came down the gangplank. He and the other performers were dismayed to discover that the vessel bore only African American mothers, who had been given cramped berths below decks. The more comfortable cabins above them had remained almost empty during the whole voyage from New York. Bullard's foreign friends embarrassed him by questioning him about this egregious example of American racism. "I had been telling everyone in all the 33 countries in which I had traveled how great our democracy was. It hurt me now to have my own French friends [realize] I had been lying." [130]

One of the "biggest thrills" of Bullard's musical career was bringing a group of jazzmen to play for Paris Post Number 1 of the American Legion when it inaugurated its new hall at 49, rue Pierre-Charron in the middle 1930s. That he had joined the post then and enjoyed the friendship of active members such as post commander Sedley Peck, James McCann, James Sparks, and others is another indication that he had never completely forsaken his native land.[131] Organized in the fall of 1919, Paris Post 1 provided services and sought jobs for members of the AEF who had decided to remain in France. Given the racism within the AEF, in the Legion's national organization, and in the Paris Post in the '20s, Bullard had not joined at that time although the Legion's membership criteria, covering American citizens bearing arms for a nation "associated with" the United States, made him eligible to do so.[132]

The financial panic in New York in October 1929 and the international depression that developed in its wake slowly began to sap the madcap energy of the Montmartre cabaret scene. As the flow of dollars diminished, the many clubs of the 9th Arrondissement fell on hard times. By 1933, even Bricktop was finding it difficult to pay her bills. Although the superrich, the big-name celebrities, and the aristocrats continued as regular customers (the "Duke and Duchess of Windsor and Lady Mendl to the very end"), the hordes of less affluent people were gone. Except for occasions such as the 1933 appearances of Duke Ellington, internationally known before coming to Paris, only half the tables in Bricktop's spacious club were occupied. In addition to her falling club revenues, the grand social affairs for which she and Bullard had been paid to provide entertainment were no longer in vogue. In the fall of 1934, Bricktop was forced to move to a smaller place on the rue Pigalle. Still, the slow draining away of customers continued, now including some of the formerly very wealthy ones.[133]

Bricktop remembered a banker reverting to the "good old days" by announcing "the party's on me" and proceeding to pay all that night's champagne bills and generously tipping the musicians, the waiters, and herself. On saying goodbye, he remarked that this was the "last tab he would be picking up in a long time." On the morrow, he "would return to the States and upon arrival be sent to jail." Bricktop read about it months later. Other good clients wrote notes marked "personal," asking her to lend them three or five thousand francs (several hundred dollars). She would lend the money, realizing it represented only a very small part of what they had spent at her club through the years. Soon, she herself knew "the scrounging existence . . . of going in and out of hock shops with her furs." By the fall of 1936, Bricktop's had closed. Until her departure from Paris three years later, she would sing and dance for pay in restaurants owned by others.[134]

Bullard did not immediately experience the economic difficulties of the 1930s. Sometime early in the decade, he did sell Le Grand Duc, but he continued to own two establishments, an American-style bar, L'Escadrille, at 5, rue Fontaine, and the nearby Bullard's Athletic Club at 15, rue Mansart. Such health clubs had proliferated in Montmartre during the interwar years, offering the cabaret patrons and entertainers an opportunity to balance their champagne-soaked bacchanalia with exercise. Bullard's gymnasium provided massage, whirlpool bathing, Ping-Pong, and boxing lessons to members who were given their own individual dressing rooms.[135] "Panama" Al Brown and Young Perez trained at Bullard's gym for their bantamweight world championship fight in Paris on February 19, 1934, in which Brown retained his crown. Bullard's old friend, Jeff Dickson—he of the 1917 two-thousand-dollar wager—had brought Brown to Paris in 1926 and then promoted many of his fights, including the bout with Perez. As much at ease with admirers like Jean Cocteau as with the half-boxer, half-musician world of Montmartre, Brown became yet another black celebrity in Paris.[136]

Bullard's bar was routinely packed as late as the summer of 1939, and his gym also enjoyed a large patronage that year.[137] His fluency in French and his cosmopolitanism brought large numbers of Parisians and non-American foreigners into his establishments, lessening the impact of the declining American patronage that affected Bricktop so drastically. In addition to professional boxers, his VIP clients at the gym in the thirties included pianist Fats Waller, trumpeter Louis Armstrong, and Wellington Koo, the Chinese ambassador to France from 1936 to 1940, along with his sons Wellington Jr. and Freeman.[138] Robert Goffin, a Belgian writer and early European aficionado of American jazz, remembered Armstrong's several months' stay in Paris in 1934. Armstrong had taken a flat on the rue Tour d'Auvergne in the 9th Arrondissement. "When the sun's dying rays gilded the dome of the Sacré-Coeur and he had finished his daily dozen at Bullard's gym," he would relax at Boudon's, a neighborhood café, discussing the jazz scene in Montmartre with other black American musicians, several of whom had married white Parisians. Goffin conveyed the high regard in which Bullard was held at the time of Armstrong's sojourn: "Montmartre . . . went wild with delight at having [Armstrong] in its midst. . . . [He] could no longer keep pace with his invitations. Counts, princes, millionaires, Josephine Baker, Bricktop, Gene Bullard . . . all sang his praises."[139]

Although the catered parties of high society were less frequent after the crash of '29, Bullard's friendship with Parisian Oscar Mauvais, the owner of the club Jardin de Ma Soeur on rue Caumartin, resulted in his being hired for one more such event in the summer of 1931. Knowing of Eugene's familiarity with Biarritz and his connection with African American performers, Mauvais asked him to arrange part of the entertainment for a party there at the Hôtel Negresco in honor of King Alphonso XIII of Spain, who had taken up residence in Paris after being exiled earlier that year by republican political insurgents.[140] An American millionaire whose daughter had married into the Spanish royal family was sponsoring the gala. Bullard's task was to put together a troupe of dancers, dress them "in the old plantation costumes of colored folk," and perform the high-stepping cakewalk.[141]

Bullard hired nineteen dancers, including an instructor, Nettie Compton, Glover's wife; and since a twentieth was needed, he joined the group in the two-hour rehearsals taking place each of the four days before the affair. Costumes were lent him by another Parisian friend, Henri Varna, since 1929 owner of the music hall Casino de Paris and producer of the 1930 musical review in which Josephine Baker introduced her signature song, "J'ai deux amours, Paris et mon pays." Bullard's troupe, "laden with champagne appeased by a lot of hot coffee," cakewalked into the grand ballroom at 3:00 A.M. to the beat of black American Hugh Pollard's band. The king and other guests were delighted, giving them three encores. The entertainers were then treated to a huge supper in the hotel's dining room, which the king visited, toasting and shaking hands with all of them. Eugene recalled that Mauvais paid the troupe well, but that Compton held out for double the sum given the other musicians.[142] A professional dancer for thirty years who had performed the cakewalk with a Negro troupe in the Ponsell Brothers' Circus as far back as 1902, the Iowa-born Compton was well credentialed.[143] Mauvais bowed to her demand.

On this occasion, Bullard's wife Marcelle was not with him in the resort town in which they had honeymooned and vacationed so often in the 1920s. After eight years of marriage, the couple had just separated. Eugene explains:

> The trouble between me and my wife started when her father died and left her his fortune. She wanted me to quit working and give all my time to sharing her life as a Parisian society woman. That would mean taking her to horse races at Auteuil or Longchamps every afternoon during the long season; escorting her to parties every night; and spending weeks at a time at fashionable resorts like Biarritz and Cannes or Monte Carlo.
>
> Like most American men who aren't sissies, I could not stand the idea of being a gigolo even to my wife. So I told her she could lead the full life of a society woman if she liked but to count me out in my working hours, because I was not going to give up earning my living.
>
> So we were seeing so little of each other that we decided to part company. We were Catholics and we were never divorced. About six years later my poor wife died.[144]

Given Bullard's insistence on paying his own way, a trait ingrained early on in life, it is not surprising that difficulties of this kind should develop. Once the romantic allure of their early relationship—hers for the heroic *poilu* and dashing aviator, his for the innocent, tender girl—had faded with the onset of parental responsibilities, both would want to bring the other into the style of life each had known before they met and fell in love. In 1928, Bullard was living at 6, passage Elysée des Beaux Arts, a location in Montmartre much closer to his clubs and the apartments of friends in the 9th Arrondissement than the couple's first residence on rue Franklin, a much more fashionable quarter. Perhaps Marcelle did not make the move with Bullard to the new address, or if she did, came to resent the less elegant neighborhood. Municipal records from several Mairies in Paris, however, do not bear out Bullard's assertions that the couple never divorced and that Marcelle had died in the late '30s. They were divorced on December 5, 1935, and Marcelle continued to live in Paris until her death in 1990.[145] The application for admission to the Federation of French Veterans of the Great War, which Bullard filled out in July 1940, a week after he arrived in New York, asked the applicant to check his marital status as *célibataire* [single], *marié* [married], or *veuf* [widower]. He typed in *divorcé*.[146]

Why Bullard would misrepresent these facts in "All Blood Runs Red" is a matter of speculation. Too important a detail to omit completely, as he did in the cases of unpleasant episodes already noted, he may have desired to render the marital breakup as a less decisive matter than it actually was. Moreover, his knowledge that he was approaching the end of his life as he wrote this section of the memoir may have deepened the Catholicism that he appears to have adopted over the long years of assimilation of French life. In any case, he stated that he did receive custody of Jacqueline and Lolita, who, in 1936, were twelve and nine years old. They were attending a convent school well to the south of Paris near Orléans,[147] receiving the best in French private education. He appears to have never told his daughters that their mother was alive. Whether this was out of embitterment toward his ex-wife for reasons left unmentioned in "All Blood Runs Red" or out of fear of losing the only real family he had known since adolescence may never be known.

In the middle and late 1930s, as Hitler posted armed forces on the Rhine in violation of the Versailles peace treaty and then absorbed Austria and conquered Czechoslovakia, Bullard saw the realization of what he had called in 1923 "the German threat of tomorrow." On at least one occasion, he had almost come to blows with German men in Montmartre after hearing racist remarks. At his gym, he flew the flags of twenty-one countries representing the nationalities of his clientele. When pugilist Walter Neusel, the promising "Blond Tiger of Germany," "kept asking [him] to fly the Nazi flag too," Bullard finally lost patience and "insisted he leave before he had to be carried out."[148]

The French military intelligence service, Le Deuxième Bureau, was closely watching the expansion of Hitlerite Germany. The strengthening of German armed forces and the development of new offensive strategies and tactics were well known to the bureau and accurately reported to the French civilian and military leadership, who unfortunately for their country failed to act on it. Where French intelligence was lacking in the 1920s through the mid-1930s was in counterintelligence. The problem was serious because by one estimate, on July 1, 1937, there were nearly 17,000 Germans in Paris and less than 500 French people in Berlin, many of these connected with the embassy and consulate. To deal with this situation, the French ministry of the interior created in 1936 a force of special commissaries of police, an organization called Surveillance du Territoire. These police officials were paired with military security officers who reported to their own headquarters in Paris. This new force was effective. By 1940, it had informed the Deuxième Bureau of the identity of most German agents operating in France as well as most "fifth columnists," French citizens supportive of Nazi Germany.[149]

Early in 1939, Bullard became part of this counterintelligence network. He was approached by a Paris municipal detective, Georges Leplanquais, who had recently been made, in Eugene's words, "Inspector Special Prés des Commissariats de la Ville de Paris." Leplanquais knew of Bullard's aptitude in the German language and asked him to eavesdrop on and engage in conversations with German patrons in L'Escadrille and his athletic club and to report back to him periodically. When assured that the security of his daughters would not be compromised, he readily assented. A twenty-seven-year-old Alsatian woman fluent in French, German, and English, Cleopatre Terrier, was assigned to work with him. Bullard had seen her in his bar hobnobbing with German patrons and, he believed, serving them as a prostitute. Only after his contact with Leplanquais and his introduction to Terrier did he realize that, contrary to appearances, she was seeking to avenge the murder of her father, a civilian, during the Great War.[150] Bullard's increased socializing with Germans in the spring and early summer of 1939 led to a near-fatal attempt on his life.

Beneath the gaiety of the cabaret culture in the interwar period, several criminal groups of Corsicans and gangsters from Marseilles and elsewhere were active in Montmartre, extorting protection money from the night-clubs and other enterprises in the area. Bricktop recalled successfully re-sisting pressure from one gang leader who wanted her to allow his pros-titutes to solicit in her club.[151] Bullard stated that he never had any trouble with these elements. However, on July 2, 1939, he entered L'Escadrille in the wee hours expecting to find the place jam-packed as was customary. Instead, he found only two patrons chatting quietly at the bar. An em-ployee nodded toward the men's restroom. Eugene opened the door into the wall-to-wall mirrored cabinet and saw one of the Corsicans, Justin Perreti, reflected endlessly in the mirrors, cursing and threatening him. Believing him drunk or doped, Bullard escorted him outside. Back in L'Escadrille, he was told by his doorman, Blink McCluskey, that the Cor-sican had threatened to kill the barman and had driven off most of the customers. Bullard then paid a visit to the nearby Café Lizeaux, the Cor-sican hangout, and explained to Perreti's brothers what had happened. The brothers dismissed the erratic behavior as a trifling matter resulting from Justin's large gambling losses on horse racing the day before. Eugene bought "drinks all around and everyone seemed reconciled." Yet back in his own place, he had to expel Justin once again. Back outside, Perreti exclaimed now that this was Bullard's "last night on earth," a remark the latter continued to regard as the empty ravings of an inebriate. Thirty min-utes later, as he was mopping up, Bullard looked up to see the trouble-maker standing in the doorway aiming a Luger at him. Trying calmly to talk the gunman down, Eugene walked slowly toward him and was able to push the weapon down just as it fired. In wrestling his assailant to the floor and knocking him unconscious with a bottle thrown to him from a customer at the bar, Bullard barely noticed the "cigarette burn" in his ab-domen. The bullet had passed through his lower abdomen and out his right side.[152]

After examining him at a hospital, his doctor believed that his internal organs must have been perforated and that he was beyond saving. He kept him under observation without food or water for twenty-four hours. Late in the day on July 3, asked how he felt, Bullard replied "hungry." His doctor, knowing of his war wounds, laughed and said, "You just won't die." He allowed Eugene to eat tiny portions of mashed potatoes and baby food. On the 4th, Bullard asked, "how can I get well without any real food? I think you want me to die." "No, no, Bullard," came the retort, "even if I did, our strongest medicines couldn't kill you." By the 5th he was permitted more substantial foods and wine, and on the 8th, in spite of his doctor's continuing doubts, he was allowed to return to his apartment, which, since his marital separation, was located one floor above his bar. In the hospital he had been showered with gifts and cards from well-wishers. As he was wheeled outside the hospital to a car, friends cheered him and did so again as he arrived home and was carried upstairs. He wept, overwhelmed by their support.[153]

"Kitty" Terrier, who had been investigating the shooting, reported that Justin Perreti, himself fiercely anti-German, had believed Bullard was a Nazi fifth columnist. In the scuffle for the pistol on the floor at the bar, Perreti had also accidentally shot himself. His brothers visited Eugene at his apartment, asking him to forget their brother's mistake, saying "they only hoped to God he'd live." Since the police had closed his bar after the incident, the Corsicans gave him money to cover his lost revenues until he could reopen. Although Bullard knew it was a bribe not to prosecute Justin, he accepted the cash. On leaving him, one of the Perreti brothers said, "On les aura,"[154] a popular anti-German oath from the Great War period meaning "we will get them."

Early in the morning of September 1, 1939, German armed forces attacked Poland. It was now clear that the policy of appeasement of Hitler by the English and French had failed. On September 3, the English and French governments, both of which had treaties with Poland guaranteeing Poland's independence, were compelled to declare war on Germany. Within days, train stations in Paris, as in August 1914, were overflowing with men freshly arrived from the provinces awaiting further orders as well as with soldiers already in service awaiting trains to the French border with Germany. As requested by the Belgian government, English armed forces began crossing the Channel to take up positions in Belgium along the Belgian-German frontier.[155]

Committed to the belief that another war should be avoided at all cost, French and English statesmen had not only appeased Hitler but also refused to prepare their own people for the possibility of a renewal of armed conflict. As the German military completed the conquest of Poland in October 1939, French and British troops remained in static defensive positions along Germany's western border, and they remained there throughout the fall, winter, and spring of 1939–40 as their leaders desperately began the process of rearmament and mobilization. During this period of *drôle de guerre,* "phony war," authorities in Paris pasted huge advertisements on billboards, one of them in Montmartre's Place Blanche near the Moulin Rouge, urging patriots to buy war bonds. Under the exhortation, which proved to be tragically false, "we will conquer because we are the strongest," these posters displayed a map depicting the vast territories governed by imperial France and England all around the globe.[156]

As a precaution against German air attacks, French authorities imposed nightly blackouts all across Paris. At sundown, darkness now fell over the fabled City of Light. For Bricktop, it was the blackouts that finally killed the Montmartre of her heyday. American consulate officials urged all U.S. citizens without urgent business in Paris to return home. Bricktop dawdled, reluctant to go back to an unfriendly homeland. Pushed by Lady Mendl and the Duchess of Windsor, who purchased her ticket on the passenger ship *Washington,* she finally did leave in late October 1939.[157] Many American entertainers had to await funds enabling them to pay for their voyages home, and others were stranded until the sailing dates of the ships on which they had booked passage.[158] Josephine Baker, a figure now revered in Paris as much as the "eternal Mistinguett," remained to entertain civilians and soldiers in blacked-out settings.[159] Bullard gave no thought to leaving. His daughters, now fifteen and twelve, were virtually French. He was committed to his espionage work and had kept his bar and gym open. Besides, he "was never too crazy about walking away from danger."[160]

During a quarter of a century of expatriation, beginning with his pre–

World War I tours with Belle Davis's Picks, Bullard had earned his livelihood as a civilian in the company of musicians, singers, dancers, and other performing artists, many of whom were close friends. Now, in the fall and winter of 1939–40, with a number of them temporarily stranded and financially straitened in Paris, he stepped forward to assist them. As he had been penniless for the first half of his life, he understood their plight. At his bar, no one in need ever had to ask for credit. He "always offered a glass of wine and had cigarettes around the tables so that no one had to be embarrassed by asking for them." The camaraderie among the black and white artists in the shrouded L'Escadrille expressed itself in song and dance around the piano. The joyful sounds heard out on the rue Fontaine attracted paying customers whom Bullard always urged, if they were able, to spend as much money as possible in order that he could continue to support those in need. With the dwindling of patrons at the bar and at his gym, he was becoming none too flush himself.[161] As fate would have it, he would never be flush again.

As his income shrank, he conceived of a way to continue his support of his hard-up friends. Les Halles, the market for fresh produce located in the heart of Paris, continued to provision the city abundantly during the "phony war," a fact boasted of in the Parisian press as resulting from France's valuing the sweetness of life in contrast to the wartime hardships, approaching famine, experienced by the German population.[162] In great profusion, meats, seafood, vegetables, and fruits were trucked and carted in daily from the countryside and seaports. The blackout, however, necessitated the closing of sales at 3:00 P.M. At 2:45, Eugene recalled, a bell rang out to warn everyone of the market's imminent closing. "Farmers would then discount [their produce] rather than cart them back into the country. It struck me that if I bought in those [last] minutes, I might afford to feed my friends."[163]

Having had to part with his car, Bullard constructed a handcart out of a wooden crate and bicycle wheels and began making lengthy midafternoon promenades down rues Notre Dame de Lorette and Montmartre, out on to the Grands Boulevards, and down boulevard de Sébastopol to what Emile Zola once called the "stomach of Paris." Making his way from the stall of one seller to the next, he gradually filled the cart with vegetables, bits of meat, and bones. On returning, he made the familiar steep ascent to rue Fontaine along streets once jammed with automobile traffic and tipsy revelers but now returned to the quiet activities of neighborhood residents—a calm before the storm. Back at L'Escadrille, his Chinese cook, Lulu, "would boil the strength out of a lot of bone into water, then add a bit of meat and all the vegetables and make the damnedest minestrone you ever saw." He was thus able to continue feeding his friends into the winter of 1939–40, when they were able to leave France, some with the financial assistance of the American consulate in Paris.[164] A handful of African Americans, including musicians Arthur Briggs and Charlie Lewis, remained with their Parisian wives and families and were later interned by German authorities governing Paris.[165]

In early 1940, with the departure of the Americans and other foreign nationals, Bullard closed his businesses in Montmartre. A wealthy American woman, a recent resident in Paris after the death of her English husband, Mrs. June Jewett James, invited him to work for her and her daughter, June, in her château in Neuilly. James V. Sparks, L. H. Cornwall, and James McCann of American Legion Post 1 in Paris had recommended him to her.[166] Just two years before, Sparks and McCann had joined a group of veterans from fourteen countries urging peace on Hitler at the latter's Bavarian retreat. Their hopes dashed, both men were now preparing for war: Sparks in remobilizing the American Ambulance Corps, McCann in sending cables to the American Legion's national headquarters in Washington, D.C., urging that the organization drop its isolationist stance and "wake up to the danger" that Hitler posed not only to Europe but also to the United States.[167]

Mrs. James, who was working with Sparks in the readying of the Ambulance Corps, encouraged Bullard to live at the château with Jacqueline and Lolita, whom, given the uncertain times, he had withdrawn from boarding school. He was glad to accept and served as chauffeur, masseur, and waiter at formal dinners. On the occasion of her donation of a number of vehicles to the French government, she hosted a formal luncheon for French and American dignitaries. Among the invitees was Dr. Gros, active in organizing the American Ambulance Corps in 1914, who remained the chief administrator at the American hospital in Neuilly. Bullard, who on occasions such as this wore an infantry dress uniform with all his medals, inevitably met his old nemesis. "Though [Gros] always pretended not to know [him], for some reason [this time] he spoke. 'Bullard, I didn't know you had the Médaille Militaire.'" Eugene could not refrain from answering, "Oh, I thought you kept all my records just as you keep the scroll issued me by the French government as it was to every member of the Flying Squadron." Gros turned on his heel and walked out of Bullard's life forever.[168]

Bullard estimates that about five weeks after this luncheon, he was ordered back to Paris by supervisors in what he now refers to as the "resistance" rather than intelligence. The German onslaught against the Low Countries and northeastern France, begun on May 10, 1940, was well under way because he mentions that Mrs. James, en route to Biarritz at this time, was encountering innumerable refugees fleeing southward. Within a week of the opening of their western campaign, highly motivated and well-led German soldiers, heavily supported by rapidly moving tank corps and tactical air support much superior to the forces opposing them, had pierced Allied defensive positions in Holland, Belgium, and France. French military leadership, set in the tactics of the previous war—maintaining strong defensive positions (as at Verdun) and gaining territory incrementally by foot soldiers—was totally unprepared for the lightning war German generals had planned precisely to avoid the stalemate on the Western Front that had led to Germany's defeat in 1918. The German army moved quickly around and over France's vaunted Maginot Line fortifications. It swiftly seized Holland, Belgium, Luxembourg, and northeastern France, unleashing a tidal wave of refugees, many of whom remembered the German occupation of 1914–18, moving toward Paris. Demoralized and in total disarray, French forces all across the north of France were captured by the hundreds of thousands. It was soon clear that Paris could not be defended. German forces marched unopposed through the Arc de Triomphe on June 14, 1940. By this time, panic had gripped the Parisian populace, several million of whom had poured out of the city's southern gate, Porte d'Orléans, joining their compatriots from the north in an even larger exodus toward the south.[169]

German Stuka dive-bombers, now flown from captured French air

bases, spread terror by bombing the columns of refugees, which were often intermixed with French troops in search of a location to regroup and
fight. On June 22, 1940, a new French government, led, in an irony of
history, by General Pétain, the hero of Verdun in 1916, agreed to a ceasefire and the absorption of Paris and all but the south of France into the
Third Reich. A German officer witnessing the French surrender remarked
that "the battle for France is over. It lasted twenty-six years." [170]

"Never one to run away from a fight," Bullard, now forty-four, threw
himself into the maelstrom in the last days of May. Evidently, clinging to
the belief that the Germans could not take Paris, he had returned to the
city, reopened his bar, and reoccupied his apartment. With "Kitty" Terrier
promising to safeguard his children, he was determined to join his old
170th Infantry Regiment, which he had heard was fighting in the vicinity
of Epinal, a town on the Moselle over a hundred miles to the east of Paris
at the southern end of the Maginot Line. Packing a knapsack containing
food and Nordhoff and Hall's two-volume history of the Lafayette Flying
Corps, he took the Paris metro to Porte d'Italie, another southern portal
of the city. From there he set out on foot in the company of other ill-
informed men looking for a fight. Marching all that day and through the
night, they arrived at Châlons, approximately half the distance to Epinal,
the next afternoon. There they met fleeing refugees who informed them
that Epinal and Bar-le-duc, so familiar from Bullard's days on *la voie
sacrée* in the first war, had fallen. "Nothing remained for [him] and [his]
weary companions but to march back to Paris—three days and nights this
time." At Porte d'Italie, gendarmes were under orders to bar any refugees
from entering the city. Unsuccessful in attempting to sneak into the city to
reassure his daughters, he headed south, where rumor had it that the
French 51st Infantry was making a stand. Sleeping in fields at night and
trudging along with the tide of refugees by day, he arrived at Chartres—
a railhead already devastated by German bombs. In Chartres, he chanced
to meet Bob Scanlon, his boxing companion in England and comrade in
the French Foreign Legion. The pair shared food and took heart in each
other's company—but not for long. Another Stuka raid chased them in
separate directions, and a bomb scored a direct hit on the crater in which
Scanlon had sought shelter. Unable to find any trace of him but assuming
him dead, Bullard, sick at heart, resumed his march south. [171]

Making his way toward Orléans via Le Mans, already abandoned by most of its inhabitants, Bullard witnessed the worst human suffering he had ever seen, and he had seen some horrible sights in the first war. He came upon a hysterical child standing beside the body of his mother "which had been cut in half as if by a guillotine." He sought to embrace the youngster and persuade him to come along with him, but the child jerked away, "his eyes crossing and uncrossing" in trauma. He moved on with the "sea of suffering"—people accompanied by their farm animals, pulling along their aging and incapacitated loved ones and meager belongings in carts and wheelbarrows. "Refined ways of life" were forgotten in the desperate struggle to survive. Women gave birth at roadside and people squatted to defecate as indifferent to passersby as the latter were to them. At the sight of people eating or clustered around a village fountain, individuals rushed forward and mobbed one another to get at the source of food and drink.[172]

On June 15, Bullard reached Orléans and offered his services at the barracks of the 51st Infantry, where Major Roger Bader, his superior officer at Verdun, was in command. Bader assigned him to a machine gun company on the south bank of the Loire River, where they would oppose German ground forces advancing from the north. His company was driven from Orléans by German artillery that night. Over the next three days and nights his unit recapitulated in microcosm the debacle that had befallen the whole French army that terrible spring: forced marches to defend the towns of Gien, Romorantin, and Poitiers were begun only to be broken off each time by news that they had already been seized by the more mobile German infantry.[173]

Bullard's participation in "the twenty-six-year" battle for France finally ended on June 18 at the village of Le Blanc, about one hundred miles south of Orléans, when the concussion of an exploding artillery shell blew him across a street and into the wall of a building. He hit head forward, but obliquely, resulting in a split and misaligned vertebra. Had he struck the wall head on, he would surely have been killed along with the eleven other French soldiers who died from the same shell. On the same day he was wounded, Charles de Gaulle, a French tank corps commander who had escaped capture, made his first radio address from London, in which he announced the creation of the Free French Movement, pledging the even-

tual liberation of France by the coordinated activities of resistance organizations within France and the Free French Army, which he was organizing in exile. Bullard was inspired by reports of the message and, had he
not been so severely wounded, would have fought on in France with the
resistance.[174]

Fearing that as a black person, French hero of the first war, and French
intelligence operative, he would be executed if captured by the racist Nazi
authorities, his commandant Bader ordered him to flee France via Biarritz.
From Le Blanc, he moved in a southwesterly direction toward Bordeaux.
He was able to get rides on vehicles, but during the intervals, he had to
walk in intense pain using as a crutch first his rifle, which he discarded
upon realizing it could only incriminate him, and then a stick. After
twenty-four hours, he arrived in Angoulême, where he staggered to a military hospital. There, Dr. H. C. de Vaux, a friend since his days as a medic
with the 170th Infantry at Verdun and as a doctor at the American hospital in Neuilly, gave him shots and wrapped his injured back. De Vaux
told him he had no choice except to move on south and out of France.[175]

With fresh water and cans of sardines, he continued on, sleeping in
fields and roadside ditches. Near Bordeaux, a French soldier gave him his
bicycle. He arrived at Biarritz in the predawn hours of June 22. At the
American consulate, a Mr. McWilliams, the consul, notified him that German military officers were already in the area and that he should shed his
uniform. Americans waiting in line for their diplomatic papers gave him
trousers and a shirt. When Bullard explained that he had no passport,
one not having been required in 1912, McWilliams, who had visited Columbus, Georgia, quizzed the French-accented black man about the ge-
ography of the place he gave as his hometown. Bullard answered correctly
that Girard and Phenix City were the Alabama towns that lay across the
Chattahoochee opposite Columbus. Since Biarritz was like the spout of
a funnel through which Americans had to pass in order to escape France,
Bullard met a number of old acquaintances at the consulate. Colonel
Sparks, who had recently arrived after a harrowing journey as leader of
American ambulance units, and Craney Gartz both confirmed his American identity.[176]

Consul McWilliams approved him for a passport, but it had to be issued by an American consular official located back up the road in Bordeaux over one hundred miles away. Before Bullard bicycled off, Gartz persuaded him to leave all his incriminating identification papers, and presumably the Hall and Nordhoff volumes, with him, except for the passport approval form. The politically left-leaning millionaire assured him that he would deliver them to his friend Roger Baldwin, the founder and head of the American Civil Liberties Union, whose office was at 31 Union Square in New York.[177] Eugene could pick them up there (as he did) when he arrived in the city.

After two more exhausting days and nights, he reached Bordeaux and collapsed at the Traveler's Aid Society. He got a few hours of fitful sleep in which he dreamed of the horrors of the past month, a period in which he had lost over twenty pounds. Shaken awake by a female employee at the Aid Society, he reflexively struck her a blow on the neck. Ashamed, he began sobbing. The woman assured him that she understood his travail and ushered him into the American consul, Henry S. Waterman, who issued his passport, paid for his photographs, and advanced him twenty dollars. Waterman would stay on at his post for over a year, assisting American stragglers escaping the German and Vichy zones in France. On his return to Biarritz, Bullard persuaded a dazed women to give up "to Heaven" the dead baby she had been carrying as if it were still alive. With the help of a French soldier's trenching tool and an elderly couple who had detached themselves from a column of refugees, he buried the child. Somewhat consoled by the sympathetic strangers, the woman watched him walk on toward Biarritz. It had seemed wrong to mount his bike and ride off. "To [his] sorrow, [he] never had the courage to look back."[178]

Back in Biarritz, Bullard spent his last night in the town whose beaches, once so welcoming to him and the rest of the Parisian-American smart set, would soon be enjoyed by German soldiers resting on the laurels of their stunning victory.[179] The next day, he accepted a ride into Spain from another old friend, Charlie M. Levy, who was driving an ambulance helping Americans leave France. Because of the heavy traffic, which reduced their movement to a snail's pace, they could only attain by nightfall the little seaport town of St. Jean de Luz. By midafternoon of the next day, they were able to reach the French frontier town of Hendaye and the International Bridge to Spain. At the bridge, Eugene encountered yet another old friend, Jacques de la Swaine, a former comrade in the Foreign Legion who was working as a Spanish customs officer. He treated Eugene to a fine meal and helped expedite his and the Levy party's passage through Spanish customs. Still, it was not until 2:30 A.M. the next morning, July 2, that they were allowed to cross into Spain. During the long wait, Bullard shared with the group bottles of wine given him by la Swaine. An "aristocratic lady" balked at partaking as a bottle was passed from mouth to mouth. "Feeling winish," Bullard told her that it was appropriate to "share microbes" since they were on the International Bridge. The woman took a swig and everyone relaxed.

In Spain, Eugene and other U.S. citizens were taken in American Red Cross vehicles to Bilbao, where they rested for several days in hotels reserved for them by that organization. To celebrate the Fourth of July, the Red Cross sponsored a dance in a hotel ballroom. It was a happy occasion until Spanish and German soldiers began cutting in on American couples on the dance floor, provoking a melee. Eugene had been serving as bartender for the occasion. For once, he stayed out of the fight, protecting the bottles of champagne and spirits. On July 7, he and the other Americans boarded a train to Lisbon. At the Spanish-Portuguese border, Spanish customs officials were confiscating currency. Bullard concealed one hundred thousand francs in his beret for a sick, elderly lady. During a search requiring that he remove the rest of his clothes, he talked boxing with an inspector who never asked him to take off his beret. On July 9, the train arrived in Lisbon. Awaiting in port was an American steamship, the *Manhattan,* captained by a U.S. Navy commander, G. V. Richardson. The U.S. State Department had ordered the ship to the Portuguese capital to pick up the seven hundred American refugees there. For Bullard and many other passengers, the departure of the *Manhattan* on July 12, 1940, marked the end of a generation and more of life in France—the end of an era.[180]

CHAPTER SIX

New York, 1940–1961

In the unseasonably cool and hazy midafternoon of July 18, 1940, the *Manhattan* slipped into New York harbor. Excepting one submarine sighting, the voyage had been uneventful. After stopping in quarantine waters off Staten Island to inoculate passengers for smallpox, the ship docked at the pier on West 18th Street. The *Manhattan* was just one of many vessels arriving with refugees from France almost daily in this period. Several days before, French modernist composer Darius Milhaud, writer Jules Romains, and expatriate American writer Julian Green had disembarked the *Excambion* with 140 other exiles. Many of Bullard's fellow passengers shared his experience of living in Paris for decades and surviving recent German bombings and strafings on the refugee routes south of the French capital. An American news photographer, Therese Bonney, covering the Battle of France spoke of "ending up like everybody else in Bordeaux." The voyagers had known too the agonizingly slow journey from Biarritz through St. Jean de Luz to Hendaye and then hours of more waiting on the International Bridge. They spoke of the ubiquitous presence of German military men along their route through Spain to Lisbon.[1]

Although physically ailing and anxious over the fate of his daughters, Bullard took heart in the appearance of the Statue of Liberty. The majestic monument revived his belief, never completely dormant, that America might live up to his hopes. However, "that burst of brightness from Miss

Liberty's torch was quickly clouded." On the pier, Jack S. Spector awaited American veterans of World War I among the new arrivals. A former commander of Paris Post No. 1, Spector had taught "Americanism" to the foreign-born children of American Legionnaires living in Paris. Evidently, as was the case with Dr. Edmund Gros, Spector's sturdy patriotism was not fully inclusive, for he had made room arrangements in New York for all members except Bullard.[2] Mitigating this slight was the gift of a small sum of money and the promise of more from Sedley Peck, Bullard's Paris American Legion friend who had also returned to the States on the *Manhattan*. The bearded, beret-wearing francophile, whose California mining company maintained a New York office, had sailed for France on the *Manhattan* on May 19 as a director of the American Volunteer Ambulance Corps. He had served under French command on the Saar front and been forced back to Bordeaux with the defeated remnants of the French army. Of the ninety-four men in his outfit, forty-one were missing and three were known to be prisoners of war.[3]

Bullard spent his first night in New York at 1829 Seventh Avenue in the apartment of a Parisian acquaintance for whom he had delivered a piece of luggage. He stayed in a room at this address for several months before renting apartments at several Harlem locations during World War II. In the late 1940s, he settled in a lodging at 80 East 116th Street, where he would reside for the rest of his life.[4] Bullard knew of Harlem as a mecca for African Americans through his connections in Paris with black entertainers and literary people like Langston Hughes. Although in marked economic and cultural decline when he moved there, Harlem still retained in its general landscape something of the beauty of the Parisian scene: the sculptured facades and low skylines of the once-elegant brownstones, the broad avenues with their magnificent views of the distant skyscrapers of midtown Manhattan, and the spaciousness of nearby Central Park. Given his straitened financial situation, which at times had him taking housekeeping jobs for French friends downtown, Bullard found the rents he paid in Harlem within his means.[5]

The area in which Bullard lived was Spanish Harlem, where the majority Puerto Rican population continued to grow throughout the years he lived there. An expatriate from ages sixteen to forty-five, he was linguistically and culturally more French than African American. "El Barrio," with its Latin accent and, near his apartment, its large outdoor public market for fresh seafood, meats, fruits, and vegetables—so reminiscent of those in Paris—may have felt more like home than the African American neighborhoods in the vicinity of Lenox Avenue and 125th Street.[6] Harlem's hometown newspaper, the *New York Amsterdam News,* proudly recognized Bullard as a "Harlemite" but one who had "gone French."[7] A resident in Harlem, Bullard was not fully of it; for the most part, his occupational and social commitments lay outside the area.

Bullard's first employment in New York was as a security guard at a U.S. Army base in Brooklyn. One day amidst the jostling of a crowd getting off a ferry on the way to work, a man focused on Bullard as the reason for his impeded movement, yelling out, "you black bastard!" Bullard knocked him down and recalls a Federal Bureau of Investigation agent intervening to prevent others in the crowd from assaulting him. The agent spoke to the crowd of the black man's exemplary record against the Germans in two wars. Bullard assumed the man knew of his exploits through a government security clearance report. With the agent's assistance, he was able to secure a higher-paying job as a longshoreman loading ships at a U.S. Navy yard on Staten Island.[8] The heavy lifting this work required was, owing to his back injury, extremely painful, but Bullard was desperate to augment his income in order to support Jacqueline and Lolita when they would arrive in New York.

Bullard's concern for his daughters in Nazi-administered Paris was heightened by the lack of any news concerning them, a situation stemming from the determination of the conquerors to seal the French capital off from the outside world. Combating his fears through action, he would play a key role in securing his children's departure from France. In Paris, he had become acquainted with the American ambassador to France, William C. Bullitt. Made ambassador in 1936, Bullitt had earned the admiration of Americans abroad by remaining in Paris for a month after its takeover to assist them in dealing with the German authorities and helping them exit the country. Called home in mid-July, Bullitt served for some months as a special advisor to President Franklin Delano Roosevelt in Washington, D.C.[9] In the fall of 1940, Bullard took the train down to

Washington to explain personally to Bullitt his daughters' circumstances and enlist his expertise on their behalf.

Bullitt promised he would take up their case and delivered. In January 1941, Eugene received two telegrams from Secretary of State Cordell Hull assuring him that American officials in Paris were issuing papers and advancing funds to transport the two youngsters, now sixteen and fourteen, along the now well-established exit route—Paris, Bordeaux, Biarritz, Hendaye, Lisbon. In late January, Hull telegraphed the joyous news that Jacqueline and Lolita were in Lisbon and ready to be repatriated. They departed on the *Exeter* and arrived on a chilly, snow-swept February 3 at Pier F at Jersey City, where their ecstatic papa gathered them up in his arms.[10]

Austen B. Crehore, president of the New York–based Lafayette Flying Corps Association, earned Bullard's eternal gratitude by driving over from his home in New Jersey to pick him up in Harlem, take him to Jersey City, and return him home with his girls. Crehore had also solicited funds from corps members to pay for Jacqueline's and Lolita's voyage. Among the sixteen American fliers for France who assisted Bullard at this time were his friends Ted Parsons, at that moment preparing for sea duty as a U.S. Navy officer; Reginald Sinclaire, his barrack roommate at the training base at Avord in 1917; and Tommy Hitchcock, a renowned polo player in the interwar years who would be killed as an American pilot in the Second World War. Through the efforts of Opal Cooper, Bullard's entertainer friend in Paris, the Negro Actors Guild also helped pay for Jacqueline's and Lolita's passage.[11] In New York, the girls lived with their father while they learned to speak English and continued their educations. They later married, Jacqueline raising a son, Richard, and Lolita, a daughter, Denise. Lolita lived in Harlem until her untimely death in 1972; Jacqueline remained in Harlem until moving with her husband to Staten Island after her father's death in 1961.

In addition to its ethnically and racially mixed native-born population, New York was home as well to hundreds of thousands of foreign nationals—individuals and families whose business and other interests in the city had made them virtual residents, sometimes over several generations. When Bullard arrived in 1940, the French colony had for many years sup-

ported a number of institutions in lower Manhattan: a French hospital at
330 West 30th Street, where Bullard would soon receive treatment; a
French school, École Maternelle Française, on West 23rd Street; and to
the east on 23rd Street, a Roman Catholic Church, St. Vincent de Paul.[12]
Founded in 1841, St. Vincent de Paul priests delivered sermons in French
into the early 1960s, and Bullard regularly attended masses there.[13] The
1940 exodus from France—including a number of artists and intellectuals
such as Bullard's old friend Moïse Kisling—enlarged the French community in New York. These newcomers established a French university in
exile, École Libre des Hautes Études, using facilities made available to
them by New York's New School of Social Research. A French bistro on
Second Avenue, La Marseillaise, also founded by the exiles, catered to
those devoted to "the France that was and will be again."[14] In 1950, the
U.S. census counted forty thousand French nationals living in the city—
a group evenly divided between French-born individuals and their American-born children and grandchildren.[15]

During the war years, Bullard's activities outside of his working life
naturally gravitated toward the French colony in lower Manhattan. Six
days after arriving in New York, he became a member of the Federation
of French Veterans of the Great War, an organization formed a few weeks
earlier in reaction to the fall of France. The group met regularly at its
headquarters on West 42nd Street. In March 1941, he entered the French
hospital for treatment of his spine and simply to rest. According to Jacqueline, he was near a nervous breakdown after his ten-month ordeal of war,
serious injury, flight, relocation, and anxiety over his daughters. While
convalescing in the hospital, he was visited by Bob Scanlon, and he saw
with a rush of delight that his old boxing and French Foreign Legion comrade had survived with only minor wounds the bomb blast at Chartres the
previous June.[16]

By the early summer of 1941, Bullard's health was restored enough to
begin, in his after-work hours and on weekends, efforts on behalf of the
New York–based section of France Forever [France quand-même]. An international organization of the Free French movement, France Forever
was created in August 1940 by Eugene Houdry, a French industrialist who
had settled in Philadelphia. Its purpose was to promote General Charles

de Gaulle, then in exile in London, as the leader of the resistance within and without France to the German occupier and the collaborationist Vichy-based French regime headed by Marshal Pétain. Directing resistance activities out of London, de Gaulle was also seeking recognition among the French people and Allied governments as the true leader of France and the man who should rightfully take power in Paris after his country was liberated. The administration of Franklin D. Roosevelt had extended diplomatic recognition to Vichy France on the theory that internal political chaos had led to France's disaster and only a strongman like Pétain could bring order. Houdry's objective in the United States was to sway public opinion in favor of de Gaulle and force the American government to change its pro-Vichy policy.[17]

France Forever's American headquarters was located in New York at 30 Rockefeller Plaza; its illustrious American sponsorship committee included historians Frederick Lewis Allen and James McGregor Burns, journalists Walter Millis and Freda Kirchwey, and industrialist Herbert Bayard Swope. Another pro-Gaullist in New York was a former patron in Bullard's and Bricktop's Paris clubs, writer Louis Bromfield. Bullard spoke for the organization before audiences in churches, clubs, union halls, and other venues in Harlem and downtown Manhattan. In a June 23, 1941, letter on France Forever stationery, he invited "friends and comrades" to hear him and several other speakers at the Blue Ribbon Ball Room on West 116th Street discuss the present situation in France. He would speak of the things he had seen while fighting in the French army and stress the point that France's failure had been one of military tactics and not political disorganization. He noted that a film would be shown demonstrating Free French activities in various parts of the world. "Our aim," he stated, "is to recruit real FREEDOM LOVING PEOPLE who are willing to fight in order to obtain it."[18]

In September 1941, he sought to recruit among African Americans. In a letter to Walter White, president of the NAACP, he explained that he had been authorized by the Free French Delegation of New York "to see if it would be possible to find colored people who would be qualified and willing to give their aid to the Free French Forces." After speaking of "the difficulties faced by colored people here in America in their effort to enlist in our own armed forces," Bullard pointed to the "Free French need for PILOTS, MECHANICS, etc." In closing, Bullard asked White to endorse a project that was "just what all of our young folks are waiting for."[19]

A few days later, Bullard sent a letter to F. D. Patterson, president of the Tuskegee Institute in Tuskegee, Alabama. "I have the assurance," he wrote, "that our boys will be able to contract an engagement with the Free French Forces of General Charles de Gaulle. We want as many aviator pilots and mechanics as we can get. It would seem that this might offer an opportunity that they have long wished for." One can assume that Bullard and his Free French associates in New York were aware that the U.S. War Department had finally approved in January of that year—after years of concerted African American lobbying—the training of a segregated black American pursuit squadron at Tuskegee and that pilots were, in fact, already training there when Bullard wrote to Patterson. Both letters imply the opportunity the Free French were offering American blacks was to fly in a number of integrated units—such as the one in which Bullard had flown in World War I—rather than the segregated ones ordered by the U.S. Army Air Corps. Perhaps Bullard was aware of White's criticism of Patterson earlier that summer in which White noted that only thirty-three blacks were among some fifty thousand American fliers then being trained. "This," he was reported to have said, "is what comes about because a Negro asked for segregation."[20]

Given the fact that the U.S. government was still neutral and extending diplomatic recognition to Vichy, neither White nor Patterson could have even considered Bullard's proposal without incurring the wrath of the Roosevelt administration—something neither could afford. White made no reply; Patterson acknowledged the letter, remarking "that Tuskegee . . . is always happy to support or do whatever it can for the furtherance . . . of worthwhile causes" and thanked Bullard "for this information regarding your work."[21] Apparently neither White nor Patterson had ever heard of Eugene Jacques Bullard, the first African American combat aviator— a fact that their correspondent chose not to mention. A stranger to American politics, Bullard was encouraged by Patterson's polite and purely rhetorical sentiments. In his own handwriting and without the editorial assistance of the New York office of France Forever, he thanked Patterson for his "kind letter" and told him that he "was expecting to have some very interesting news for our young men. . . . I am sure that with your coloboration [sic] this will make history for many." He closed in fine French epistolary style, "I beg to offer you my sincere salutations."[22]

On April 4, 1942, the French war veterans were permitted to participate with American military units in the Army Day parade down Fifth Avenue. Bullard was strong enough to carry the tricolor in a color guard that also presented the American flag, and for the first time in the States, the banner of the Free French. Meanwhile, Eugene and his Gaullist friends continued to argue France Forever's case in New York from 1941 through 1944. In 1940, when they began their work, Vichyite and other anti-Gaullist factions were quite strong in the city. The Free French movement in the States was hindered by the public relations gaffe of a de Gaulle emissary to Washington who was quoted in the August 24, 1942, issue of *Life* magazine that Mistinguett, Georges Carpentier, Maurice Chevalier, and thirty other notables might be shot after the war for alleged collaboration with the Germans.[23] Nevertheless, Bullard and his France Forever associates were gratified to observe the swelling of pro-Gaullist sentiment within the New York French colony. Support for the general grew as well in the New York media and public opinion. The Republican mayor of New York, Fiorello La Guardia, an early de Gaulle backer, encouraged a huge Bastille Day celebration in 1943 for the general—allowing 44th Street between Second and Third Avenues to be closed off for festivities.[24]

The first large and enthusiastic Bastille Day celebrated anywhere since 1939, the occasion was made more joyous by news of the successful Allied operations in Sicily and press reports that the Vichy government had banned all traditional observances in France for security reasons. For two days and the night of July 14, multitudes of French and native New Yorkers danced, drank champagne, sang "La Marseillaise," and raised up the tremendous cheer "Vive de Gaulle!" As onlookers, Bullard and his children would have thoroughly enjoyed the event, which the *New York Times* reported as a bona fide French "Quartorze juillet": "it could have been—for twenty-four hours—Montmartre and the rue de Clichy. (At least the cobble stones were the same.)" Uptown at Hunter College, France Forever staged a rally at which speakers such as playwright Henri

Bernstein were openly critical of the Roosevelt administration's continued anti-Gaullist stance.[25]

On June 18, 1944, France Forever commemorated the fourth anniversary of de Gaulle's call for resistance with a Fifth Avenue parade and a mass at St. Vincent de Paul. A month later, having finally received Roosevelt's muted blessing in Washington, the general made a triumphal visit to New York. Paraded through reportedly tumultuous crowds, the Free French leader was met by a beaming La Guardia at City Hall. Among a number of other appearances, the general spent half an hour at the headquarters of France Forever, thanking some two hundred members and guests for their efforts on his behalf.[26] Six weeks later, with the liberation of Paris and the subsequent installation of de Gaulle as the French national leader, Bullard's active participation with France Forever came to a satisfying conclusion. He would remain a member of the organization, read its magazine *France amerique,* and maintain memberships in other New York–based French societies until the end of his life.

Through the goodwill of Austen Crehore, Bullard also stayed in touch in the postwar years with other Americans whose love for France continued from afar. Since the 1930s, Crehore had been organizing reunions of Americans who, like himself, had flown for France in the Great War.[27] He felt that the glare of publicity that had always surrounded the Lafayette Escadrille—the one French-commanded squadron containing only American pilots—had obscured the valor of those Americans flying in units in which most of the pilots were French.[28] One suspects too that Crehore knew of Edmund Gros's prejudicial treatment of Bullard. In any case, Crehore always made sure that all the Lafayette Corps fliers, including its one black man, were invited to the association's informal reunions in lower Manhattan.

These were thoroughly enjoyable affairs as the several score attendees swapped war stories, reminisced about France, and recalled fallen comrades and those who had died since the war. The conversations took place around a large banquet table on which was served a leisurely paced meal. Several courses of food were washed down with fine wines and postprandial coffee and brandy. The dinners took place, appropriately enough, at the Lafayette Hotel at University Place and 9th Street, "a little corner of Paris in New York" as a reporter wrote in a story of the association's last meal at the hotel before it closed a few weeks later. At this March 1949 reunion, talk turned to "stories of Eugene Bullard of 80 East 116th Street, who was present." Someone remembered that Tommy Hitchcock had once asked Bullard why he had come from Georgia to fight the Germans in 1914. "Well, I don't rightly know," he was quoted as saying, "but it must have been more curiosity than intelligence." Bullard showed the journalist his business card as a vendor of French perfumes. On the line below his name was the phrase, "First Known Negro Military Pilot."[29]

During World War II and after, Bullard and his daughters paid visits to his cousin James Bullard, who had left Richland, Georgia, where Eugene had stayed with him in 1911, to live in New York. They also traveled to Newport News, Virginia, to see his older sister Pauline and her family. Eugene's cousin Daisy Bullard Thomas came from Cleveland to attend these reunions (and Pauline's funeral in the 1950s) and remembered Bullard wearing a beret and speaking with a pronounced French accent. She never could understand what Jacqueline and Lolita were saying. Thomas, who recalled her young cousin's leaving home in Columbus and his father's attempt to get the American government to return him from France, had heard no more of him until the late 1920s, when a relative in Cleveland showed her a press clipping indicating that he owned a club in Paris patronized by the Prince of Wales.[30]

Shortly after World War II, Bullard traveled to his hometown, Columbus, Georgia, to try to locate other family members. He made this trip with sorrow and trepidation, for he knew he would not find his oldest brother, Hector. Bullard had learned not long after arriving in Europe that Hector had been lynched for trying to assume ownership of a farm inherited from his maternal grandmother, a Creek Indian. White squatters on the peach farm near Fort Valley, Georgia, had hanged him when he insisted on pressing his claim. In Columbus, Bullard failed to come into contact with anyone in his immediate family. Moreover, he could hardly recognize the Rose Hill neighborhood in which he had roamed as a youngster. A public housing project, the George F. Peabody Apartments, constructed in 1940, had obliterated the Bullard homes on Talbotton Avenue and 26th Street—indeed most of 26th Street itself had completely disappeared in the urban renewal.[31] During his brief stay, Bullard would have learned of the courage of Primus King, a local black barber, roughed up and made the subject of death threats for attempting to vote and in so doing exposing the injustice of the Southern institution of the "whites only" Democratic Party primary. King had infuriated local officials at the Muscogee County courthouse by appearing before them on Independence Day, 1944.[32] Repelled by the continuance of entrenched Jim Crow beliefs and practices in the locality, Bullard hurried back north. If he attempted to get in touch with his father's employer and benefactor, W. C. Bradley, who lived until July 1947, he makes no mention of it in "All Blood Runs Red."

As millions of blacks had discovered in migrations to the North earlier in the century, Bullard would find New York, while not as overtly hostile to black aspirations as the South, a place by no means free of racism. Two years after his arrival in New York, he received an invitation to attend a dinner of Paris Post No. 1 Legionnaires at the Paris Hotel on 97th Street. Several days before the event, he found in his mail an anonymous letter— postmarked "Jamaica, New York, November 22, 1942"—that politely told him not to appear because "your extended sojourn abroad has perhaps made you forget that in the states white and colored don't mix at social functions." The correspondent advised that "it would be to your advantage not to attend the dinner on Monday night or to join in any social activities of the Post in the future." Bullard mailed a copy of the letter to Jack Spector, liaison officer of the Paris Post in New York. To his dismay, he received no reply.[33]

In the late summer of 1949, Bullard found himself at the center of the worst episode of Northern white violence perpetrated against blacks and Jews in the immediate post–World War II era, a violence described by the African American *Pittsburgh Courier* as one of the "blackest and most shameful spectacles in American history."[34] Bullard was beaten by police officers during the episode, and photographs of the beating were published in several New York newspapers and have reappeared in several books since.

The beating took place in the midst of mob violence accompanying a protest against an outdoor concert given by actor, singer, and political activist Paul Robeson near Peekskill, New York, in upper Westchester County, thirty miles north of Harlem. A Rutgers College honor student and star football player, Robeson became an internationally known dramatic actor and singer in the interwar years. He used his celebrity effectively to publicize the cruelty and irrationality of American racism.[35] Finding no hope in mainstream American politics for dealing with discrimination and the continuing horror of lynching, Robeson became a radical and sojourned in the Soviet Union with his wife, Essie, and son, Paul Jr., in the mid-1930s. He came to admire the Soviet Union, seemingly so free of the racial bigotry against which he raged in the United States. With many other leftists, he refused to credit the stories of mass executions of Russian citizens carried out by Soviet dictator Joseph Stalin during the 1930s. By the end of World War II, Robeson's admiration for the Soviet Union had grown. The Soviet Red Army, after all, had played the major role in destroying the Nazi regime—a regime that had slaughtered millions in the name of Aryan racial supremacy.[36]

Like others on the American left, Robeson was critical of President Harry S. Truman's "Cold War" and military containment of the Soviet state. In 1948, believing that peaceful relations were possible, he supported the Progressive Party, whose presidential candidate was Henry A. Wallace. A strong proponent of federal civil rights laws, Wallace had been fired from Truman's cabinet two years earlier for opposing his policy of toughness toward the Soviets. After Truman's election in 1948, Robeson attended the Congress of World Partisans of Peace held in Paris in April 1949. There he gave a speech in which he stated that "the wealth of America had been built on the backs of white workers from Europe . . . and on the backs of millions of blacks." "We are resolved," he declaimed, "to share it equally among our children. We shall not put up with any hysterical raving that urges us to make war on anyone. . . . We shall not make war on the Soviet Union."[37]

At the time Robeson spoke, the American red scare hysteria, the fear of communist infiltration throughout American society, was well developed. Director of the Federal Bureau of Investigation J. Edgar Hoover, the House Un-American Activities Committee, and President Truman's Loyalty Review Board were vying to see who could expose the most American communists and "fellow travelers," those sympathetic to communist causes. Although never a Communist Party member himself, Robeson's work for international peace and for civil rights in America led him to associate with American leftists, some of them communists. When an Associated Press wire story, reporting on his Paris speech, misquoted him as saying, "It is unthinkable that American Negroes would go to war on behalf of those who have oppressed us for generations against a country [the Soviet Union] which in one generation has raised our people to the full dignity of mankind," Robeson became a figure of contempt for everyone on the American political spectrum, from Cold War liberals, including most black leaders, to right-wing extremists.[38]

On three previous occasions, Robeson had given concerts—the proceeds going to civil rights groups—without incident in a park near Peekskill. With the announcement of another concert for August 27, 1949, sponsored by a New York leftist group, People's Artists, led by novelist Howard Fast, militant reactionaries in the Peekskill area mobilized to prevent the event from taking place. A mob composed of American Legionnaires, Veterans of Foreign Wars, and local Negrophobes and antisemites—Jews were prominent concert organizers and Paul Robeson Jr. had recently married a Jewish woman—blocked the entrance into the concert area and started screaming the usual epithets, "nigger," "kike," "commie," and so on. The automobiles of Robeson fans were stoned and several people were dragged out of their cars and beaten. Police on the scene arrested no one. Robeson's friends were able to hide him on the floor of a car and return him to New York City.[39]

The concert had been planned as a benefit for the Harlem chapter of the American Congress on Civil Rights. African Americans, progressive labor unionists, and war veterans rallied to Robeson's call for holding a concert on Sunday, September 4, at a site near the intended location of the aborted one. On August 30, an audience estimated from three to five thousand people filled the Golden Gate Ballroom in Harlem and crowded before loudspeakers placed outside in the street. They heard Robeson rededicate himself to "the America of the true traditions; to the American abolitionists, of Harriet Tubman, of Thaddeus Stevens, of those who fought for my people's freedom." Peekskill, he declared, had provided "a glimpse of

American storm troopers in action." [40] He urged his listeners, described by the *New York Amsterdam News* as "Robeson fans, Communist Party leaders . . . [and] rank and file Harlemites . . . representing all shades of political opinion," to support him in "going on the offensive." "We'll have our meetings and our concerts all over these United States. . . . And we'll see that our women and our children are not harmed again!" "The surest way to get police protection," he concluded, "is to have it very clear that we'll protect ourselves, and good. . . . I'll be back with my friends at Peekskill." The large crowd roared its approval and marched spontaneously up Lenox Avenue to 135th Street. [41]

On the morning of September 4, several thousand union members and war veterans—some armed with baseball bats—formed lines near the performance area to ensure the safety of Robeson, other singers such as Pete Seeger, and the thousands of spectators who gathered to hear the concert. When the entertainment began at 2:00 P.M., the volunteer security guards moved away from the sole road into the park in order that they might better protect the singers and the audience. It would now be up to some nine hundred Westchester County and New York state police to protect the late arrivals from the anti-Robeson forces which, as they had promised, were forming to demonstrate against the rescheduled event. [42]

Of the estimated twenty to twenty-five thousand people who heard the concert, approximately one-third were African American, many of them arriving in specially chartered buses from Harlem and other points in Manhattan. Similar in temperament to Robeson in his habitual disinclination "to walk away from a fight," Bullard boarded one of these buses, which arrived at the scene after the concert had begun. Police ordered the drivers to park outside the area where the event was occurring; passengers would have to breach the crowd of several thousand counterdemonstrators. Bullard left his bus and walked directly to the entrance of the park outside of which police were stationed to keep order. As Paul Robeson Jr., then twenty-one years of age and an eyewitness, recalls: "Bullard was a small man, but he carried himself with an air of remarkable composure and authority. At the entrance to the park, a bystander said something to him and Bullard turned to respond." Then, as Robeson remembers, "a Westchester County sheriff's deputy rebuked Bullard and Bullard answered the rebuke. At that point, the deputy, joined by another and two state police troopers, began clubbing Bullard who threw up his arms to protect his head and fell backward to the ground."[43]

The incident was documented photographically in pictures appearing in the *New York Daily Mirror* and *New York Amsterdam News* the next day. Confronting his assailants, Bullard is shown neatly dressed in dark slacks and a white dress shirt. Photographs of him on the ground reveal his beret, which he always wore when outdoors, lying at his feet. The captions to the pictures identify him as a World War I aviator. There is no mention of what happened after he hit the ground. According to Robeson Jr., Bullard got up, brushed himself off, and pushed his way determinedly through the crowd and on into the park to hear the rest of the concert.[44]

Bullard's explanation of the episode, given the next day in the *Amsterdam News,* was that "he resented having a man spit in his face and spat back. At that moment, he was spun around by police who began to club him." He said that he had been given the officers' badge numbers and might use them against them. The newspaper reported that he had suffered numerous bruises and had been cut on the left elbow.[45] The *Amsterdam News* printed the story of another Harlem man, Emmett Ely, who was bused in late to the concert and appears to have witnessed Bullard's beating. He arrived at the entrance to the grounds at 3:00 P.M. and said police did little to stop anti-Robeson demonstrators from throwing rocks at late arrivals. "The police themselves," he reported, "were very hostile [to the concert-goers]" and "seemed particularly to try to provoke the husky-looking Negroes." When a "colored fellow got hit by protesters and turned around to cover himself, the police would strike him. . . . One fellow . . . was knocked down by a police lieutenant. . . . Instead of the police picking at the crowd, they hit him. On the ground they jabbed him with sticks." Ely reported to the paper the badge numbers of the two deputies and one of the state troopers; he stated that like most of the riders on the buses, he was not a communist, but had gone to Peekskill to defend the right of freedom of assembly.[46]

On leaving the grounds after the concert, many spectators in cars and buses were injured by stones thrown through windshields and windows by counterdemonstrators. Police made several token arrests but failed to stop the violence. Many bus drivers refused to board their vehicles, and people like Ely spent hours making their way as unobtrusively as possible to a local train station in order to return to Harlem. A driver of a bus carrying black children back to New York from a visit to the Franklin D. Roosevelt Library at Hyde Park had the misfortune of driving through Peekskill in the postconcert hours. Mobs stoned the bus, broke windows, and cut a number of the children.[47]

The next day, Robeson called a press conference to protest the attacks at the library of the Council on African Affairs, a body he chaired, on West 26th Street. Bullard appeared with fifteen other people, most of them, like him, bandaged, to testify against the police brutality aimed especially, in their view, at African Americans. Bullard said he was a disabled veteran of two foreign wars and that he had been knocked down and beaten by police for trying to enter the concert grounds.[48] Two days later, New York State District Attorney George M. Fanelli reported to Governor Thomas E. Dewey on the Peekskill affair. He praised the police forces for preventing worse violence and asserted that "all those seeking to attend the concert gained admission without hazard." The first indication of threatened disorder, Fannelli claimed—a claim rebutted by the photographs of Bullard's beating and Ely's testimony—came when the first of the Robeson followers' cars attempted to leave the concert area at 4:00 P.M.[49]

Progressive groups mobilized again to demand that Dewey reject Fanelli's "whitewash" and undertake a more thorough and less politically biased investigation. When Dewey refused, Bullard and other witnesses to the Peekskill violence spoke on September 10 in White Plains, New York, before a crowd of Westchester County "unionists, churchgoers, Negro, and civic organizations"—groups that were joining forces to "demand a federal inquiry under the civil rights statutes."[50] Ultimately, no interest in the matter was shown by the Truman administration.

For Robeson, Peekskill foreshadowed a period in which he was not only blacklisted by the entertainment industry in the States but also banned from going abroad by the U.S. State Department, which, in 1950, refused to issue him a passport. While his lawyers contested this action, Robeson, although continuing to lash out against U.S. foreign policy and racism, drifted toward deep depression. He was recovering his emotional equilibrium when the Supreme Court ruled in 1958 that the government could not restrict an individual's right to travel because of political convictions. He promptly journeyed to Europe, still a sanctuary for African Americans, where he performed and spoke before audiences as large and appreciative as any he had seen since debuting as a youthful sensation in the late 1920s.[51]

In the immediate aftermath of Peekskill, sporadic acts of violence against Jewish residents in that locality continued.[52] Bullard himself may have been a victim of this abiding bigotry. As a salesman of French perfumes, he often had to resort to public transportation when plying his trade since he could not always afford to own a car. According to Carisella and Ryan in *The Black Swallow of Death,* Bullard boarded a bus in the Peekskill Mountains and was ordered to sit in the back by the driver. Bullard refused and as a result of the ensuing fisticuffs, the aging warrior—now in his mid-fifties—lost most of the sight in his left eye.[53] Because of this condition, he began wearing eyeglasses; the first photograph of him wearing them was taken in 1952.

Bullard was deeply disheartened by these incidents. He was shaken especially by the mob violence at Peekskill that had injured so many innocent people. This was the North, yet, as in the case of most Southern lynchings, the horror of which remained sharp in his memory,[54] the justice system seemed indifferent to if not complicit in the stone-throwing and beatings. In 1950–51, he sojourned in Paris seeking to re-establish himself as a club owner. He stayed for some months in Montmartre with Jocelyn Bingham, his friend from his "golden years" before the war. Receiving no compensation—after extended litigation—for the loss of his clubs, Bullard was unsuccessful in his bid to relocate.[55] In this he was not alone, for Bricktop, even with considerable financial backing from her old friends, found too many empty tables to sustain her club, which she had reopened briefly on the rue Fontaine in 1950.[56] After two decades of economic depression, German occupation, an unsatisfactory peace, and considerable postwar anti-Americanism in Paris, Montmartre could not return to what it once had been, a playground for the worldly and eccentric rich. Although Bullard gave up on the idea of living in Paris permanently, he did travel in Europe in 1952, serving as a translator and advance man for Louis Armstrong and his band.[57]

For the most part, Bullard's last years were spent in quiet pursuit of

his livelihood and the enjoyment of his family and friends. Richard, Jacqueline's son, remembers his grandfather as a "gentle, soft-spoken man"
who "slept like a baby" when the two shared a bedroom. Richard also
recalls visits to the New York home of Armstrong, whom he called "Uncle
Louie."[58] Bullard maintained an "inner exile" in New York in the 1950s.
He continued to attend the meetings of various French societies and read
the publications of his World War I military units. He visited with old
Paris friends such as Paul Damski, a Lithuanian Jew who had used Bullard's gym on rue Mansart to train boxers and now lived in New York as
a wholesale jeweler and diamond dealer.[59]

French authorities maintained their ties to Bullard. In 1954, he was invited with all expenses paid to participate with other French war veterans
in Bastille Day ceremonies in Paris. Before a large group of onlookers, the
bespectacled Bullard, wearing a civilian trench coat, placed flowers and
relit the eternal flame at the tomb of the unknown soldier beneath the Arc
de Triomphe.[60] In January 1956, an old friend, Hubert Cournal, a black
pilot in the French air force, visited Harlem while en route as a represen-
tative of France to political ceremonies in the Dominican Republic. The
Martinican-born and much-decorated flier told reporters that he "was
happy to be in Harlem for the first time [meeting] his American brothers
of color." Bullard hosted a private champagne party in Cournal's honor
at his 116th Street apartment.[61]

On October 9, 1959, his sixty-fourth birthday, he was made a chevalier
(knight) of the Legion of Honor, a French governmental body that recog-
nizes distinguished military and civilian service to France. It was his fif-
teenth decoration bestowed by France. In formal ceremonies at the French
consulate on Fifth Avenue, Consul Raymond Laporte pinned the Legion
of Honor medal on the lapel of Bullard's suit coat. In attendance were his
daughters and many friends in New York's French colony, including actor
Charles Boyer, whom he had known since working with him in France
Forever.[62] According to a French newspaper story on the event, Bullard
had been proposed for membership in the Legion of Honor as far back as
1933. The piece quoted his touching acknowledgment of the honor in
words spoken, of course, in French: "I have served France as best I could.
France taught me the true meaning of liberty, equality, and fraternity. My

services to France can never repay all I owe her."[63] The day before the ceremony, Bullard's award had been toasted at a special meeting of the Federation of French War Veterans. Interviewing Bullard there, Anthony Shannon recorded Bullard's reflection on his life: "You might say I touched all
the bases. Not much more you can do in 65 years."[64]

After the ceremony at the consulate, Violette Marzan, a nurse who had
served with the First French Army commanded by General de Gaulle in
1944 and 1945, hosted a luncheon for Bullard at her fashionable Manhattan residence. Eight other French friends, among them French diplomat Henri Goiran, raised glasses of champagne and applauded as he cut
a birthday cake. Alfred Jodry, an acquaintance of Bullard's since World
War I and a founder in 1940 of the New York Post No. 1 of the French
War Veterans, took photographs on this occasion. His short hair thin-
ning and graying at the temples, Bullard, elegantly dressed in a dark suit
and tie, smiles broadly, relishing the warm admiration of his dear companions.[65]

In late April 1960, Charles de Gaulle visited the United States as president of France. After meeting with President Dwight D. Eisenhower in
Washington to plan for a forthcoming summit conference with Soviet
leader Nikita Khrushchev in Paris, de Gaulle flew to New York to pay his
respects to the city that had received him so warmly in July 1944 and then
again in 1945 after Germany's surrender—an occasion on which Mayor
La Guardia had officially proclaimed him as an honorary citizen of the
city. A cheering and confetti-throwing crowd estimated at one million
lined Broadway to greet de Gaulle's motorcade as it moved from lower
Manhattan to midtown.[66]

After speeches at City Hall and the Waldorf-Astoria Hotel, de Gaulle
ended his day by attending a reception at the Seventh Regiment Armory
on Park Avenue organized by the French community. Some five thousand
French locals and several Americans notable for their service to France
were invited by General and Madame de Gaulle to attend. Just before 6:
00 P.M., de Gaulle's entry into the armory triggered thunderous cheers.
More than three hundred children from local French schools waved their
nation's tricolor as the general led the singing of "La Marseillaise." After
a brief speech, the French chief of state embraced dignitaries at the dais

and nearby tables and then walked down the long center aisle to shake hands with his excited countrymen.⁶⁷ An invited guest, Bullard participated in the festivities as a member of the color guard. Seated at a table for VIPs near de Gaulle, Bullard, wearing his French Legionnaire's dress uniform and cap, received the warm embrace of the man to whom he had rallied in France's darkest hour.⁶⁸

Whereas the "white" New York dailies were filled with stories and photographs of de Gaulle's visit, the *New York Amsterdam News,* preoccupied with the burgeoning civil rights struggle in the American South and the struggles of emergent nations in Africa and Asia, gave no reportage whatsoever on the French frenzy downtown. However, in the upper left corner of the weekly's April 30, 1960, issue, there appeared a small photograph of Bullard, in his bemedaled Legionnaire's uniform, kissing the outstretched hand of an attractive and fashionably attired lady. The caption read: "THAT GALLIC CHARM (A L'AMERICAN) [sic] Jacques Eugene Bullard [sic], Harlemite and former flier who was a member of the honor guard that welcomed General Charles de Gaulle, gives it the old world flourish as he greets another American who went French, the nonpareil Jo Baker, at a reception for the French leader at the 7th Regt. Armory." ⁶⁹

Always a hard-working man fully engaged in the activity before him, Bullard had given little thought to leaving a record of his singular life. If there had been little newspaper or magazine interest in his story during his years in New York, the reason in part was because he himself had drawn so little attention to it. When approached by a reporter at the 1949 Lafayette Association banquet, for instance, he had answered questions matter-of-factly and without exaggeration—as his business card stated, he was the first "known" Negro military aviator. Covering Bullard's party for Hubert Cournal, the *New York Amsterdam News* writer could only say that Bullard was "reportedly" the only Negro among the Americans flying for France in World War I.⁷⁰ Even Richard Reid, his grandson, did not know he had been a pioneer in black aviation until after his death.⁷¹

Over the years, Ted Parsons had urged Bullard to write a memoir. In early 1959, while working as an elevator operator at Rockefeller Center in midtown Manhattan, he decided to do so. Since he had never formally learned to write in English (or for that matter in French), he would need an assistant. Through an acquaintance, a member of Manhattan's Unitarian Church of All Souls, he was introduced to Louise Fox Connell, who also belonged to this congregation. A widow since 1949 of writer and Hollywood scenarist Richard Connell, Mrs. Connell was herself a well-published author. She had fought bigotry since her student days at Barnard College, when she campaigned against antisemitism on that campus. When she later became aware of the prejudice against American blacks, she worked for racial justice through participation in the NAACP and many other biracial organizations.

Intrigued by Bullard's saga, impressed by his native intelligence and resourcefulness, and stirred by his battles against racism, the sixty-nine-year-old woman agreed to help him organize his autobiography and offered her services as an editor. Connell paid for the services of a typist. Without Connell's labors—which would include a decade-long campaign to find a publisher for his work—Bullard's remarkable career would never have entered into the public domain. Two years before the publication of Carisella and Ryan's *The Black Swallow of Death,* the author of a book on World War I aviators was writing that he had not been able to identify the American Negro in the French air service mentioned by several people.[72]

From the beginning of her collaboration, Connell made clear that she desired no "money payment for herself now or at any future time," and that her interest lay solely in "furthering a cause dear to me" by "publicizing the first rate achievements of individuals belonging to unappreciated races." Bullard would later request that Connell, should he die before the completion of the work, "please finish my biographie [sic]." He asked her to share any profit that might come from it with his grandson, Richard Reid, and his granddaughter, Denise Robertson. He hoped that the money might help pay for their educations.[73] Before he began writing his first draft, Bullard told Connell his life's story. From her notes, she typed a thirteen-page outline, sketching the various phases of his experiences upon which he would elaborate in his manuscript. The outline concluded in 1940.[74] Evidently, Bullard did not feel his final years in New York City were worth recording.

In the spring of 1959, drawing on memory and his large collection of photographs and documents, Bullard began penciling in his large, bold script his recollection of his early years in Georgia. Writing on legal-sized sheets of paper, he would periodically bring completed sections to Connell at her apartment on East 91st Street, where she would begin editing and readying the copy for typing. Bullard's writing often kept him up late into the night. One note to "Dear Madame Connell," enclosed with a section covering the First World War, has "Tuesday 3 A.M." written at the top of the page.[75] In February 1960, Ted Parsons, who was critiquing sections of the manuscript sent him by Connell, suggested naming the work "All Blood Runs Red," a title that implied Bullard's underlying theme, the equality of the races.[76] Then in retirement, Parsons had risen to the rank of rear admiral in the U.S. Navy during and after the Second World War.[77]

While working with Bullard on his composition, Connell sought to create some advance publicity for the work. Shortly after Bullard's award of membership in the Legion of Honor, she sent Eleanor Roosevelt, widow of the former president, press clippings about the ceremony and her outline of Bullard's life. In mid-October of 1959, Roosevelt thanked her for the information and promised to write about Bullard in her long-running syndicated column, "My Day." The two-hundred-word piece appeared in thirty-nine newspapers two weeks later.[78] On the day of the de Gaulle visit to New York six months later, Connell sent out a press release summarizing Bullard's adventures and noting that Bullard was in the process of writing a book about them. In the first paragraph of the release, she mentioned that he would be a Guard of Honor and color bearer at the reception that evening for the French president.[79] No New York newspaper, excepting the *Amsterdam News,* which sent a photographer, used the release. A week later, Dabney Horton, a writer whom Connell was trying to interest in rewriting the Bullard manuscript, wrote her about that "gawd-awful publicity release." "I can't believe much of it," he wrote, "especially [the part] about the color guard."[80] The inability of Horton, a well-informed, worldly New York writer, to credit Bullard's participation in the armory reception suggests why Bullard's story did not become more widely known until years after his death. Bullard's adventures, which as Anthony Shannon had noted "made the daydreams of Walter Mitty look pale by comparison,"[81] were either too unbelievable or, given the French connection, too difficult to substantiate to interest American editors and publishers, white or black. It took Connell six years after Bullard's death to interest *Ebony* in publishing a long piece based on the memoir, and no book publisher would touch the project until 1972, when Marlborough House agreed to take Carisella and Ryan's version of it.

If much of the print media was uninterested in the Bullard story, the producers of the National Broadcasting Company's "Today Show" were intrigued with their building's black elevator operator who came to work wearing military decorations on his Rockefeller Center uniform. On December 22, 1959, the program's host, Dave Garroway, invited Bullard to appear on camera to tell how he had earned the medals which, during the interview, Garroway displayed on a board for close-up viewing. Bullard spoke of his services to France in two wars as Garroway listened, his facial expressions reflecting astonishment and delight. The Bullard interview generated hundreds of letters congratulating NBC for giving the adventurer the opportunity to tell his story. For the network and Garroway, still reeling from the recent exposure of the rigged game show "Twenty One" and the downfall of Professor Charles Van Doren, a frequent "Today Show" guest and friend of Garroway, Bullard's straightforward tales of valor provided a refreshing and welcome respite.[82]

In early 1961, Connell sent completed portions of the Bullard manuscript to Herbert Malloy Mason Jr., associate editor of *True: The Man's Magazine,* published in New York. Author of a recent book on the Lafayette Escadrille, Mason was aware of Bullard's stint in the French air corps and was eager to meet the man. In the last year of Bullard's life, Mason saw him on several occasions and later wrote about him in a 1965 book about notable French fliers in the Great War.[83] Invited by Bullard to his 116th Street apartment for a luncheon, Mason wrote that the outside of the building was "ramshackle and discouraging," its "hallways smelling of boiled cabbage and fifty years of neglect." Inside the apartment, however, the evidence of the occupant's vitality and industry were everywhere. Beneath the ceiling "dripping" with World War I vintage model airplanes, the walls were covered with photographs, plaques, paintings, and documents. The floor "was given over to bookcases, potted plants, a radio, trunks, tables, chairs." The windowsills were filled with more plants. Perhaps revealing Bullard's appreciation of the qualities of quiet strength and compassion, a four-foot-tall colored pasteboard cutout of Marshal Matt Dillon stood atop the refrigerator.[84]

Besides Mason, Bullard had invited to lunch several other interesting friends. One of them was Leland LeSalle Rounds, an American pilot in the service of France whom Bullard had known during World War I. Rounds, then a banker, had been a U.S. diplomat and was decorated for his service in Oran, Algeria, during the Second World War. Other friends in the company were French count Edward de Pianelli, an author and former commander in the resistance in southern France, and Roger Bader, Bullard's former commander at Verdun and again, in 1940, at Orléans. During the meal prepared and served by the host, "the conversation never flagged." When Mason departed, Bullard and Bader were bent over a map of Verdun, deeply absorbed in a "rapid fire conversation in French" about the German infantry attack on Fort Douaumont in February 1916.[85]

In April 1961, Mason joined Bullard at a Franco-American military ceremony at the statue of Lafayette on Union Square—an occasion for which Bullard served as a flag bearer. A photograph, the last taken of Bullard, shows him standing beside the statue and the wreath of flowers he had just placed at its base. After the ceremony, Mason accompanied his friend for several stops on an uptown-bound subway car. "Even in case-hardened Manhattan," Bullard, dressed neatly in his khaki and proudly clasping the furled French tricolor in "his huge black fist," was "an object of wide-eyed curiosity."[86]

Early in 1961, Bullard began experiencing stomach pains that he believed to be caused by ulcers. His daughters and friends finally persuaded him to submit to medical tests at the Metropolitan Hospital. At the beginning of August, his examining doctor, Elio F. Vieira, discovered an advanced case of intestinal cancer.[87] Bullard finished writing his memoir on August 15, the last page of which, written in his own hand before editing, read: "I would like to offer my humble thanks to those that's [sic] still living and a sincere prayer for those who have passed on for the human kindness and help that they have shown in time that I so need [sic] it." He listed the men who helped bring his daughters to New York and thanked Connell, without whom "I would never have been able to finish my story." The last lines are: "May God bless the United States et Vive La France pour toujoure [sic] et Mercie [sic] Dieu."[88]

On August 18, he entered Metropolitan for treatment. Experimental anticarcinogenic drugs and infusions of blood donated by friends such as Violette Marzan and members of the Federation of French War Veterans failed to arrest the spread of the disease.[89] Georges Ittel and his wife, long-time French friends of Bullard in New York, visited him frequently at the hospital. Toward the end, Ittel, president of the Croix de Guerre Association in America, presented the warrior with a framed diploma of the society and a framed formal letter of gratitude from its French president. Bullard told the Ittels that he was not afraid of dying, saying, "God is my friend. He has always been my friend."[90] When Mason visited, Bullard joked, "Man, if I had as many needles stickin' out of me as I've got stuck in me, I'd look like a porcupine." When the invalid opened his pajama top to reveal the twelve-inch surgical scar on his chest, Mason was "sickened by the knowledge of what that meant." However, "there came awe" as well, for the physique "belonged not to a 67-year-old man dying of cancer but to a prizefighter at the apex of his career."[91]

A frequent visitor to his ward in Metropolitan, Louise Connell was with Bullard during the day of October 12, the last day of his life, when he required an oxygen tube and was in and out of consciousness. She was able to cheer him with news that his manuscript was completely edited and typed. Recovering briefly from a difficult spell of breathing and noting Connell's anguish, Bullard was able to remove the tube, and whisper, "Don't fret honey, it's easy."[92] After receiving all the sacraments from Reverend Father Joseph O'Brien of St. Vincent de Paul church,[93] Bullard expired at just after 10:00 P.M. As Mason wrote so aptly thirty-five years ago, "He died as he had lived—just as game as hell."[94]

At 10:00 A.M. on October 17, a requiem mass was celebrated for Bullard at St. Vincent de Paul. According to the *New York Amsterdam News,* hundreds of New Yorkers were in attendance, including members of the Federation of French War Veterans, France Forever, the Verdun Society, and American Legion Paris Post No. 1. After the mass, the French veterans organization led a long procession of cars to the burial plot in the cemetery at Flushing, New York, in the borough of Queens.[95] His body was interred in grave No. 7, Section C, Plot 53. A simple one-foot square slab, bearing his name and the year of his birth and death, marks his final resting place.[96]

Epilogue

The contrast between Eugene Bullard's unrewarding years of toil and trouble early and late in life in the United States and his quarter-century of much-heralded achievement in France illustrates dramatically what American blacks have always known but whites have often denied or forgotten: the crippling disabilities imposed on the descendants of Americans of African ancestry. Jim Crow laws and the innumerable discriminatory social behaviors and institutions they sanctioned in the North as well as the South prevented millions of blacks from participating in what Gunnar Myrdal identified over fifty years ago as the American Creed: the widely propagated belief that citizens of this country should enjoy the freedom to rise in life as far as their talents might take them.

Although his strengths of character, intelligence, and enterprise enabled Bullard to transcend to some degree the virulent white racism of turn-of-the-century Georgia, he realized as a young man that no matter how well he behaved and dressed, how much useful knowledge he acquired, or how hard he strove to improve himself, his racial identity would frustrate his efforts to make good on these qualities. English gypsies told him that the color line was virtually nonexistent in Britain. Bullard and thousands of other black expatriates found this to be true, not only in that country but also in France. This was because citizens of these nations were free of the historic burden of three centuries of slavery and segregation in their homelands and free also of the various and ever-mutating doctrines of black racial inferiority, handed down generation after generation to legitimize the American caste system of white over black. Uncomprehending French men and women looked on in dismay as white Americans—military and civilian—segregated, scorned, and physically abused their black compatriots on French soil during and after World War I.

In France, Bullard's athletic, martial, and entrepreneurial abilities, and his exuberance, a spirit that the horrors of war and confrontations with racists never dampened for long, brought him the friendship of many remarkable people: soldiers and statesmen of the first rank as well as celebrities of many nationalities in art, entertainment, and sport. A multilingual cosmopolite, he was a leading figure in the American expatriate community of interwar Paris. The single most notable exploit of his career, however, was daring to learn to fly and then doing so in combat in the rickety wooden and canvas airplanes of the French air service during the Great War.

He is rightly esteemed today as a pioneering combat pilot, even though his activity in this sphere was of short duration and he was not especially gifted. In the very act of flying he was doing something influential white Americans insisted no black man could ever do. African Americans were prohibited by the U.S. Army from joining the Air Corps during World War I—even as mechanics. In the late 1930s, in spite of the flights of Bessie Coleman and the combat flying of John C. Robinson in the Italo-Ethiopian War, it remained the conventional wisdom of authoritative whites that "blacks could not fly." That American white men would not give colored people the opportunity to fly—a potent symbol of escape from oppression—was widely known and resented by African Americans. Richard Wright's protagonist, southside Chicagoan Bigger Thomas, muses on this particular disability several times in Wright's 1940 novel *Native Son*. Only after a widespread publicity campaign and intensive congressional lobbying did the War Department signal early in 1941 its intention to train black pilots in the Army Air Corps—segregated training that began at Tuskegee Institute in the summer of that year and produced a number of outstanding combat pilots in World War II.

As an aviator in 1917, Bullard was a "bad example" in terms of conventional American racial stereotypes, which held that blacks could not succeed in jobs requiring technical skills. American authorities were able to terminate his service in the French air corps, and the white American media made virtually no mention of his career as a pilot until after his death. The publication of Carisella and Ryan's *The Black Swallow of Death* in 1972 has gradually brought about an appreciation of Bullard's air achievement. Thanks to men and women of goodwill, future generations will know of him. Today, he is recognized with a memorial bust in the National Air and Space Museum of the Smithsonian Institution; on a mural of aviation pioneers at the St. Louis Airport; in exhibits at the U.S. Air Force Museum in Dayton, Ohio, and at Gunter Air Force Base, Montgomery, Alabama; and with plaques at the Georgia Aviation Hall of Fame in Warner Robins, Georgia, and at the Metropolitan Airport in his hometown of Columbus, Georgia. On September 14, 1994, the U.S. Air Force promoted Bullard posthumously to the rank of second lieutenant, and on October 9 of that year, Georgia Governor Zell Miller declared a "Eugene Bullard Day."

Eugene Bullard was a singular individual who from a young age was encouraged by his father to believe that he was destined to experience an especially notable life. Yet many black Columbusites who stayed at home, like their brethren throughout the country, also led remarkable lives and built communities powerful enough to begin the destruction of Jim Crow during Bullard's declining years. Bullard's two lives, the one in America and the other in France, illustrate the colossal spiritual, social, and economic waste to this nation caused by the tenacious denial to black people of their inalienable rights to life, liberty, and the pursuit of happiness.

Notes

Introduction

1. P. J. Carsella and James W. Ryan, *The Black Swallow of Death* (Boston: Marlborough House, 1972).

2. Stanley Rothenberg to P. J. Carisella and James W. Ryan, January 28, 1971, Louise Fox Connell Papers, Schlesinger Library, Radcliffe College. Connell befriended Bullard in 1959, edited and arranged for typing his handwritten memoir as he brought sections of it to her, and sought to find a publisher for the completed manuscript throughout the 1960s. Correspondence and memoranda related to the publishing of *The Black Swallow of Death* are among her papers.

3. David Manning White, President, Marlborough House, to Stanley Rothenberg, March 10, 1974, Connell Papers. Of the many journalistic pieces based on *The Black Swallow of Death,* the most widely distributed is Irving Wallace, David Wallechinsky, and Amy Wallace, "The Black Swallow," *Parade Magazine* (September 26, 1982): 19. Interest in Bullard has revived with the publication of Jamie H. Cockfield's "All Blood Runs Red" in *Legacy: A Celebration of African-American Culture, American Heritage Magazine* special edition (February/March, 1995), which is based largely on Carisella and Ryan's book.

4. Louise Fox Connell to Kenneth Littauer, April 14, 1959, Connell Papers.

5. Darryl Pinckney, "Promissory Notes," *New York Review of Books* 42 (April 6, 1995): 41.

6. Eugene J. Bullard, "All Blood Runs Red: My Adventurous Life in Search of Freedom," (hereafter ABRR), manuscript in possession of Richard Reid and Jacqueline O'Garro, 1961, "Adventures in Atlanta."

Chapter 1. Columbus, Georgia, 1895–1906

1. Twelfth Census of the United States, 1900, Bulletin 72.

2. John S. Lupold, *Columbus, Georgia, 1928–1978* (Columbus: Columbus Sesquicentennial, 1978), 1–43; Joseph B. Mahan, *Columbus: Georgia's Fall Line "Trading Town"* (Northridge, Calif.: Windsor Publications, 1986), 31–63; James Pickett Jones, *Yankee Blitzkreig: Wilson's Raid through Alabama and Georgia* (Athens: University of Georgia Press, 1976), 126–44.

3. Lupold, *Columbus, Georgia,* 45–49; Randall Castleton, "The Problem of Reconstruction in Columbus, Georgia, in Early 1866," Columbus State University Archives, 1990.

4. De jure segregation would develop in the twentieth century. See John Hammond Moore, "Jim Crow in Georgia," *South Atlantic Quarterly* 66 (fall 1967), 554–55.

5. C. Vann Woodward, *Tom Watson: Agrarian Rebel,* 2d ed. (Savannah: Beehive Press, 1973), 186–209, 316–32.

6. Journalist and Columbus historian Billy Winn has written about the 1896 case in "Mob Violence Led to Deaths of Many Blacks," *Columbus Enquirer,* January 28, 1987, A-6.

7. Winn's seven-part series on the 1912 lynching, "Incident at Wynn's Hill," appeared in the *Enquirer* between January 25 and January 31, 1987.

8. "Pistol Duel in Public Road Between White Man and Negro," *Columbus Ledger,* January 18, 1903, 1; "Mr. Elliot's Side of the Shooting," *Ledger,* January 19, 1903, 1; "A Good Thing for the County Says Judge Redd," *Ledger,* January 20, 1903, 1.

9. "Boston Negro Given Job," *Columbus Ledger,* January 13, 1903, 3; "City Brevities," *Ledger,* March 13, 1903, 8.

10. "Address to the People of the United States Delivered at a Convention of Colored Men, Louisville, Kentucky, September 24, 1883," in Philip S. Foner, ed., *The Life and Writings of Frederick Douglass,* 5 vols. (New York: International Publishers, 1975), 4:378.

11. ABRR, "Violence."

12. Ibid.

13. Ibid.

14. In a notarized letter (in possession of the author) of August 24, 1915, William Bullard certified that L. F. Humber, a man also born and raised in Stewart County, "knew me and my father."

15. Helen Eliza Terrell, *History of Stewart County,* 2 vols. (Columbus: Colum-

bus Office and Supply, 1959), 1:313–14; telephone conversations between the author and Daisy Bullard Thomas, March 14, 1989, and November 1, 1991.

16. Terrell, *History of Stewart County,* 1:425, 466.

17. Telephone conversation between the author and Daisy Bullard Thomas, November 1, 1991. The *Columbus City Directories* for 1912 and 1914 support Thomas's recollection during this conversation that "around 1912," when she was working for a "Mr. Charles Jordan, an employee of the water works at his home," she would occasionally visit with Dr. Bullard, who "lived a few blocks away." Daisy Thomas is listed as a laundress (1912) and a cook (1914); Charles Jordan is listed as a cashier for the Columbus Water Supply Company living at 1235 Third Avenue; and Dr. Bullard's address was 1408 Third Avenue. The 1912 directory also bears out Thomas's memory that Eugene's father, William, was working for the wholesale drygoods firm Power and Baird at this time.

18. Conversation between Daisy Bullard Thomas and Caroline Corner, December, 1991. At that time, Corner was collaborating with the author in gathering materials for a documentary film project. She sent me a transcript of her conversation, which took place in Thomas's Cleveland apartment.

19. Ibid.

20. "Dr. W. L. Bullard Dies of Apoplexy," *Columbus Enquirer-Sun,* May 19, 1925, 1. That William L. Bullard's father, Lewis, was a brother of Wiley Bullard is established in Eleanor D. McSwain, *Abstracts of Some Documents of Twiggs County, Georgia* (Macon, Ga.: National Printing Company, 1972), 263, 267, 309; and Kathleen Jones Carswell, "Collections of Twiggs Countians Here and There" (unpublished manuscript, 1973, pp. 43, 44), in the Bradley Memorial Library Genealogy Room, Columbus, Ga.

21. Mary Hart (Mrs. Sewell) Brumly to the author, March 24, 1993. A family genealogist, Mrs. Brumly is the granddaughter of Dr. Bullard.

22. Ibid; "Dr. W. L. Bullard Dies of Apoplexy," 1, 4.

23. ABRR, "Violence"; telephone conversation between the author and Daisy Bullard Thomas, November 14, 1991.

24. Terrell, *History of Stewart County,* 1:1, 5, 39–54.

25. Daniel L. Littlefield Jr., *Africans and Creeks: From the Colonial Period to the Civil War* (Westport, Conn.: Greenwood Press, 1979), 84–134; Michael D. Green, *The Politics of Indian Removal: Creek Government and Society in Crisis* (Lincoln: University of Nebraska Press, 1982), 150–51, 206 n. 4.

26. ABRR, "Run-Away Child."

27. Marriage Records, Marriage Book C, Stewart County Courthouse, Lumpkin, Ga.

28. Twelfth Census of the United States, 1900, Schedule No. 1, Population, Muscogee County, Georgia, 304A.

29. Ibid.; William Bullard to U.S. Department of State, August 9, 1915, in possession of the author. In ABRR, Bullard repeatedly errs in giving his birthdate as October 9, 1894. The *Columbus Magazine* of July 31, 1941, 6, contains a 1900 photograph of such a house on 27th Street—a house lived in by Charity Wiggins, mother of Blind Tom, a sightless slave boy of musical genius who would become an internationally known concert pianist.

30. *Columbus City Directory, 1894,* 270; conversation between author and Alfonso Biggs, June 3, 1988.

31. Terrell, *History of Stewart County,* 2:386, 414, 652; Mark L. Berger, "Bradley, W. C.," *Dictionary of Georgia Biography,* 2 vols. (Athens: University of Georgia Press, 1983), 1:111–12.

32. Twelfth Census of the United States, 1900, Schedule No. 1, Population, Muscogee County, Georgia, 304A.

33. The 1900 census gives "washer woman" as Josephine's employment. The noted African American historian John Henrik Clarke grew up in Columbus a generation after Eugene Bullard. Clarke's mother was also a washerwoman. He remembers how much better it was washing for affluent whites than poor ones: the clothes were less dirty, detergent was often supplied, the "bundles" might be dropped off and picked up, and there might even be a tip (Barbara Eleanor Adams, *John Henrik Clarke: The Early Years* [Hampton, Va.: United Brothers and Sisters Communications, 1992], 8–9).

34. *Columbus City Directory, 1894,* 270.

35. Annie H. Canady to author, September 26, 1988, and December 17, 1993. The school records of the Bullard children, noting the schools they attended and their dates of attendance, were compiled for the author by Ms. Canady, Records/Microfilm Specialist of the Records Department of the Muscogee County School System. A photograph of the 28th Street School was made available to me by Alfonso Biggs. Comparative salary figures may be found in Katherine Hines Mahan and William Clyde Woodall, *A History of Public Education in Muscogee County and the City of Columbus, Georgia, 1828–1976* (Columbus: Muscogee County Board of Education, 1977), 152–60.

36. Quoted in Becky Matthews, "The Development of Secondary Education for Black Students in Columbus, Georgia, 1920–1932," Columbus State University Archives, 1990.

37. Conversation between Corner and Daisy Thomas, December 1991.

38. Record of death of Josephine Bullard, August 24, 1902, Columbus Depart-

ment of Health; "Local Laconics," *Columbus Enquirer-Sun,* August 26, 1902, 8; Riverdale Cemetery Records, Columbus. The cemetery records do not, however, indicate the site of her unmarked grave.

39. *Columbus Enquirer-Sun,* August 26, 1902, 8.

40. ABRR, "Violence."

41. Ibid. The author has found no evidence for Bullard's assertion that his father's family came from Martinique and arrived in Georgia by way of Mississippi. In the 1900 federal census, William gives his parents' birthplaces as South Carolina. Eugene began saying he had Martiniquan ancestry while he was serving with French military forces during the Great War.

42. Ibid.

43. Ibid.

44. Ibid.

45. Ibid. Since he was dredging up memories some sixty years old, it is not surprising that Eugene Bullard's estimation of the dates and sequence of events of his early life is often inaccurate. In ABRR, he wrote that his mother died in 1899 instead of 1902 and that he was five and Pauline twelve at the time, instead of seven and seventeen. In other places in the memoir, he indicated that he ran away from home as early as age six and stowed away on the merchant ship at age ten. That a child this age—and a small one at that (fully grown, Eugene was a slender five-feet-seven inches tall)—could possess the requisite physical and mental strength for such activities seems unlikely. And since his last school record is dated June 1906, he could not have left Columbus permanently until he was at least eleven years old (Canady to author, September 26, 1988).

It is difficult to establish conclusively when the clash between William Bullard and his foreman as well as its traumatic denouement occurred. However, circumstantial evidence suggests that these events took place in 1903 or 1904, several years, not months, before Eugene left his family and Columbus. In the early part of the century, the city directories of Columbus were published in even-numbered years. The 1902 directory is the last one in which William Bullard is listed as an employee of W. C. Bradley and a resident at 2601 Talbotton Avenue. Oddly enough, the 1904 directory includes neither an address for William nor an address for his oldest son, Hector; it is the only directory of the era in which addresses are not given for these men—William is listed by address and employer until 1921, Hector until 1908. The 1904 directory cites another occupant at 2601 Talbotton Avenue and records William Bullard as a driver for the Kern and Loeb Company.

It is possible that the death of Josephine Bullard occasioned the move away from 2601 Talbotton Avenue in 1903–4. Also, Bullard's memory of his father's tenure with a railroad company is not sustained by information in the directories. Through the last entry for William Bullard in 1921, his occupation is consistently given as drayman or driver with local merchants. However, it seems telling that William Bullard, having been with W. C. Bradley for over a decade, was no longer with him in 1904.

Moreover, Eugene recalled that a colored neighbor, a Mrs. Butler, provided meals and motherly comfort to the Bullard youngsters in the absence of their father after the visitation of the mob to the family home. The 1904 directory records a colored Fannie Butler living with her husband, John, on Talbotton Avenue; John Butler's occupation is recorded as a drayman for the W. C. Bradley Company. The couple is listed as living in rural Muscogee County in 1902, and they are not listed in 1906 and 1908 (*Columbus City Directories,* 1902, 1904, 1906, 1908). Enrollment records of the Muscogee County School District indicate that Eugene was withdrawn from first grade in February 1902 (no reason is given) and that he did not reenter school as a second grader until September 1904 (Canady to author, September 26, 1988).

46. Answering a request for information from a *Columbus Enquirer* columnist who had seen Eugene's obituary in an October 1961 wire service story, Henry Walker recalled that the Bullard family was living on 26th Street, not Talbotton Avenue, when Eugene Bullard ran away; this information is consistent with the 1906 city directory and Muscogee County School records that give William's address on 26th Street. Walker's memory was consistent with Eugene's in ABRR in recalling that Eugene was called "Honey" by his father and "Gene" by his siblings and friends, and that the night he ran away from home, he hid from his father in a gypsy camp in East Highlands, several blocks from home. What does not appear in the memoir was Walker's "understanding" that "'Honey' Bullard left after being severely whipped by his father. . . . Gene's father had tied his hands to his knees and put a 'stock' between his arms before giving him the beating." (Conversation between Corner and Daisy Thomas, December, 1991; Luke Teasley, "Who Knows Bullard, Negro Hero?" *Columbus Enquirer,* December 12, 1961; Teasley, "J. Bullard, Negro Hero Identified," *Enquirer,* December 14, 1961, 5.)

Chapter 2. Youthful Vagabond, 1906–1912

1. An enumerator for the 1910 (thirteenth) U.S. census recorded in April of that year a fifteen-year-old black male, Eugene Bullard, residing at a boarding house and working at a sawmill in Thomasville, Georgia, a town close to the Florida border. There is no mention of Thomasville or sawmill employment in ABRR.

2. ABRR, "Run-Away Child," "Adventures in Atlanta." Bullard accurately recalls the depot as "the big white terminal station."

3. *Columbus Ledger,* May 18, 1903, 6.

4. ABRR, "Run-Away Child."

5. Konrad Bercovici, *Gypsies: Their Life, Lore, and Legends* (1928; reprint, New York: Greenwich House, 1983), 224; H. E. Wedeck, *Dictionary of Gipsy Life and Lore* (London: Peter Owen, 1973), 116–17, 118–19, 236–37, 371, 426; Thomas Acton, *Gypsy Politics and Social Change: The Development of Ethnic Ideology and Pressure Politics among English Gypsies from Victorian Reformism to Romany Nationalism* (London: Routledge and Kegan Paul, 1974), 46–47.

6. ABRR, "Gypsies and Other Good Whites."

7. Ibid. Bullard remembers the phrase *"mong, chevy, mong"* [beg, child, beg], a traditional gypsy usage (see *Wanderers of the World* [Washington, D.C.: National Geographic Society Special Publications, 1970], 14). The name "Jamesy" suggests that Eugene gave his middle name, James, as his first name, perhaps to foil the efforts of his father to retrieve him.

8. ABRR, "Gypsies and Other Good Whites." While the author was conducting research in the Terrell County Court House in Dawson, Georgia, in August 1991, Mrs. Nancy Fryer, Clerk of the Probate Court, recalled that her grandmother frequently pointed out to her the "old gypsy campground" at this site.

9. ABRR, "Gypsies and Other Good Whites." A reference in *Lee County, Georgia: A History* (Atlanta: Wolfe, 1983), 456–57, and a telephone conversation between the author and Nora Moreland Allen, July 1993, provided some information on a Travis Moreland of Leesburg and his horse farm at the turn of the century.

10. ABRR, "Gypsies and Other Good Whites."

11. Ibid.

12. Ibid.

13. Ella Christie Melton and Augusta Griggs Raines, *History of Terrell County* (Roswell, Ga.: Wolfe, 1980), 652. Obituary notice, *Dawson News,* February 17, 1920.

14. Ibid.

15. ABRR, "Gypsies and Other Good Whites." John Angling Turner's obituary notice states that "Ange Turner numbered his friends by his acquaintances" (*Dawson News,* December 16, 1948, 1). In ABRR, Bullard refers to him as "Ange" and Raymond Turner as "baby" or "little Raymond."

16. ABRR, "Gypsies and Other Good Whites."

17. Melton and Raines, *History of Terrell County,* 652.

18. ABRR, "Big Horse Race."

19. Ella Christie Melton, "History of Terrell County," Terrell County Court House, 1940, unpaginated; "The County Fair Was a Big Success," *Dawson News,* November 2, 1910, 1.

20. "Sporting Contests at Fair," *Dawson News,* November 1, 1911, 14; "Half-mile Running Race," *Dawson News,* October 25, 1911, 14; "Negroe's Day," *Dawson News,* October 28, 1911, 12.

21. Robert J. Jakeman, *The Divided Skies: Establishing Flight Training at Tuskegee, Alabama* (Tuscaloosa: University of Alabama Press, 1992), 55. The much-ballyhooed flight, however, was prevented from taking place by a dispute over the promoter's fee for Peters.

22. ABRR, "Big Horse Race." Eugene Bullard is not mentioned in the *Dawson News*' coverage of the horse race. Two "half-mile running races, straight dash" were reported for Wednesday, October 25, and Friday, October 27. Both were won, it was reported, by Steve Cocke on Happy Jack and I Win, respectively. In the Friday race, Angling Turner's horse, listed as Gay Boy, was reported finishing second, but the jockey was not named, the only such omission in the paper's reportage. Given the racial taboos of this period and their effects on journalistic protocol, it is difficult to reconcile the newspaper's reporting with Bullard's account in ABRR that he won the two races. Several interpretations are possible: his victories went unmentioned; his exultation at being allowed to represent the Turner family in the races caused him to remember himself as their winner; or he raced in contests simply not covered in the paper. In any case, because there was no Terrell County Fair in 1912 and because records show that Bullard was in England during fall 1913, the *Dawson News*' reportage does confirm that Eugene was with the Turners as late as fall 1911, when he was 16 years old, not 10, as he gave his age at the time of the races in the memoir ("Sporting Contests at Fair," "Races of Various Kinds Occurred Each Afternoon," *Dawson News,* November 1, 1911, 14).

Melton, in her 1940 unpublished history of Terrell County, observes that the Women's Library Association organized "the first fair [since the 1870s] in 1910" (as well as the fairs in 1911 and 1913) and gives the revenues obtained from each. In 1912, she notes, a school fair was held as a benefit for city and county schools (Melton, "History of Terrell County," "Library Association, 1907–1924"). The *Dawson News* of October and November 1912 reported no activities of the kind taking place in 1910 and 1911. Bullard gives his age as nine when he left the gypsies (ABRR, "Gypsies and Other Good Whites").

23. ABRR, "Wild Man and Wild Horse." Melton and Raines note that trains of

the Central of Georgia Railroad had been passing from Macon through Dawson and on to Eufaula since 1858 (*History of Terrell County,* 101).

24. ABRR, "Wild Man and Wild Horse." After recalling these events of a half-century earlier, Eugene adds parenthetically that "when I returned to New York [in 1940 where James Bullard was then living] . . . I learned [from him] the name of the man who'd whipped me. It was David Dewitt Drew. His brother, Charles, killed him a year later." The *Dawson News* of November 1, 1911, 2, contains a story that, even if it does not confirm the exact chronology of the whipping episode described in ABRR, does indicate its occurrence in the period when young Bullard was with the Turners:

BROTHER SHOT BROTHER DEAD
The Drews Fell Out About Their Automobile
Sunday afternoon, Chief of Police, W. E. Hiers received a telephone message requesting him to be on the lookout for Charles Drew, who had killed his brother, Dewitt Drew, and left in an automobile.
It seems that the Drews owned an automobile and the disagreement arose over the possession of the car. Young Charles Drew asserts that his brother, Dewitt Drew, was advancing upon him in a threatening manner when he fired, first in the air, then at his brother point blank. . . . Charles Drew, who is only about 19, was arrested Sunday afternoon in Americus and taken back to Richland.

25. ABRR, "Wild Man and Wild Horse."

26. ABRR, "Boy Hoodlums."

27. Ibid. The Atlanta directories of 1911 and 1912 list a Charles Butler at 288 Decatur Street, a foreman with the Georgia Railway and Electric Company.

28. ABRR, "Boy Hoodlums."

29. Ibid.

30. Ibid. Bullard gives the tailor's name as "Rothchilds." The 1912 Atlanta directory lists no Rothschilds but does list under "tailors" a Benjamin Rosenfeld with a shop at 25 E. Alabama Street.

31. ABRR, "Boy Hoodlums."

32. Ibid.

33. ABRR, "Riding the Rails."

34. Ibid.

35. Ibid. Alexander Crosby Brown, *Newport News: 325 Years* (Newport News: Newport News Golden Anniversary Corp., 1946), 57–64. Norfolk's development as a major seaport in the 1880s was also due to its access to cheap coal.

As late as 1960, coal was the "largest single commodity handled at the port" (*Ports of America: History and Development* [American Association of Port Authorities, 1961, 127–28]; ABRR, "Stowaway—Age 10").

36. ABRR, "Stowaway—Age 10."

37. Ibid. Bullard's imperfect recollection of his travels from Atlanta to Norfolk makes it difficult to retrace his path. Yet his account contains enough clues to sort out how and when he made his fateful trip. He remembers leaving the Butlers and the Hugheses wearing "all my clothes on under my overalls"—those garments amounted to "two shirts, two union suits, and the pair of new pants" (ABRR, "Boy Hoodlums"). This would rule out summertime, with its suffocating heat and humidity in the Deep South, as the time of his departure. And if, as evidence indicates, Eugene left Atlanta in late February of 1912, such bundling would have been necessary, since it was unseasonably cold along his route at that time ("Hasty Departure Made by Spring," *Atlanta Constitution,* February 22, 1912, 8). The paper reported highs and lows in the 30s over the next five days, running a front-page story on February 23 headlined "22 Steamers Driven Ashore by Furious Gale, Worst Since 1879 in Norfolk Area." On the night of March 3, a snowstorm developed over the Hampton Roads, causing a ship collision in the crossing between Newport News and Norfolk (*Newport News Times Herald,* March 4, 1912).

Bullard recalls that the Atlanta train station from which he departed was located "below a main street" and "all trains had to pass under an overhead bridge in the heart of" the city. Given his distinct memory of his two arrivals in Atlanta at Terminal Station, "the big white building," it is evident that Eugene left for Virginia from Union Station in what today is "Underground Atlanta." In 1912, Seaboard Air Line Railway (SAL) passenger trains departed there at 8:55 P.M. daily for New York, with connections to Portsmouth and Norfolk, Virginia. It seems likely that the vagabond "rode the rods" on this train. During the night, he must have missed a switching of cars bound for Norfolk at the junction town of Norlina, N.C., near the Virginia border, and remained on the train as far north as the vicinity of Richmond, where he stayed with the Hughes family. (ABRR, "Riding the Rails"; "Railway Schedules," *Atlanta Constitution,* May 12, 1912, 8A; Peter Maiken, *Night Trains: The Pullman System in the Golden Years of Rail Travel* [Chicago: Lakme Press, 1991], 110, 127.)

On leaving Richmond a week later, he would have indeed been confused about which train to take, since the depot was a complex affair, accommodating trains of both the SAL and the Chesapeake & Ohio (C&O) Railways. Bullard recalls the Richmond station as situated at the "lower end of Main Street" (ABRR, "Riding the Rails"). Maiken notes that "the SAL and the C&O . . . shared the Main Street Station, which the two roads had built just after the turn of the century." The structure's "large elevated train shed made it one of the South's most distinctive depots" (*Night Trains,* 111). Fortuitously, the train Eugene climbed beneath was an express of the C&O traveling east that would carry him to its terminus in Newport News. Bullard remembers arriving at Newport News at dusk (ABRR, "Riding the Rails"). The C&O schedule in the *Newport News Times Herald* for March 2, 1912, shows trains arriving there daily at 5:30 and 7:30 P.M.

Despite Bullard's mention in ABRR of the ship *Matherus,* a search of the shipping pages of the *Newport News Times Herald,* the *Norfolk Virginian-Pilot,* the *Norfolk Landmark,* and the *New York Times* from November 1911 to February 1913 reveals no ship by the name *Matherus* in or out of either port. An exhaustive list ("Eldredge Shipping List for the Hampton Roads," n.d.) of ships—big and small—out of these ports compiled by Edwin Eldredge and deposited in the Mariner's Museum in Newport News also records no ship of that name. Ships reported in the *New York Times* with similar names, such as the *Matheran* and the *Materam,* did not visit the Hampton Roads and were owned and based in England, and their routes did not take them into the North Sea or Baltic Sea. However, there is reported in the Newport and Norfolk newspapers a ship by the name of *Marta Russ,* which, having loaded 235 tons of bunker coal, left Norfolk for Dunkirk in the late afternoon of Monday, March 4, 1912. ("Shipping Report," "Maritime Miscellany," "With the Shipping," *Virginia Pilot and the Norfolk Landmark,* March 6, 1912.) Built in 1899, the ship was owned by Ernst Russ of Hamburg, its home port. Its captain, a man named Westphal, and crew were German. (*Lloyd's [of London] Register,* "Steamers, 'Mar,' 1912–1913"; also *Deutsche Lloyd's [of London],* 1911, "Steamers, 'Mar–Mat,'" Mariners' Museum Library, Newport News, Virginia.) The sailing date conforms roughly to Bullard's estimation of the amount of time between leaving the Turners' home sometime in late 1911; it is evident that his time with the Butlers in Atlanta was only a matter of several weeks and that he was with the Hughes family for only one week. The March 4, 1912, departure also accommodates his recollection of the amount of time he spent in Glasgow and Liverpool after being put ashore in late March by Captain Westphal in Aberdeen, Scotland. He recalls spending his first Christmas abroad in Liverpool, which would have been Christmas 1912.

Whether Eugene rendered the ship's name from hearing the sailors pronounce it or from seeing it painted on the vessel, it would have been easy for him to transpose *Marta Russ* into "Matherus." Moreover, his use of the name in the memoir is based on a recollection of the name he had written on a matchbox that was no longer in his possession. He might simply have misremembered how he had written it down.

What of the ship he boarded at Newport News on which he traversed the

Hampton Roads to Norfolk? The *Newport Daily Press,* in its shipping news of Saturday, March 2, 1912, reported that an English steamer, *Powhatan,* had loaded a supply of fuel coal at the Newport docks and was sailing for London via Norfolk. This was probably the ship from which Eugene disembarked at Norfolk in order, as destiny would have it, to meet the crew of the *Marta Russ,* which sailed, as he correctly remembered, on a Monday.

38. ABRR, "Boy Hoodlums"; Jerry Robinson, *The Comics: An Illustrated History of Comic Strip Art* (New York: Putnam, 1974), 32; Robert C. Harvey, *The Art of the Funnies* (Jackson: University Press of Mississippi, 1994), 4–7; Arthur A. Berger, *The Comic-Stripped American* (New York: Walker, 1973), 19–34; Shirley Glubok, *The Art of the Comic Strip,* (New York: MacMillan, 1979), 35.

39. ABRR, "Stowaway—Age 10," "Love and a Life Purpose." At many points in ABRR, beginning with the sale of his goat but not his goat cart, Bullard takes pains to account for how he paid his way through life.

Chapter 3. Vaudevillian and Boxer in Britain and France, 1912–1914

1. ABRR, "Stowaway." The ship's dimensions are given in *Deutsche Lloyd's [of London],* "Steamers, 'Mar–Mat,'" 1911.

2. Ibid. An article dealing with the prosecution of stowaways on transatlantic voyages appears in the *London Times,* June 25, 1912 (early edition), 8.

3. Ibid.

4. Ibid.; ABRR, "Adventures in Atlanta."

5. ABRR, "Stowaway."

6. Ibid.; Will Irwin, "Flashes from the War Zone," *Saturday Evening Post* (July 15, 1916), 13.

7. ABRR, "Prize Fighting Days." By examining Brown's well-documented travels in pursuit of his boxing career, it is possible to approximate the dates of Bullard's moves from town to town within Britain, movements which, as is the case of his youthful travels in Georgia, are difficult to determine from the memoir, with its conflicting estimates of length of stays in various locations. (The reader should again bear in mind that the memoirist in the first section of ABRR was attempting to recall events occurring forty to fifty years earlier.) The Dixie Kid had come to Europe for the first time in 1905. Although he had returned to fight in the States, by 1911 he was back in Europe, boxing mostly in England with an occasional match in Paris.

A schedule of all Brown's matches—listing opponents, venues, and dates through 1914—was published in that year. It reveals that he had been fighting in

Liverpool and other provincial English towns from January to April 1913. His last fight in Liverpool for that year was April 10. He did not fight again until he scored a fourth-round knockout against an opponent in London on October 13, 1913. He won again in two successive matches in London before crossing the English Channel to fight in Paris on November 28, 1913 (*Boxings's Book of Records Up to June, 1914,* n.d., 65). This date is significant, for it is the same one that Bullard recorded in ABRR for his first fight in Paris with the Brown group. Since he was in Dawson, Georgia, in 1911, crossed the Atlantic in March 1912, and spent his first Christmas in Liverpool, it is clear that he first met the Dixie Kid in early 1913. In ABRR, Bullard recalls living in London with Brown and his family at a "Mrs. Carter's boarding house" at "Number 2, Coram Street, Russell Square." The fact that "Samuel Carter, apartments" is listed at that address in the London city directory (Holborn Borough) only in 1912 and 1913 is further evidence that Bullard was there in the summer and fall of 1913. The author consulted these directories (*The Post Office of London Directory for 1912 and 1913*) in the Archives of the Borough of Holborn in June 1990.

8. "Dixie Kid: l'ex-champion du monde poids welters et ses deux jeunes espoirs," *La Boxe & les boxeurs,* January 21, 1914, cover.

9. ABRR, "Prize Fighting Days." In the memoir, Bullard misspelled Burge as "Berge." Fred Dartnell, *"Seconds Out!": Chats about Boxers, their Trainers and Patrons* (New York: Bretano's, 1924), 203.

10. ABRR, "Prize Fighting Days."

11. Scanlon's account of his life appears in Nancy Cunard's *Negro Anthology* (1934; reprint, New York: Negro Universities Press, 1969), 339. Scanlon's name heads the fight card for matches at London's Wonderland ring on September 18, 1909 ("Boxing," file at John Johnson Collection of Printed Ephemera, Bodleian Library, Oxford University). Langford appears in a May 1909 photograph fighting in the ring at the National Sporting Club in London's Covent Garden in Maurice Golesworthy, *Encyclopedia of Boxing* (London: Hale Press, 1960), 129.

12. "Many Negroes in England—Thousands of them Flocking to that Country," *Dawson [Georgia] News,* September 16, 1908, 6.

13. Tony Martin, ed., *Sport in Britain: A Social History* (Cambridge: Cambridge University Press, 1989), 91.

14. White American and English minstrel entertainers are discussed and photographed in Benny Green, ed., *The Last Empires: A Music Hall Companion* (London: Pavillon, 1986), 181–82; Ernest Short, *Fifty Years of Vaudeville,* rev. ed. (Westport, Conn.: Greenwood Press, 1978), 147–48; John Lehmann, *Holborn: An Historical Portrait of a London Borough* (London: MacMillan, 1970), 166;

Raymond Mander and Joe Michinson, *British Music Halls,* rev. ed. (London: Gentry Books, 1974); S. Theodore Felsted, *Stars Who Made the Halls* (London: T. Werner Laurie, 1946), 55–58. Williams' career and triumph in England are taken up in Douglas Gilbert, *American Vaudeville: Its Life and Times* (New York: Dover, 1963), 282–87.

15. "Many Negroes in England," *Dawson News.*

16. Joe Laurie Jr., *Vaudeville From Honky-Tonks to the Palace* (1953; reprint, Port Washington, N.Y.: Kennikat Press, 1973), 137.

17. Black vaudevillian Bert Williams once commented to the American Jewish singer Eddie Cantor, "it wouldn't be so sad, Eddie, if I didn't still hear the applause ringing in my ears" (quoted in John E. Dimeglio, *Vaudeville U.S.A.* [Bowling Green, Ky.: Bowling Green University Popular Press, 1973], 114). Michael Rogin has recently made clear the enormous influence of blackface minstrelsy as content in early American motion pictures. These films, he argues, advanced a new concept of nationalism—a cultural pluralism accepting as Americans the recently immigrated European Jews at the expense of African Americans, who were held in traditionally servile roles. See Rogin, *Blackface, White Noise: Jewish Immigrants in the Hollywood Melting Pot* (Berkeley: University of California Press, 1996).

18. "A Question of Colour," *Holborn and Finisbury Guardian,* November 28, 1913, 8.

19. "The Mayor of Battersea," *The Crisis* 7 (March 1914), 224–25.

20. Marshall Stearns and Jean Stearns, *Jazz Dance: The Story of American Vernacular Dance* (New York: Macmillan, 1968), 250–53. The *Holborn and Finisbury Guardian* of January 5, 1913, 5, carries a story pertaining to black music hall performers living on Coram Street.

21. Henry T. Sampson, *The Ghost Walks: A Chronological History of Blacks in Show Business* (Metuchen, N.J.: Scarecrow Press, 1988), 108, 114, 160, 211, 212, 231, 284, 313, 406 (on page 405 of this work, there is a photograph of Davis and one of her Picks); Laurie, *Vaudeville,* 137; Will Marion Cook, "Clorindy, The Origin of the Cakewalk," *Theater Arts* 31 (September 1947), 65; Eric Midwinter, *Old Liverpool* (Plymouth, U. K.: David & Charles, 1971), 37–38.

22. Jeffrey T. Sammons, *Beyond the Ring: The Role of Boxing in American Society* (Urbana: University of Illinois Press, 1988), 34–40; Robert Jakoubek, *Jack Johnson* (New York: Chelsea House, 1993), 64–65, 71.

23. Sammons, *Beyond the Ring,* 40–45.

24. Ibid.; Randy Roberts, *Papa Jack: Jack Johnson and the Era of White Hopes* (New York: Free Press, 1983), 126–29.

25. ABRR, "Prize Fighting Days"; Dartnell, *"Seconds Out!,"* 176; Golesworthy,

Encyclopedia, 42; Alexander Johnston, *Ten—And Out! The Complete Story of the Prize Ring in America* (New York: Ives Washburn, 1928), 269–70.

26. Golesworthy notes that the BBBC did not allow a black man to fight for a British title until September 1947 (*Encyclopedia,* 58); Roberts, *Papa Jack,* 128–29.

27. Dartnell, *"Seconds Out!,"* 175.

28. Golesworthy, *Encyclopedia,* 33; Dartnell, *"Seconds Out!,"* 173. French boxing historian Pierre Cangioni celebrates Langford in his *La fableuse histoire de la boxe* (Paris: Editions O.D.I.L., 1977), 198.

29. Bullard remembers his fight taking place at the Elysées Montmartre (ABRR, "Prize Fighting Days"). The Dixie Kid's bout of this date was at the Premierland arena ("Dixie Kid battu par Demlen," *La Boxe & les boxeurs,* December 3, 1913, 5112.

30. Jakoubek, *Jack Johnson,* 38–41; Sammons, *Beyond the Ring,* 36–37.

31. Elizabeth Hausser, *Les Evénements vus par la presse, 1900–1919* (Paris: Editions de Minuit, 1968), 118.

32. Ibid., February, 1908, 291. The widely circulated French pictorial newspaper *Illustration: Journal universel* of February 22, 1908, carried the story of this fight along with a dramatic black and white drawing, photographic in effect, of McVey standing "in the pose of a victorious gladiator" over his fallen foe. Parisian high society, men and women in elegant evening dress, are shown seated at ringside.

33. This information is given in the McVey-Jeanette fight program found in the "Boxing" file of the Johnson Collection of Printed Ephemera, Bodleian Library. The program cover features exotic sketches of the two fighters on the program, their African facial features exaggerated. These sketches in which racial difference is clearly being appreciated rather than disdained is suggestive of Paul Colin's famous poster promoting the 1925 "Revue Nègre" and reminds us that the *culte des nègres* in France had pre–World War I origins.

34. "Boxing," Johnson Collection; Hausser, *Les Evénements vus par la presse,* 325.

35. Hausser, *Les Evénements vus par la presse,* 325.

36. Alexis Philouenko, *Histoire de la boxe* (Paris: Criterion, 1991), 226. Bob Scanlon asserts that he had begun training the young Carpentier in 1908 in Cunard's *Negro Anthology,* 340.

37. Items in "Boxing" file of the Johnson Collection.

38. "Toujours l'invasion Américaine," *La Boxe & les boxeurs,* December 3, 1913, 5132.

39. "Bernard contre Blink MacCloskey [sic]," *La Boxe & les boxeurs,* December 3, 1913, 5132.

40. ABRR, "Prize Fighting Days."

41. Ibid.

42. ABRR, "Dream Come True."

43. Ibid.

44. "Recognize Jack Johnson," *New York Times,* May 7, 1914, 9. Several months later, Johnson would retain his title in a bout with Frank Moran, which took place on the eve of the assassination of the Archduke Ferdinand of Austria. At ringside were celebrities whom Eugene, because of his heroism for France in the coming war, would know personally in the Paris of the '20s: Mistinguett, the Dolly Sisters, and the Princess de Polignac (Stephen Longstreet, *We All Went to Paris: Americans in the City of Light* [New York: Macmillan, 1977], 293).

45. ABRR, "Dream Come True."

46. Ibid.

47. Ibid. Bullard uses the phrase "in search of freedom," which became the subtitle of ABRR, in connection with memories of his second stay in Atlanta when he wondered if he had been "wrong to leave them [the gypsies]" instead of waiting for them to return to England.

48. Anthony Shannon, "U.S. Adventurer Wins 15th French Decoration," *New York World Telegram,* October 9, 1959.

49. ABRR, "Dream Come True."

Chapter 4. A Hero in the Great War

1. Andre Kaspi and Antoine Mares, *Le Paris des étrangers depuis un siècle* (Paris: Imprimerie nationale, 1989), introduction.

2. James Weldon Johnson, *Along this Way: The Autobiography of James Weldon Johnson* (1933; reprint, New York: Viking, 1968), 209.

3. ABRR, "Foreign Legion." Interestingly, Bullard here recalls correctly his birth year as 1895, the only time he does so in the memoir.

4. Douglas Porch, *La Légion étrangère, 1831–1962* (Paris: Fayard, 1994), 399, 765.

5. ABRR, "Foreign Legion."

6. Phillippe Conrad and Arnaud Laspeyres, *La Grande Guerre* (Paris: Editions Presse, 1989), 100–101.

7. ABRR, "Heroism and Comedy," "Trophy Troubles." In *La Grande Guerre,* p. 101, there is a photograph of German soldiers captured after this battle.

8. William O. Bullard to Secretary of State, August 10, 1915, U.S. State Department Records, National Archives. I am indebted to Jamie Cockfield, professor of history at Mercer University, for making available to me copies of U.S. government documents pertaining to William and Eugene Bullard. At the urging of Professor Cockfield, officials in the U.S. Air Force agreed to grant posthumously a second lieutenancy to Eugene Bullard on September 14, 1994. In validating Bullard's case, Air Force historians found a number of Bullard-related items in the National Archives and sent copies of them to Cockfield, who in turn sent them on to me. I shall cite such materials hereafter as U.S. Air Force–Cockfield documents.

9. ABRR, "Two Thousand Dollar Bet."

10. Alvey A. Adee, Second Assistant Secretary, U.S. Department of State, to William O. Bullard, August 16, 1915, Air Force–Cockfield documents.

11. Terrell, *History of Stewart County*, 1:52–54, 1:508–15; "L. F. Humber," "W. C. Bradley," *Columbus City Directories*, 1884, 1888, 1914.

12. William O. Bullard to Secretary of State, August 24, 1915; Robert Lansing to William G. Sharp, American Ambassador to France, September 4, 1915, Air Force–Cockfield documents.

13. Paul Ayres Rockwell, *American Fighters in the Foreign Legion, 1914–1918* (Boston: Houghton-Mifflin, 1930), 159. Rockwell's chapter on the 170th at Verdun is entitled "Les hirondelles de la mort."

14. Bullard, it should be made clear here, never called himself "the Black Swallow of Death." Indeed, in ABRR, he mistranslated *hirondelles* as "chimney swifts" instead of "swallows." Since he regretted having to take human life, the sobriquet associating him with death would have been offensive to him and, in fact, has only been used to refer to him since being coined in a 1967 *Ebony* magazine piece and taken over by Carisella and Ryan as the title of their book (ABRR, "170th Infantry—Regimental Citation"; Mary Smith, "The Incredible Life of Monsieur Bullard," *Ebony* 23 [December 1967]: 120–28). Louise Fox Connell, who edited ABRR and endeavored to have the manuscript published after Bullard's death, protested to James Ryan the title he and Carisella had chosen. To her mind, it suggested "death by the hideous black plague . . . the black death" (Connell to Ryan, November 19, 1971, Connell Papers).

15. S. L. A. Marshall and the editors of *The American Heritage History of World War I* (New York: Simon and Schuster, 1964), 176.

16. ABRR, "Verdun."

17. Bernadette E. Schmitt and Harold C. Vedeler, *The World in Crucible, 1914–1919* (New York: Harper and Row, 1984), 124–25.

18. Patrick Facon, *La Grande Guerre et ses lendemains, 1914–1935* (Paris:

Larousse, 1985), 43; Adrian Gilbert, *World War I in Photographs* (London: Orbis, 1986), 72–73 (Gilbert asserts that "2,500,000 shells supported the opening assault"); ABRR, "More About Verdun."

19. ABRR, "Base Hospital"; Cunard, *Negro Anthology,* 340. The horror of the Battle of Verdun is conveyed in photographs in Gilbert's and Facon's books as well as Yves Buffetant, *Verdun: Images de l'enfer* (Paris: Tallandier, 1995), 113–16. See also *1916: Année de Verdun* (Paris: Charles-Lavauzelle, 1996), the recent work published by the French Ministry of Defense on the occasion of the eightieth anniversary of the battle. In the preface, historian Antoine Prost observes that Verdun marks a transgression of the limits of the human condition (12).

20. Marshall, *American Heritage History of World War I,* 176.

21. ABRR, "First Negro Pilot."

22. Marshall, *American Heritage History of World War I,* 176. The author visited the site of the Battle of Verdun in August 1994.

23. Schmitt and Vedeler, *The World in Crucible,* 127.

24. ABRR, "Base Hospital."

25. Ibid. Gerard Chauvy's *Lyon autrefois* (Lyon: Horvath, 1993), 20, 90, contains photographs of the train station and a ward of the Hôtel Dieu.

26. Andre Gibert et al., *Visages du Lyonais* (Paris: Editions de Horizons de France, 1952), 170, contains a photograph of the huge exterior of the Hôtel Dieu.

27. ABRR, "Decorations and Honors."

28. Irwin, "Flashes from the War Zone," 12–13. Bullard retained a copy of this piece and refers to it without criticism, indeed pridefully, in ABRR.

29. Ibid. Bullard was either so indifferent to or oblivious of racial stereotypes that he told Irwin he'd eaten so much *singe* [monkey], the *poilus* term for their beef stew rations, that he might start climbing trees.

30. Ibid.

31. ABRR, "More About Verdun."

32. Irwin, "Flashes from the War Zone," 12–13.

33. "Remise solennelle de décorations," *Lyon républicain,* June 27, 1916, 3. Bullard's name is listed among "les soldats" [the soldiers] in the last paragraph of this column.

34. Chauvy, *Lyon autrefois,* 125.

35. "L'Actualité lyonnaise," "On demande des Mariannes," *Lyon républicain,* June 24, 1916, 4. The requests for Mariannes occurred daily in these weeks in the *républicain.* The patriotic fervor is also evident in the bimonthly *Lyon passe-partout,* July 26, 1916.

36. "Le 14 juillet à Lyon," *Le Nouvelliste de Lyon,* July 15, 1916, 2. In ABRR, Bullard refers to Place Bellecour as Place d'Armes, its name after World War I.

37. Ibid.

38. "La fête de la France," *Lyon passe-partout,* July 26, 1916, 1.

39. "La fête nationale à Lyon," "Le défilé," *Lyon républicain,* July 15, 1916, 2.

40. ABRR, "Decorations and Honors."

41. Ibid.

42. Ibid.

43. Henri Troyat, *Kisling, 1891–1953* (Turin, Italy: Jean Kisling, 1982), 11, 28. The building at 3, rue Joseph Bara, remains today a studio, appearing much the same as when Kisling worked there.

44. ABRR, "Decorations and Honors."

45. E. Benezit, *Dictionnaire critique et documentaire des peintres, sculpteurs,* 8 vols. (Paris: Librarie Grund, 1960), 8:731.

46. Liliane Grumwald, *Claude Cattaert, Le Vél' D'Hiv, 1903–1959* (Paris: Ramsay "image," 1979), 54–57. The authors dedicate their work to Dickson and two other directors of the Vélodrome d'Hiver. "Jeff Dickson Missing," *New York Times,* July 25, 1943, 27.

47. Billy Kluver and Julie Martin, *Kiki's Paris: Artists and Lovers, 1900–1930* (New York: Abrams, 1989), 74–79, contains a lengthy discussion and many photographs of Kisling and his associates in the period when Bullard visited him. See also "Montparnasse," *Dictionnaire de Paris* (Paris: Librarie Larousse, 1964), 349; Maurice Sachs, *The Decade of Illusions: Paris, 1918–1928* (New York: Knopf, 1933), 106, 127; Troyat, *Kisling,* 48–64.

48. Sachs, *Decade of Illusions,* 106.

49. Philip M. Flammer, *The Vivid Air: The Lafayette Escadrille* (Athens: University of Georgia Press, 1981), 71–72.

50. Roland Penrose, *Picasso: His Life and Work,* 2d ed. (New York: Schocken, 1962), 193.

51. Arlen J. Hansen, *Expatriate Paris: A Cultural and Literary Guide to Paris of the 1920s* (New York: Arcade, 1990), 122. In ABRR, Bullard mentioned La Rotonde as a drinking spot he patronized, but he erred in believing the scene of the two-thousand-dollar wager to be La Coupole, which did not open until 1927.

52. ABRR, "Two Thousand Dollar Bet." According to Dickson's son, Andy, Dickson did not arrive in France before the fall of 1917 (letter to author, Dec. 15, 1999). The bet was probably made in early 1919 over whether Bullard *had flown* in 1917.

53. Ibid.

54. Ibid.

55. Charles Christienne, *L'Aviation française, 1890–1919* (Paris: Atlas, 1988), 166–67. Bullard incorrectly spelled "Girod" as "Girard" several times before getting it right in a final mention in ABRR.

56. ABRR, "Two Thousand Dollar Bet." This is the first time in ABRR that Bullard uses his middle name; he was christened Eugene James Bullard but only used the name after rendering into the French "Jacques" during the war, another indication of how fully he was assimilating into French life. The names Eugene and Bullard have their identical French equivalents in spelling although not, of course, in pronunciation. (In his certified letter to the State Department of August 24, 1915, William Bullard gives his son's name as Eugene James Bullard.)

57. ABRR, "Two Thousand Dollar Bet." Bullard believed he was the recipient of the last letter Genet wrote before being killed in combat on April 16, 1917. After the war, he sent the letter to Genet's mother and received a grateful note in return.

58. Walt Brown Jr., ed., *An American for Lafayette: The Diaries of E. C. C. Genet* (Charlottesville: University of Virginia Press, 1981), 100.

59. ABRR, "Two Thousand Dollar Bet."

60. James R. McConnell, *Flying for France: With the American Escadrille at Verdun* (New York: Doubleday, 1917), 142. McConnell was killed in action shortly before the United States entered the war. In ABRR, Bullard did not discuss to any great extent his training by the French as a student pilot. Indeed, perhaps because of his bitterness over his abrupt severance from the air service, he wrote virtually nothing about the thrilling experience of flight—neither as a learner nor as a trained pilot capable of performing acrobatic aerial maneuvers.

61. James Norman Hall and Charles Bernard Nordhoff, *The Lafayette Flying Corps,* 2 vols. (Boston: Houghton-Mifflin, 1920), 2:317–19.

62. McConnell, *Flying for France,* 143–52.

63. Edwin C. Parsons, *I Flew with the Lafayette Escadrille* (New York: Arno Press, 1972), 67.

64. ABRR, "Twice Killed Rabbit." The French newspaper *La Presse* of July 12, 1919, noted that at Navarre's funeral a number of boxers and other sports personalities were present. For some reason, Carisella and Ryan (189–91) substitute the name of Charles Nungesser for Navarre as Bullard's leave-time buddy.

65. Christienne, *L'Aviation française,* 142.

66. Herbert Molloy Mason Jr., *High Flew the Falcons: The French Aces of World War I* (Philadelphia: Lippincott, 1965), 67.

67. Ibid., 68–69.

68. Flammer, *The Vivid Air*, 48–49; Christienne, *L'Aviation française*, 142.

69. Mason, *High Flew the Falcons*, 74–76.

70. ABRR, "Twice Killed Rabbit." Bullard ranked Chez le Pere Lebas as his favorite among the many drinking places he had known, from cities all across Europe and North Africa to the "honky-tonks" in Harlem.

71. Ibid.

72. Ibid.; ABRR, "Two Thousand Dollar Bet." This date and his breveting number is registered in a file on Bullard at the document center at Le Bourget Airport. The document center holds the records of the Aéro Club de France, the organization responsible early in this century for establishing guidelines and certifying the competence of pilots in both civilian and military service. See Christienne, *L'Aviation française*, 87–92, and *Jane's All the World's Aircraft* (New York: Anco, 1919), 216a.

73. ABRR, "Two Thousand Dollar Bet."

74. Basil Woon, *The Paris That's Not in the Guide Books* (New York: Brentano's, 1926), 40.

75. ABRR, "Two Thousand Dollar Bet."

76. Ibid. Bullard misremembers "Robertson" as "Robinson."

77. "Foreign [News]," *The Crisis* 15 (January 1918), 145.

78. Jakeman, *Divided Skies*, 323. Schuyler, a *Pittsburg Courier* journalist, made reference to Bullard in a letter to the editor rebutting Kenneth Brown Collings' gratuitous remark that "Negroes cannot fly—even the bureau of Air Commerce admits that." Collings' argument in his essay, "America Will Never Fly," in the July 1936 issue of the *American Mercury*, p. 292, was that, given the mental and physical skills required for flying, few Americans would want to fly. Those wanting to should be rigorously tested, he concluded. Schuyler's rebuttal carried too far, claiming that Bullard had "brought down a flock of German planes," but curiously erred in stating that "Bessie Coleman was the first American Negro to successfully fly a plane." Earlier, Bullard and several black civilian pilots before him had flown, as Jakemen shows in his book.

79. McConnell, *Flying for France*, 152–57.

80. Hall and Nordhoff, *Lafayette Flying Corps*, 2:21.

81. Ibid.

82. ABRR, "First Negro Pilot." At Avord, Bullard witnessed the nose dive crash of Lawrence "Red" Scanlon into the roof of the camp's bakery and the disbelief of the French captain when Eugene translated the unscathed, flour-covered trainee's first postcrash words: "It was me." A photograph of the plane embedded in the roof—which touched off a brief *crise du pain* in the camp—appears in the Hall

and Nordhoff work; Scanlon survived several more crashes before being released from the service (Hall and Nordhoff, *Lafayette Flying Corps,* 1:425–26). The photograph of Bullard and Sinclaire appears in Jamie Cockfield, "Eugene Bullard, America's first black military aviator; flew for France during World War I," *Military History* (February 1996), 10. Navarre's wearing of the silk stocking on his head is noted in Ezra Bowen, *Knights of the Air* (Alexandria, Va.: Time-Life Books, 1980), 80, and Edward Jablonski, *The Knighted Skies: A Pictorial History of World War I in the Air* (New York: Putnam, 1964), 92. Jablonski notes that Navarre's nonconformist dress and attractive "sensual mouth and heavy-lidded eyes made him a favorite in Paris," even as he shocked authorities during his convalescent leaves there.

83. ABRR, "First Negro Pilot." A photograph in Hall and Nordhoff, *Lafayette Flying Corps,* 1:151 records this moment.

84. ABRR, "First Negro Pilot," "In the Air," "It Couldn't Happen to Me."

85. ABRR, "It Couldn't Happen to Me," "Turned Down by My Country."

86. ABRR, "Turned Down by My Country," "It Couldn't Happen to Me."

87. ABRR, "It Couldn't Happen to Me," "Prejudice Again."

88. ABRR, "Prejudice Again."

89. Hall and Nordhoff, *Lafayette Flying Corps,* 1:69–71; "Dr. Gros Headed Neuilly Hospital," *New York Times,* October, 18, 1942, 53.

90. See Gros' introduction to James Norman Hall, *High Adventure: A Narrative of Air Fighting in France* (Boston: Houghton-Mifflin, 1918), ix; Hall and Nordhoff, *Lafayette Flying Corps,* 1:71. An indication of his conservative patriotism, Gros would drop his membership in the American Legion in protest of resolutions passed at its national convention in 1922—resolutions attacking the Harding Administration's failure to support a retirement pension for soldiers and for its inadequate medical programs and personnel dealing with veterans of the Great War. Marquis James, *A History of the American Foreign Legion* (New York: William Green, 1923), 239–76. "Dr. Gros Headed Neuilly Hospital," *New York Times.*

91. ABRR, "First Negro Pilot," "In the Air," "Prejudice Again."

92. ABRR, "Turned Down by My Country," "Princes and Heels"; Flammer, *The Vivid Air,* 172. It is clear from sources such as *Lafayette Flying Corps,* Hall and Nordhoff's two-volume study of all the Americans who flew for France, and *The Vivid Air,* Flammer's history of the fabled all-American squadron flying under French command, that many of these American pilots who knew Bullard genuinely liked him. In addition to Hall's remarks in his letter, he and Nordhoff write that "there was scarcely an American at Avord who did not know and like Bullard.

He was a brave, loyal, and thoroughly likeable fellow, and when a quarrel with one of his superiors caused his withdrawal from aviation, there was scarcely an American who did not regret the fact" (1:151).

It seems evident that some of these comrades would have told him about the discrimination practiced against him by a superior, as Bullard said they did in ABRR. On the issue of his being withheld from combat, the information in Hall and Nordhoff indicates that Bullard's close friend, John R. Russell, with whom he completed his flight training, was breveted six weeks later than Bullard yet was sent to the front two weeks earlier (1:97, 151). Another friend at Avord, Reginald Sinclaire, Bullard's *sous-chef,* was at the front a month sooner than Eugene from the date of being breveted (1:431).

93. ABRR, "Turned Down by My Country"; Flammer, *The Vivid Air,* 172–74; Memorandum from Commander-in-Chief to Chief of the French Mission on the subject of Americans in French Aviation Service, October 21, 1917, Air Force–Cockfield documents.

94. ABRR, "Turned Down by My Country," "Princes and Heels." While not discrediting all of Bullard's charges of prejudicial acts against him by Gros, Carisella and Ryan in *Black Swallow* (192–97) do not believe that Gros was responsible for his removal from the French air service; indeed, they find incredible that "white Americans in wartime Paris could still practice their age-old prejudices." Drawing from remembrances of "many former wartime acquaintances of Bullard's . . . including Reginald Sinclaire," they offer another explanation: in returning by foot to his base after a leave, Eugene tried to hitch a ride on a French troop truck carrying soldiers. Rebuffed and angered by racial taunts, he grabbed an individual off the vehicle, who turned out to be a French lieutenant, and struck him. The officer's report of Eugene's action led to his punishment, his "clipped wings," as Carisella and Ryan refer to this episode. If this other incident did occur—and Sinclaire does not refer to it in his "recollections" of Eugene forwarded to the authors at the time of writing and printed by them as a footnote—how could those other unnamed former wartime acquaintances who testify to it be certain that this was what led to the punitive action allegedly taken by the French Air Corps leadership? Unable to believe his beloved France would cashier him, Bullard, Carisella and Ryan imply, found it more comforting to conclude that "the enemy was the same old one who had haunted him at home and still followed in his footsteps overseas" (197).

In analyzing this dispute between the memoirist and Carisella and Ryan one must note the discrepancies between Bullard's account of his months in the air service and the documentation. Bullard says that his fellow pilots Edmund Genet and Victor Chapman had warned him about Gros' efforts to pressure the French to keep him out of combat, yet both men had died in action before he was breveted (Hall and Nordhoff, *Lafayette Flying Corps,* 2:320). Once at the front, Bullard believed he remained in air combat for France through December 1917 and into January 1918 and gives the date of his argument with the French officer as January 13, 1918 (ABRR, "Prejudice Again"); French documents give his termination date in the air and his transfer back to the 170th Infantry as November 16, 1917 (Jamie Cockfield, "The Black Icarus: Eugene Bullard in the Dawn of Military Aviation," *Over the Front* 9, no. 4 [winter 1994]: 17). Adding to the confusion and perhaps suggesting that both Bullard's memory and the documents may be in error is evidence in Hall and Nordhoff that gives extensive information on all those Americans who, like themselves, flew for France. Drawing on information gathered in 1919 from other American pilots as well as from French records, they report Eugene's last day at the front as November 11, 1917, but also say that he was not transferred to the 170th until January 11, 1918. That Bullard himself was not their source is indicated by their comment that from the date of his transfer "all trace of him has been lost" (1:151).

In spite of these errors, which Bullard could have avoided had he carefully consulted his copy of *The Lafayette Flying Corps,* and in spite of the fact that he admits that in his direct confrontations with Gros both during and after the war the doctor steadfastly and coolly denied any prejudicial actions toward him, there is substantial circumstantial evidence that Gros and doubtless other Americans were prejudiced toward the black airman and were responsible for Bullard's aborted service as a pilot. In his February 1918 introduction to Hall's *High Adventure* (xi–xii), Gros observes that he had personally "examined every candidate medically and morally" who had become a pilot in the Lafayette Escadrille and the Lafayette Flying Corps, and that he had been "associated with this group of American volunteers from the very beginning." Tommy Hitchcock remembers being examined personally by Gros in his office, as he believed every candidate was, and being pronounced "medically and morally fit" (quoted in Nelson W. Aldrich Jr., *Tommy Hitchcock: An American Hero* [Gaitherburg, Md.: Fleet Street, 1984], 64). If these statements are true, Bullard would have been the only American to have entered the Flying Corps through purely French military channels and as such, quite likely, was an annoying anomaly to Gros who, according to Bullard, did not even inform him of the pay the white Americans were receiving out of his office. At the time of the transfer physicals, Gros no doubt knew that Bullard would be grounded in the American air corps and delegated to subordinates the unpleasantness of formally carrying out a meaningless examination.

Additional support for Bullard's suspicion of Gros comes from Edwin C. "Ted" Parsons, one of the other American pilots flying for France whom Bullard cites as a friend and supporter both during the war and throughout his life (ABRR, "First Negro Pilot"). Scion of a wealthy old New England family and educated at Exeter Academy and the University of Pennsylvania, Parsons, like Bullard, had rebelled against his father, in Parson's case by refusing to enter the family's prosperous insurance business in Springfield, Massachusetts. Before the war, he had gone to the American west, where he had worked on a ranch, in a mine, and on Hollywood movie sets, and learned to fly airplanes. In 1913, he and a friend were hired by Pancho Villa to train some of his officers as aviators. Warned of Villa's impending attack on the United States, Parsons left Mexico and returned to the east, where he learned that there were Americans flying for France in the Great War. He worked his way across the Atlantic as an assistant veterinarian on a ship transporting horses. In France, he joined the American Ambulance Corps and, like others in that capacity, found his way into French aviation in April 1916, serving with the Lafayette Squadron (Flammer, *The Vivid Air,* 110–11).

Parsons was one of those American fliers, impatient with months of bureaucratic delays, who chose not to be transferred from French to American squadrons when such a transfer was finally effected (Flammer, *The Vivid Air,* 180–81). Perhaps Parsons' adventurous and maverick spirit fostered his appreciation and steadfast support for Bullard. Bullard himself wondered in his memoir whether Parsons' sympathetic encouragement as a flier did not stem from the fact that Parsons knew of Gros' prejudicial actions, although Bullard admits that Parsons never told him so directly. However, it was Parsons, he related, who informed him of the 1928 ceremony in the Paris suburb of Garches involving the unveiling of a monument commemorating the dead American aviators who had flown for France. Dr. Gros had invited everyone from the Lafayette Flying Corps except Bullard. Parsons somehow knew this and came by Eugene's nightclub to pick him up and take him to the ceremony. In his war memoir, Parsons qualifies his brief tribute to Gros by observing that during the war "we didn't always see eye to eye with him" and "frequently . . . thought that possibly he was engineering considerable publicity for his own benefit" (ABRR, "Princes and Heels"; Parsons, *I Flew with the Lafayette Escadrille,* 14).

In the 1950s, it was Parsons, then an admiral in the U.S. Navy, who encouraged Bullard to write his memoir and who also suggested its title, "All Blood Runs Red." (Parsons to Bullard, April 6, 1959; Parsons to Louise Fox Connell, February 8, 1960, Connell Papers. The assertion that Bullard had the French translation of "all blood runs red," *tout sang qui coule est rouge,* painted on his Spad is an invention of Carisella and Ryan.) By the time Eugene died in October 1961, Parsons had read the typewritten manuscript in its entirety. Significantly, although he was highly critical of it stylistically and for its obsession, in his view, with racial injustice, Parsons is silent on the question of Bullard's charges against Gros. His silence is telling since he had known Gros well both in the Ambulance Corps and as the individual who handled the passage of Americans into the French air service. If he had disagreed with Bullard's judgment on Gros, surely he would have used it as an example of the memoir's too-great concern for racial injustice as opposed to being the book Parsons wanted, namely, a rags to riches story stressing courage and adventure. (Parsons to Connell, February 8, March 10, 1960, Connell Papers.)

95. Richard M. Dalfiume, *The Desegregation of the U.S. Armed Forces* (Columbia: University of Missouri Press, 1969), 16–19; Jack D. Foner, *Blacks in the Military in American History* (New York: Praeger, 1974), 120–23; Morris J. MacGregor and Bernard C. Nalty, *In the United States Armed Forces: Segregation Entrenched, 1917–1940* (Wilmington, Del.: Scholarly Resources, 1977), 4:108.

96. Allen J. Greer, Lt. Colonel, Camp Funston, Kansas, Bulletin No. 35, March 28, 1918, reproduced in MacGregor and Nalty, *United States Armed Forces*, 277.

97. David Levering Lewis, *When Harlem Was in Vogue* (New York: Knopf, 1980), 13–14; Willie "The Lion" Smith with George Hoefer, *Music on My Mind* (New York: Da Capo, 1975), 75–76.

98. ABRR, "Love and a Life Purpose"; Elizabeth de Graumont, *Souvenir du monde, 1890–1940,* quoted in Louis Chevalier, *Montmartre du plasir et du crime* (Paris: Editions Robert Laffont, 1980), 312.

99. Carisella and Ryan, *Black Swallow,* 266.

100. James Norman Hall, who entered the French air service at approximately the same time as Bullard, observed that during training and even after being breveted "a pilot continued to wear the dress of his former service." There was no standard dress uniform. "As for the Americans, they follow individual tastes. . . . Some of them, with an eye to color, salute the sun in the red trousers and black tunic of the artilleryman" (Hall, *High Adventure,* 15–16). Hall and Nordhoff (*Lafayette Flying Corps,* 1:151) comment on Bullard's "breeches of vivid scarlet" and "black tunic." French musician Leo Vauchant remembers a French pilot in a Montmartre café wearing a pink uniform (Vauchant interviewed in Chris Goddard, *Jazz Away from Home* [New York: Paddington Press, 1979], 263).

101. The quotation from the *Columbus Ledger* is printed in *The Crisis* 15 (November 1917), 32.

102. ABRR, "Prejudice Again." The Fontaine du Berger was erected as a military camp in 1875 (A.-G. Maury, *Histoire des communes de Puy-de-Dôme* [Paris: Editions Horvath, 1987], 352–55).

103. ABRR, "Prejudice Again," "Zelli's Zig Zag Band"; Charles H. Williams, *Sidelights on Negro Soldiers: A Special Investigation of Conditions Among Negro Soldiers in the World War* (Norwood, Mass.: Ambrose Press, 1923), 73. Johnson beat Blink McCloskey on points on April 3, 1918, in Madrid; it was his only fight that year (*Jack Johnson, in the Ring and Out* [London: Proteus, 1977], Appendix 1).

104. ABRR, "Prejudice Again"; Hausser, *Les Evénements vus par la presse,* 737.

105. Carisella and Ryan, citing French military records now located at the Archives de l'Armée, Château Vincennes, give this date on page 199.

106. See page 70.

107. William E. B. Du Bois, "Documents of the War," *The Crisis* 18 (May 1919), 16.

108. Ibid. Du Bois printed first the document in the original French and then in its translation into English.

109. Du Bois printed, as one of his "Documents of the War," Greer's letter of December 6, 1918, to Tennessee senator Kenneth D. McKellar in which he makes these charges (*The Crisis* 18 [May 1919], 19).

110. Du Bois, *The Crisis* 17 (March 1919), 218–23.

111. Du Bois, *The Crisis* 18 (May 1919), 12–13.

112. Du Bois, *The Crisis* 17 (March 1919), 222–23.

113. Du Bois, *The Crisis* 17 (April 1919), 268.

114. Du Bois, *The Crisis* 18 (June 1919), 63. The stanza can be translated as "Onward patriots! / The day of glory has arrived! / Against us tyranny's / Bloody banner has been raised!"

115. "Le Boxeur Dixie Kid tué d'un coup de poing," *Le Matin,* May 29, 1919, 3; "Faits divers," *Le Temps,* May 29, 1919, 4; "Un peu fort," *La Presse,* May 29, 1919, 3.

116. The detail about the role of the newspaper vendor is in *Le Matin,* May 29, 1919, 3.

117. Ibid.

118. Daniel Cousin, "Sports divers," *La Presse,* May 30, 1919, 3.

119. Fred R. Moore to Emmett J. Scott, June 2, 1919, Air Force–Cockfield documents.

120. *New York Age,* June 14, 1919, 1; *Chicago Defender,* June 14, 1919, 11; *Washington Eagle,* June 14, 1919.

121. War Department cablegram from Thos. C. Cook to Military Attache, American Embassy, Paris, June 16, 1919, Air Force–Cockfield documents.

122. Telegram from Mott in Paris to Military Intelligence Branch, War Department, Washington D.C., June 18, 1919, Air Force–Cockfield documents.

123. Chevalier (*Montmartre du plasir*, 323) notes the frequency of assaults by drunken white American soldiers and sailors on blacks in Montmartre in the years 1919–21—acts of violence that always provoked disgust and indignation on the part of the local population, who took the side of the blacks.

Chapter 5. Man of Montmartre, 1919–1940

1. Jean Gravigny, *Montmartre en 1925* (Paris: Editions Montaigne, 1924), 12–13.

2. Andre Warnod, *Le vieux Montmartre* (Paris, 1913); Pierre Macorlan, *Montmartre souvenirs* (Paris, 1946); Francis Carco, "Promenade a Montmartre," *La Revue de Paris* (February 1922), 854–63; Jerrold Seigel, *Bohemian Paris: Culture, Politics, and the Boundaries of Bourgeois Life, 1830–1930,* (New York: Viking, 1986), 338–40.

3. Albert Flamond, "Sur un toit," *La Revue de Paris* (July-August 1924), 702–5.

4. This address is given as Bullard's in a January 6, 1923, page-one story about Bullard in the *Chicago Defender*.

5. ABRR, "Zelli's Zig Zag Band"; Goddard, *Jazz Away From Home,* 24.

6. Alain Hardel, *Strass: En remontant les bas résille du music hall* (Paris: Jean-Claude Simoën, 1977), 64; Stearns, *Jazz Dance,* 97–98.

7. Frank Driggs and Harris Lewine, *Black Beauty, White Heat: A Pictorial History of Classic Jazz, 1920–1950* (New York: William Morrow, 1982), 206; Jacques Damase, *Les Folies du music hall à Paris* (Paris: Editions Spectacles, 1960), 8–9.

8. A reproduction of this *Post-Dispatch* article, "Ragtime by the U.S. Army Band Gets Everyone 'Over There,'" appears in Robert Kimball and William Bolcom, *Reminiscing with Sissle and Black* (New York: Viking, 1973), 67–68.

9. John Chilton, *Sidney Bechet: The Wizard of Jazz* (New York: Macmillan, 1987), 81. For singer Ada Louise "Bricktop" Smith, "tips were it—the butter on the bread, the rent on the room, the new dress" (Bricktop with James Haskins, *Bricktop* [New York: Atheneum, 1983], 94).

10. ABRR, "Zelli's Zig-Zag Band."

11. Roi Ottley, *No Green Pastures* (London: John Murray, 1952), 87–88; Michel Fabre, *From Harlem to Paris: Black American Writers in France, 1840–*

1980 (Urbana: University of Illinois Press, 1991). In his *Paris Noir: African-Americans in the City of Light* (New York: Houghton Mifflin, 1996, 36), Tyler Stoval analyzes the appeal of Paris for African Americans from World War I to the present day. Of the first generation, he finds in Bullard a "fascinating" and significant figure.

12. Jean Prasteau, *La merveilleuse aventure du Casino de Paris* (Paris: Denoël, 1975), 88.

13. Among the African Americans who lived in France for extended periods in the 1920s, only Claude McKay, so far as I am aware, perceived that by rewarding and encouraging assimilation in metropolitan France, French leaders facilitated their colonial rule by "Frenchifying" the brightest and the best among the native peoples in their empire (McKay, *A Long Way from Home* [New York: Arno Press, 1969], 277–81). Enthralled by the experience of living in a land without a color line, even Du Bois, during his visit to France in 1918–19, could actually celebrate French imperialism (David Levering Lewis, *W. E. B. Du Bois: Biography of a Race, 1868–1919* [New York: Henry Holt, 1993], 565–69). However, by the time of the second Pan African Congress in 1921, Du Bois had become openly critical of French imperialism (Manning Marable, *W. E. B. Du Bois: Black Democrat* [Boston: Twayne, 1986], 104–5).

14. Williams, *Sidelights on Negro Soldiers,* 204; Foner, *Blacks in the Military,* 124.

15. ABRR, "Zelli's Zig-Zag Band." In the cursory and understated manner that typifies the highly condensed postwar section of his memoir, Bullard simply stated "I knew Maître Robert Henri, one of France's most influential lawyers at that time." The *Grand Larousse universel* (1989), 8:5227, explains that the lawyer was called [*dit*] Robert Henri, as Bullard does in his memoir. However, in print, the same source makes clear, his name appears as Henri-Robert.

16. "Henri-Robert," *Larousse du XX siècle* (Paris: Librairie Larousse, 1928), 1001; "Henri-Robert," *Dictionnaire de biographie française* (Paris: Librairie Letouzey et Ane, 1989), 26:954; "L'Affaire Cattaui-Humbert," *L'Illustration: Journal universel,* February 21, 1903, 102; "M. Henri-Robert," *Le Figaro,* June 1913, in Fernand Payen, ed., *Anthologie des avocats français contemporains* (Paris: Bernard Grasset, 1913), 17–21; Elizabeth Hausser, *Paris au jour le jour,* March 26, 1906, 225; January 8, 1908, 117; February 4, 1908, 290; "Henri-Robert," *Dictionnaire national des contemporains* (Paris: Editions La Jeunesse, 1936); Hausser, November 25, 1915, 580; May 22, 1916, 598; October 26, 1916, 610; March 7, 1917, 627; "Les américains chez nous, ouvrons aux Sammies les foyers français," *Le Matin,* December 27, 1917, 1.

17. "Henri-Robert," *Dictionnaire de biographie française,* 26:954.

18. ABRR, "Zelli's Zig-Zag Band"; Gravigny, *Montmartre,* 153.

19. ABRR, "Zelli's Zig-Zag Band."

20. Ibid.; Al Laney, *Paris Herald: Incredible Newspaper* (New York: Appleton-Century-Crofts, 1947), 193–95.

21. ABRR, "Zelli's Zig-Zag Band"; Gravigny, *Montmartre,* 155.

22. Gravigny, *Montmartre,* 155; Laney, *Paris Herald,* 195.

23. ABRR, "Love and a Life Purpose"; Langston Hughes, *The Big Sea: An Autobiography* (1940; reprint, New York: Hill and Wang, 1963), 152–53.

24. Laney, *Paris Herald,* 195; Basil Woon, *Paris,* 244–45.

25. ABRR, "Zelli's Zig-Zag Band."

26. Carisella and Ryan, *Black Swallow,* 204, 222.

27. Ibid.; Bricktop, *Bricktop,* 118.

28. Carisella and Ryan, *Black Swallow,* 204, 220–22.

29. ABRR, "Zelli's Zig-Zag Band."

30. Ibid.

31. P. J. Carisella interviewed Cooper in May 1970. Cooper remembered "Dixie," "Gene's old pal from London days," as Dixie Walker (Carisella and Ryan, *Black Swallow,* 222). Surely, Cooper meant Aaron Lester Brown, the "Dixie Kid," not the Brooklyn Dodger outfielder of the late 1940s, the most adamant Dodger in opposing Jackie Robinson's joining the ballclub in 1947.

32. ABRR, "Zelli's Zig Zag Band."

33. *Chicago Tribune European Edition,* January 2, 1923, 1.

34. Don C. Seitz, *The James Gordon Bennetts* (Indianapolis: Bobbs-Merrill, 1928), 374.

35. Richard O'Connor, *The Scandalous Mr. Bennett* (New York: Doubleday, 1965), 314–19; *Chicago Tribune European Edition,* January 2, 1923, 1.

36. *Chicago Tribune European Edition,* January 2, 1923, 1.

37. "Voice of Americans in Europe," *Chicago Tribune European Edition,* January 5, 1923, 4.

38. "French Hero, Georgia Born, Whips White Bully in Paris," *Chicago Defender* (national edition), January 6, 1923, 1.

39. Doris Rich, *Queen Bess: Daredevil Aviator* (Washington, D.C.: Smithsonian, 1993), 32–37.

40. "A Letter from Mr. Bullard," *Chicago Tribune and New York Daily News European Edition,* May 24, 1923, 1. A record of the Tribunal Correctionnel de la Seine, "Bullard contre Dabbadie Maurice procès en diffamation" dated July 3, 1923, suggests that Bullard filed for a monetary award in addition to the right of rebuttal. The tribunal ruled, however, that there was not enough evidence to pur-

sue the case. This record was found by the author at the Archives de Paris, July 21, 1992.

41. Albert Curtis, "Bullard, French Ace, Wins 'Truth Fight,'" "Court Ends 'Dirty Ways' of Tribune," *Chicago Defender,* June 16, 1923, 1, 3.

42. "A Letter from Mr. Bullard," *Chicago Tribune and New York Daily News European Edition.* Fernando Jones recalls his connection with Belle Davis in an interview with Charles Lejay in the journal *Paris Music Hall* (May 15, 1926).

43. Rich, *Queen Bess,* 44, 127.

44. Gravigny, *Montmartre,* 109.

45. This story described in a French newspaper is printed in translation in "Colored Frenchmen and American 'Métèques,'" *Literary Digest* 78, no. 9, September 1, 1923, 41.

46. "Informations diverses, les etrangers en France," *Le Temps,* August 2, 1923, 3; Gratien Candace, "Préjugé de couleur: Il est temps que cela cesse," *L'Homme libre,* August 11, 1923, 1. In this piece, Gratien notes that he had called on the Quai D'Orsay for its statement in the press.

47. Candace, "Préjugé de Couleur." See also the front-page story in *La Presse,* "Français de couleur molestés, l'attitude de certains étrangers est intolérable," August 7, 1923.

48. Georges de la Fouchardiere writing in *L'Ocurre,* quoted in "Colored Frenchmen and American 'Métèques,'" 44.

49. Candace, "Préjugé de Couleur," 1.

50. "Colored Frenchmen and American 'Métèques,'" 44.

51. Quoted in Andre Kaspi and Antoine Mares, *Le Paris des étrangers depuis un siècle,* 162. Perhaps influenced by Garvey, however, Touvalou would soon begin espousing the anticolonial cause of black Africa, lose favor with the French government, and become disenchanted with France (Ottley, *No Green Pastures,* 107–8).

52. ABRR, "Zelli's Zig-Zag Band."

53. Ibid.

54. Ibid.; Sheridan Morley, *A Talent to Amuse: A Biography of Noel Coward* (New York: Doubleday, 1969), 94, 168.

55. ABRR, "Zelli's Zig-Zag Band"; Madame Wellington Koo with Isabella Taves, *No Feast Lasts Forever* (New York: Quadrangle, 1975), chap. 14.

56. ABRR, "Zelli's Zig-Zag Band." In her autobiography, Gloria Swanson identifies Gartz as a close friend and describes the man, his life in Paris, and his political views in some detail. Gloria Swanson, *Swanson on Swanson* (New York: Random House, 1980), 103–6, 145, 178–79, 221–43.

57. ABRR, "Love and a Life Purpose." The names of Marcelle and her parents appear exactly as Bullard gives them here (except for the aristocratic "de" in the mother's and father's name) on the death record of Marcelle registered at the Mairie of the 20th Arrondissement in Paris.

58. ABRR, "Love and a Life Purpose." Marcelle's birthdate of July 8, 1901, is registered at the Mairie of the 2nd Arrondissement. A copy of the *extrait des minutes des actes de naissance* was obtained by the author in July 1992. The author has found no information about the social backgrounds of the Straumanns. In contemporary France, Straumanns, according to a telephone book database examined in 1992, live almost exclusively in lower Alsace-Lorraine—an area with a heavy Jewish and Protestant population. Professor Michel Fabre, a Professor of African American studies at the University of Paris, has speculated that M. Straumann may have been Jewish, his wife Catholic—a circumstance that would explain why the couple would have no difficulty accepting the mixed marriage of their daughter and why there was no reporting of the wedding and gala reception in the society pages of the Parisian newspapers.

59. ABRR, "Love and a Life Purpose."

60. This address is given in "Bullard Former U.S.A. Subject, Weds Paris Girl," *Chicago Defender* (national edition), September 1, 1923, 1.

61. ABRR, "Love and a Life Purpose."

62. Ibid.

63. ABRR, "Big Gamble—Night Club Owner"; Ralph Trevill, *Days and Nights in Montmartre and the Latin Quarter* (London: Herbert Jenkins, 1927), 60.

64. Hughes, *The Big Sea,* 144–57.

65. Foner, *Blacks in the Military,* 121.

66. ABRR, "Big Gamble."

67. Ibid.; Hughes, *The Big Sea,* 148; Bricktop, *Bricktop,* 117–18. When Bullard wrote the post–World War I section of his memoir, his health was deteriorating and, one senses, he simply wrote down his memories as they occurred to him, making little effort to structure them in chronological or any other order.

68. Bricktop, *Bricktop,* 86, 117–18.

69. Ibid., 119.

70. ABRR, "In the French Underground."

71. Ibid.; *Jet* 21 (November 2, 1961): 7.

72. Florence E. Gilliam, *France: A Tribute by an American Woman* (New York: Dutton, 1945), 145–46; Ernest Hemingway, *The Sun Also Rises* (1926; reprint, New York: Scribners, 1970), 62–64. For an interpretation of Hemingway's interest in Bullard see Frederick J. Svoboda, "Who Was That Black Man?: A Note on

Eugene Bullard and *The Sun Also Rises,*" *The Hemingway Review* 17, no. 2 (spring 1998), 105–10.

73. Bricktop, *Bricktop,* 89–90, 108, 130; George Eells, *The Life that He Led: A Biography of Cole Porter* (New York: Putnam, 1967), 82–84.

74. ABRR, "Big Gamble."

75. Ibid.; Stearns, *Jazz Dance,* 97–98; "Dooley and Dodo," *Time* 41 (May 10, 1943): 68–70; Jack Salzman et al., "Wilson, Arthur Eric Dooley," *Encyclopedia of African-American Culture and History,* 5 vols. (New York: Simon & Schuster, 1995), 5:2857–58.

76. ABRR, "Big Gamble."

77. Hughes, *The Big Sea,* 159.

78. Ibid., 159–60; Ernest B. Speck, "Henry Crowder: Nancy Cunard's 'Tree,'" *Lost Generation Journal* 6, no. 1 (summer 1979): 6–8; Anita Loos, *Gentlemen Prefer Blondes* (1925; reprint, New York: Liveright, 1963), 93–128. Loos recalls her visits to Paris in 1921 and 1925 in her autobiography, *A Girl Like I* (New York: Viking, 1966), 225–38, and in her book about silent film stars Constance and Norma Talmadge, *The Talmadge Girls: A Memoir* (New York: Viking, 1978).

79. ABRR, "Big Gamble." Tucker spent the Christmas season of 1922 in Paris with the Dolly Sisters and recalls the "fizz water at Zelli's making [her] very happy." She perfomed in Paris in 1928 (Sophie Tucker, *Some of these Days* [New York: Doubleday, 1945], 251–55). Robinson was in Paris in the spring and summer of 1924 (Edward G. Robinson with Leonard Spigelgass, *All My Yesterdays: An Autobiography* [New York: Hawthorn, 1973], 77). In making her French films, Swanson was in and out of Paris frequently in 1924–25 (Swanson, *Swanson on Swanson,* 221–43).

80. ABRR, "Big Gamble"; David A. Yallop, *The Day the Laughter Stopped: The True Story of Fatty Arbuckle* (New York: St. Martin's Press, 1976), 289. Yallop agrees with the 1922 jury verdict that found Arbuckle innocent in the controversial case; Damase, *Les Folies de music hall à Paris,* 25–26.

81. ABRR, "Big Gamble."

82. *Histoire d'un roi: Les Mémoires de son Altesse Royale Le Duc de Windsor* (Paris: Amiot-Dumont, 1951), 240–45; Keith Robbins, ed., *The Blackwell Biography of British Political Life in the Twentieth Century* (London: Alden Press, 1990), 138–39.

83. In her notebooks of daily events Bricktop recorded her first meeting with the Prince as October 29, 1926; the next day she gave him a lesson in the Black Bottom (Box 4, Folder 1, Ada "Bricktop" Smith Papers, ScM 85–65, Archives, Schomburg Center for Research in Black Culture). While entertaining at a private

party in London in 1933, Duke Ellington recalls the Prince playing drums with his band (Edward Kennedy Ellington, *Music is My Mistress* (New York: Doubleday, 1973), 84–85; *Histoire d'un roi*, 244; Bricktop, *Bricktop*, 116–17; Goddard, *Jazz Away from Home*, 36, 194, 206–12, 218–19.

84. ABRR, "Big Gamble."

85. Bricktop, *Bricktop*, 81–82. Blues singer Alberta Hunter, who had known Bricktop years earlier in Chicago and who also became a popular entertainer in Paris after her arrival in 1927, alleged that Bullard's call for a performer was meant for her. Bricktop, she claimed, stole the notice off a public bulletin board in their Harlem rooming house. Since Bricktop says Richardson had to reach her in Washington, D.C., where she was staying briefly with her mother, and Bullard makes no mention of the issue in ABRR, one doubts the accuracy of the allegation. Frank C. Taylor with Gerald Cook, *Alberta Hunter: A Celebration in Blues* (New York: McGraw-Hill, 1987), 70.

86. Bricktop, *Bricktop*, 87.

87. Ibid., 88–89; Hughes, *The Big Sea*, 161–63.

88. Gravigny, *Montmartre*, 172.

89. Bricktop, *Bricktop*, 90–93.

90. F. Scott Fitzgerald, *Babylon Revisited and Other Stories* (1931; reprint, New York: Scribners, 1960), 210–30. In this story the protagonist recalls dissipations in Zelli's and Bricktop's. In a draft of an unpublished fiction entitled "World's Fair," Fitzgerald makes reference to a drunken evening at the Grand Duc where "near us," among many others, "discernible through the yellow smoke of dawn," was Josephine Baker. Cited in Arthur Mizener, *The Far Side of Paradise: A Biography of F. Scott Fitzgerald* (Boston: Houghton-Mifflin, 1949), 181, 183.

91. Bricktop, *Bricktop*, 95–98.

92. Ibid., 95, 98–99.

93. Kisling's 1924 oil painting *Kikki de Montparnasse* is reproduced in Troyat, *Kisling*, 284.

94. Bricktop, *Bricktop*, 100–107. In her notebooks, Bricktop records her first party at the Porters' as May 3, 1926; she gave Charleston lessons to Porter at a soirée hosted by Elsa Maxwell at the Ritz Hotel on May 10, 1927 (Box 4, Folder 1, Ada "Bricktop" Smith Papers).

95. ABRR, "Big Gamble."

96. Charles Schwartz, *Cole Porter: A Biography* (New York: Dial Press, 1977), 44–48, 62–65.

97. Bricktop, *Bricktop*, 118–19. According to some, Bricktop could use foul language too. Hunter, who didn't like her—perhaps out of professional rivalry—recalls her yelling raucously from the street up to the apartments of acquaintances,

"Hey bitches, whatcha doing?" If there were no answer, a "kiss my ass" would follow. Taylor, *Alberta Hunter,* 130.

98. Bricktop, *Bricktop,* 11–52, 130.

99. Hughes, *The Big Sea,* 157, 171–76, 181–83.

100. Bricktop, *Bricktop,* 84.

101. Fabre, *From Harlem to Paris,* 120–22.

102. Gwendolyn Bennett, "Wedding Day, A Story," *Fire!! A Quarterly Devoted to Younger Negro Artists* 1, no. 1 (1926): 25–28.

103. See the 1927 photograph of Bullard at the drums with the band inside Zelli's reproduced in Driggs and Lewine, *Black Beauty, White Heat,* 210, as well as with the band outside of Zelli's in Carisella and Ryan, *Black Swallow,* 205. A photograph of a "gentler" Bullard taken in 1928 is in his file at the document center of Le Bourget Airport in Paris; the author has a copy in his possession.

104. ABRR, "Love and a Life Purpose."

105. Bricktop, *Bricktop,* 88.

106. Ibid., 145.

107. Ibid., 127; Taylor, *Alberta Hunter,* 90–91; Goddard, *Jazz Away From Home,* 19; "French Actor Objected to Zeal of American Negro Boxer as Villain," *New York Times,* January 9, 1928, 2.

108. Andre Demaison, "Jazz William's," *Jazz: L'Actualité intellectuelle,* March 15, 1929, 175.

109. Phyllis Rose, *Jazz Cleopatra: Josephine Baker in Her Time* (New York: Doubleday, 1989), 8–9, 18–19.

110. Ibid., 120–27.

111. Ibid., 100–101; William Wiser, *The Crazy Years: Paris in the Twenties* (New York: Atheneum, 1983), 157–58.

112. Jack Rennert, *100 Posters of Paul Colin* (New York: Images Graphiques, 1977), especially the introduction.

113. B. J. Kospeth's article of January 20, 1929, notes the wide use of this term, several years earlier, by Parisians conveying their "unbounded enthusiasm" for "Negro dancers, singers, and jazz bands" (Hugh Ford, ed., *The Left Bank Revisited: Selections from the Paris Tribune, 1917–1934* [University Park: Pennsylvania State University Press, 1972], 201). For the historians, see François Bédarida's treatment of the years 1914–31 in *Histoire du peuple français: Cent ans d'esprit républicain* (Paris: Nouvelle Librarie de France, 1989), 288–89; Marcel Renhard, *Histoire de France,* 2 vols. (Paris: Librairie Larousse, 1954), 2:430; and Robert Aron, *Les grandes heures de la Troisième République* (Paris: Librarie Perrin, 1968), 152–54.

114. Bricktop, *Bricktop,* 108–10.

115. The *Bottin* (city directory) for Paris in 1931 gives 39, rue Fontaine as the address for "Chez Josephine Baker, cabaret dansing."

116. Bricktop, *Bricktop,* 110.

117. Jacqueline O'Garro, Eugene Bullard's oldest daughter, remembered Baker as her occasional baby sitter in a conversation with the author, November 17, 1988.

118. Chilton, *Sidney Bechet,* 75–81.

119. Sidney Bechet, *Treat It Gentle* (London: Twayne, 1960), 149.

120. Driggs and Lewine, *Black Beauty, White Heat,* 210. In the 1927 photograph inside Zelli's on this page, Compton can be made out at the piano, chomping on a big cigar.

121. Chilton, *Sidney Bechet,* 83–84; Bechet, *Treat It Gentle,* 150–52.

122. Speck, "Henry Crowder," 6–8.

123. ABRR, "Princes and Heels." Although Eugene listed Bechet as a friend in ABRR, he did not comment on this episode, an omission consistent with his inclination not to burden his brief narrative of his Paris years with unpleasantries.

124. Bechet, *Treat It Gentle,* 153.

125. Ibid., 153–54.

126. Ibid., 156.

127. Ibid., 154.

128. An AEF veteran, Burr interspersed work on Wall Street in the 1920s with "a number of European trips and the general life of *bon vivant*" ("Courtney Burr, Producer, Dead," *New York Times,* October 18, 1961, 45; ABRR, "Princes and Heels").

129. ABRR, "Princes and Heels."

130. Ibid.

131. Ibid. The *Paris Post*'s building at this address was constructed in 1935 ("U.S. War Museum for Paris," *New York Times,* July 25, 1935, 2; "France Decorates Peck," *New York Times,* February 28, 1933, 5). A Californian, Peck is pictured in the *American Legion Monthly* representing the *Paris Post* in a parade at the Legion's national convention in Miami in 1934 (*American Legion Monthly* 18, no. 2 [February 1935], 57). Hailing from Indianapolis, Sparks married a Frenchwoman and practiced dentistry in Paris in the interwar years ("Hitler to Receive Visiting Veterans," *New York Times,* February 16, 1937, 17). James L. McCann, a native of Tuscaloosa, Alabama, is listed as a national executive committeeman representing France, 1936–52, in Raymond Moley Jr., *The American Legion Story* (New York: Meredith, 1966), 413.

132. The *American Legion Weekly Magazine* (it became a monthly in 1927)

began appearing in 1919 with the creation of the "Legion in Paris" organizational meetings of that year. In 1919, the issues are sprinkled with cartoons belittling African American soldiers of the AEF. Typical is the caricature in the August 22, 1919, issue of a coal-black American replete with protuberant lips and large white eyes, responding to a suspicious British officer, "Dis am de American Army, Suh!" A Negro subscriber denounced such "insulting and opprobrious" references to blacks in the November 7, 1919, issue but the caricatures continued well into the 1920s. This is one example of how the characters of theatrical blackface comedy reinforced negative stereotypes of African Americans in the United States. On the other hand, as James Weldon Johnson has pointed out (quoted in Sampson, *Blacks in Blackface*, 4), minstrel companies provided not only employment but "an essential training and theatrical experience, which, at the time, could not have been acquired from any other source." Men like Bullard's friend Opal Cooper used minstrelsy as the springboard to a "legitimate" theatrical career. See Harry T. Sampson, *Blacks in Blackface: A Source Book on Early Black Musical Shows* (Metuchen, N.J.: Scarecrow Press, 1980), 4, 188–92.

The Legion's constitution and eligibility section are printed in the *American Legion Weekly*, December 5, 1919, 1.

133. Bricktop, *Bricktop*, 190, 194–96. Andre Patry in *Les années folles à Paris* (Montreal: Humanitas-nouvelle optique, 1990), 25, estimates that as many as 400,000 North and South Americans had been lost to the Parisian entertainment industry in the year 1931 alone.

134. Bricktop, *Bricktop*, 194, 198–206.

135. See the advertising poster for the gym reproduced in Carisella and Ryan, *Black Swallow*, 206, which contains this information. Louis Chevalier discusses the vogue of health clubs in interwar Montmartre in *Montmartre du plaisir et du crime*, 361–65.

136. The advertising poster notes that the two fighters prepared at Bullard's gym. The date of the fight is given in Bob Burrell, *Who's Who in Boxing* (New Rochelle, N.Y.: Arlington House, 1974), 31. See also Eduardo Arroyo, *"Panama" Al Brown, 1902–1951* (Paris: J. C. Lattes, 1982), 163–64. Janet Flanner's appreciation of Brown as a singer and dancer in Paris in the '30s is in Flanner, *Paris Was Yesterday, 1925–1939* (New York: Viking, 1972), 182–83. Interestingly, Bullard's American Legion pal in Paris, James Sparks, was beaten by a mob in Marseilles when he declared with one other judge that Brown had defeated a local favorite in a fifteen-round bout ("French Fight Fans Attack U.S. Judge," *New York Times*, July 11, 1932, 16).

137. ABRR, "In the French Underground."

138. ABRR, "Zelli's Zig-Zag Band." Fats Waller's 1932 stay in Paris is detailed in Charles Fox, *Fats Waller* (New York: Barnes, 1960), 39–43. William Tung, in *V. K. Wellington Koo and China's Wartime Diplomacy* (New York: St. John's University Press, 1977), 6–7, discusses Koo's pre–World War II diplomatic career; Huges Panassié, *Louis Armstrong* (New York: Scribners, 1971), 18, notes that Armstrong was in Paris in 1932.

139. Robert Goffin, *The Story of Louis Armstrong* (New York: Allen, Towne, and Heath, 1947), 298–303.

140. ABRR, "Big Gamble"; Vincente R. Pilapil, *Alfonso XIII* (New York: Twayne, 1969), 198–99; Sir Charles Petrie, *King Alfonso XIII and His Age* (London: Chapman and Hall, 1963), 230–33. In his memoir, Bullard recalls seeing the Prince of Wales playing tennis with Charlie Chaplin during this sojourn in Biarritz. Chaplin's autobiography confirms that this was in 1931 although the Prince was in the company of Lady Furness, not, as Bullard remembers, Wallis Simpson, whom the Prince did not meet until several years later (Charles Chaplin, *My Autobiography* [New York: Simon and Schuster, 1964], 362–64).

141. ABRR, "Big Gamble."

142. Ibid.; Stearns, *Jazz Dance,* 369; Prasteau, *La Merveilleuse Aventure,* 184–211.

143. Stearns, *Jazz Dance,* 71.

144. ABRR, "In the French Underground."

145. The Passage Elysées des Beaux Arts address is indicated on Bullard's application for a new issue of his flying certificate (Bullard File, Document Center, Le Bourget Airport; *Extrait des minutes des actes de mariages,* Mairie of 10th Arrondissement). A copy of the extract indicating the divorce of Eugene Bullard and Marcelle Eugénie Henriette Straumann on this date was obtained at the Mairie of the 10th Arrondissement on December 11, 1991. A copy of the record of death of Marcelle E. H. Straumann on the 18th of February, 1990, was obtained at the Mairie of the 20th Arrondissement on July 20, 1992. Copies of both documents are held by the author. A neighbor of Marcelle Straumann in the last years of Marcelle's life said that Marcelle thought her former husband and daughters had died during World War II.

146. "Demande d'Admission," Federation of French Veterans of the Great War, July 24, 1940. On his application for readmission to the Federation of June 15, 1955, however, he gave his marital status as widower. "Widowed" is the term appearing on his death certificate. Copies of these documents were sent to the author by Roger Cestac, president of the Federation, on November 14, 1988.

147. ABRR, "In the French Underground."

148. Ibid.; "Walter Neusel, 56, German Boxer Dies," *New York Times,* October 10, 1964, 29.

149. Philip John Stead, *Second Bureau* (London: Evans Brothers, n.d.), 9–26. An organizational chart of the French intelligence services as of August 1939 indicates that police "commissaires" were gathering counterintelligence information for the French Ministry of the Interior. The chart is published in Roger Faligot and Rene Kauffer, *Histoire mondiale du renseignement, tome 1: 1870–1939* (Paris: Robert Laffout, 1993), 403–4. This source (462–64) demonstrates that French intelligence had warned its government of the impending German attack on May 1, 1940.

150. ABRR, "In the French Underground."

151. Chevalier, *Montmartre du plaisir,* 432–39, discusses the Corsican criminal groups in Montmartre in the late '30s. See also Bricktop, *Bricktop,* 167–70.

152. ABRR, "In the French Underground."

153. Ibid.

154. Ibid.

155. Albert Blanchard et al., *Des Années-mémoire 1939* (Paris: Bayard Presse, 1991), 44–45.

156. *Histoire de France illustrée, 1936–1945* (Paris: Larousse, 1985), 58.

157. Bricktop, *Bricktop,* 202–6.

158. Ibid. On the other hand, frustrated over being told she was "too refined" to work in the United States, Alberta Hunter wrote the State Department on May 1, 1940, begging for a renewal of her passport. The Department wisely rejected her request (Taylor, *Alberta Hunter,* 150–51).

159. Blanchard, *Des Années-mémoire 1939,* contains a photograph of Baker performing at the Casino de Paris in December 1939. Jacques Marseille and Daniel LeFeuvre reproduce a photograph from *Le Petit Parisien* of March 12, 1940, showing Baker entertaining British soldiers in Paris (*1940, Au jour le jour* [Paris: Albin Michel, 1989], 46).

160. ABRR, "Invasion."

161. Ibid.

162. Ibid.; quoted in Christien Regeau, *La Drôle de guerre: Images de la France et des français, september, 1939, à mai, 1940* (Paris: Herme, 1990), 70.

163. ABRR, "Invasion." Regeau observes that at Christmas 1939, les Halles were open only during the day and sales ended between 2:30 and 3:30 P.M.

164. ABRR, "Invasion."

165. Bricktop, *Bricktop,* 203. Arrested on October 17, 1940, Briggs was sent to a camp in the Parisian suburb of Saint-Denis, where he spent four years orga-

nizing musical entertainments enjoyed by both the inmates and the German commandant (Rudolph Dunbar, "Trumpet Player Briggs Freed After Four Years in
Nazi Camp near Paris," *Chicago Defender,* September 23, 1944).

166. ABRR, "Invasion"; "Mrs. June J. James is Saved as Air Yacht Dives into
Sea," *New York Times,* January 26, 1933, 9.

167. "Hitler for Peace, He Tells Veterans," *New York Times,* February 18,
1937, 13. Sparks's role in rebuilding the Ambulance Corps is mentioned in "Ambulance Plans Pushed," *New York Times,* September 20, 1939, 19; Thomas A.
Rumer, *The American Legion: An Official History, 1919–1989* (New York:
Evans, 1990), 231–32.

168. ABRR, "Invasion." The French government awarded the Croix de Guerre
to Sparks, Gros, and other Americans involved in ambulance duty during the
Battle of France. The Vichy government later recognized these awards. See "12
Americans Decorated," *New York Times,* August 22, 1940, 4; "Vichy Awards
Croix de Guerre," *New York Times,* October 11, 1941, 8. Edmund Gros returned to the States in the fall of 1940. He died at West Chester, Pennsylvania
two years later ("Dr. Gros, Headed Neuilly Hospital," *New York Times,* October 18, 1942, 53).

169. The Battle of France from the opening of the German campaign on
May 10 to the ceasefire agreement of June 22, 1940, is described on a day-by-day
basis in Jacques Benoist-Mechin, *Sixty Days that Shook the West: The Fall of
France, 1940* (New York: Putnam, 1963).

170. *World War II: The War Chronicles,* video, part 1 of 7, The History Channel, 1995.

171. ABRR, "Millions Flee from Death."

172. Ibid.

173. Ibid.; ABRR, "Orleans—The Last Stand." Orleans and smaller towns in
its vicinity such as Gien were devastated by German aerial bombing from June 14
through June 16. German ground forces captured the area on the 16th and 17th
(Jacques Bonnet et al., *Histoire d'Orléans de son terroir, tome III, de 1870 à nos
jours* [Roanne: Horvath, 1982], 198–202). Bonnet's work and Yves Durand, *Le
Loiret dans La Guerre, 1939–1945* (Roanne: Horvath, 1983), 14–23, contain
many photographs that graphically document the ferocity of the German assault
on the lingering French resistance along the Loire.

174. ABRR, "Orleans—The Last Stand."

175. Ibid.

176. Ibid.; "U.S. Ambulance Unit Reaches Bordeaux," *New York Times,*
June 23, 1940, 21.

177. "Americans Report Nazis Fill Spain," *New York Times,* July 19, 1940, 10; ABRR, "Orleans—The Last Stand." Bullard does not mention or was unaware that Baldwin was the founder and director of the American Civil Liberties Union.

178. ABRR, "Orleans—The Last Stand"; "Consul Waterman Active," *New York Times,* May 23, 1941, 9.

179. German soldiers are pictured relaxing on "la Grande-Plage de Biarritz" in the summer of 1940 in Francis Sallaberry, *Quand Hitler bétonnait la Côte Basque* (Bayonne: Harriet, 1988), 24.

180. ABRR, "International Bridge—One More River to Cross"; "Liner Bringing 798 Here," *New York Times,* July 18, 1940, 12.

Chapter 6. New York, 1940–1961

1. "Celebrities Forced to Flee France Arrive Here by Way of Lisbon," *New York Times,* July 16, 1940; "Liner Bringing 798 Here," *New York Times,* July 18, 1940, 12; "Americans Report Nazis Fill Spain," *New York Times,* July 19, 1940, 10.

2. ABRR, "America the Beautiful with Fear and Love." Spector's teaching of Americanism is cited in M. B. Deschler's letter to editor, *New York Times,* May 4, 1936, 18.

3. A photograph of Peck appears with story "Ambulance Men Sail for Europe," *New York Times,* May 19, 1940, 28. Peck's experience in the Battle of France is in "Americans Report Nazis Fill Spain," 10.

4. Manhattan telephone books, white pages, 1941–49. Bullard's first listed address at 80 East 116th Street is in the 1949 book, p. 214 (Microfilm Reel #62, New York Public Library). It is possible that he was there in 1947, for although that year's directory does not give his address, his phone number was the same one that appeared for the rest of his life at 80 East 116th Street. Before 1947, he had himself listed as E. Bullard; after 1947, he appears as Eugene Jacques Bullard.

5. See introduction by John Henrik Clarke in Clarke, ed., *Harlem: A Community in Transition* (New York: Freedomways, 1970), 8; Jervis Anderson, *This Was Harlem: A Cultural Portrait, 1900–1950* (New York: Farrar Straus Giroux, 1982), 307–50.

6. *Manhattan Communities: Population Characteristics* (New York: Bureau of Statistical Services, Research Department, The Community Council of Greater New York, 1950, 1955, 1959). These statistical studies showing the growing Puerto Rican population in Bullard's neighborhood in these years are on microfilm in the Schomburg Center for Research in Black Culture. See the discussion of the

public marketplace, said to "express most vividly the Latin-American character of the locality," in the Federal Writers Project, *New York City Guide* (1939; reprint, New York: Octagon Books, 1970), 266–67. For discussions of Bullard's immediate neighborhood see Hope MacLeod, "Rent Jungle in a Little Spanish Town," *New York Post,* February 6, 1959; and Patricia Cayo Sexton, *Spanish Harlem* (New York: Harper and Row, 1965).

7. *New York Amsterdam News,* April 30, 1960, 1.

8. ABRR, "America the Beautiful."

9. Ibid.; Julian G. Hurstfield, *America and the French Nation, 1939–1945* (Chapel Hill: University of North Carolina Press, 1986), 4–12.

10. ABRR, "America the Beautiful." See the photograph in Carisella and Ryan, *Black Swallow,* 248. See also "Ocean Travelers," *New York Times,* February 3, 1941, 9; "Traveler Reports Italian Defections," *New York Times,* February 4, 1941, 9.

11. ABRR, "America the Beautiful."

12. Federal Writers Project, *New York City Guide,* 154.

13. In a telephone conversation, July 8, 1997, Father Maurice Carroll of St. Vincent de Paul told the author that parts of the mass at the church were spoken in French until the early 1960s. Having come to the church in the 1980s, he had no knowledge of Bullard.

14. *Fighting France Year Book, 1944* (New York: France Forever, 1944), 127; Hurstfield, *America and the French Nation,* 100. Pianist Arthur Rubenstein, an old Paris friend of Kisling's, recalls the artist's years of exile in New York and Hollywood in his memoir *My Many Years* (New York: Knopf, 1980), 488–89.

15. The census figure is cited in "City's French Colony Roars Salute to de Gaulle," *New York Times,* April 27, 1960, 21.

16. *Fighting France Year Book, 1943* (New York: France Forever, 1943), 111; ABRR, "America the Beautiful."

17. Hurstfield, *America and the French Nation,* 50–51; Raoul Aglion, *Roosevelt and De Gaulle* (New York: Free Press, 1988), 17–21.

18. This letter and copies of other Bullard-related documents in the New York files of the Federation of French War Veterans were sent to the author by the late Roger Cestac, president of the FFWV, in October and November 1988. I am much indebted to him for his helpfulness.

19. The Bullard letter to White is located in the NAACP Papers in the Library of Congress, Group II, Series A, Box 647, U.S. Army Air Corps General Folder. Copies were made available to the author by the Library and by Professor Robert J. Jakeman of Auburn University, who found it while researching *Divided Skies.*

20. The Bullard letter to Patterson is located in the Patterson Papers, GC 1941, "Bro-By," Tuskegee University Archives. I thank Professor Jakeman for sending me a copy and also copies of the letters cited in the following two notes. White's attack on Patterson is cited in Robert J. Norrell, *Reaping the Whirlwind: The Civil Rights Movement in Tuskegee* (New York: Knopf, 1985), 47.

21. Patterson Papers, GC 1941, "Bro-By."

22. Ibid.

23. *Fighting France Year Book, 1942* (New York: France Forever, 1942), 44; *Fighting France Year Book, 1943,* 111. On this page, there is a photograph of Bullard with his French comrades taken during the parade. The *Life* photograph of the Free French emissary and the caption in which he is quoted are reproduced on page 6 of the photograph section in Aglion, *Roosevelt and De Gaulle.*

24. "French Add a Little Bit of Paris to Old New York for Bastille Day," *New York Times,* July 15, 1943, 13.

25. Ibid.; "Bernstein Assails Foes of De Gaulle," *New York Times,* July 15, 1943, 13.

26. *Fighting France Year Book, 1945* (New York: France Forever, 1945), 136; Frank S. Adams, "New York Crowds Acclaim de Gaulle in Whirlwind Day," *New York Times,* July 11, 1944, 1, 17.

27. "A. B. Crehore Dies, Insurance Man," *New York Times,* August 22, 1962, 34.

28. Flammer, *The Vivid Air,* 232.

29. Mac R. Johnson, "Lafayette Pilots Say Adieu to Lafayette Hotel," *New York Herald Tribune,* March 13, 1949, 34. A photograph of Bullard at the banquet table appears in Smith, "Incredible Life of Monsieur Bullard," *Ebony* 23 (December 1967): 122.

30. Telephone conversation between author and Daisy Bullard Thomas, November 1, 1991; transcript of conversation between Thomas and Caroline Corner, Cleveland, Ohio, November, 1991.

31. Bullard discusses Hector's lynching in ABRR, "Runaway Child." The author has been unable to uncover documentation of this tragedy. Architectural drawings of the Peabody Apartments project and maps held by the Columbus State University Archives reveal the changes brought about in the Rose Hill neighborhood in 1940.

32. King filed suit in federal court for denial of his constitutional right to vote. On March 6, 1946, the 5th U.S. Circuit Court of Appeals in New Orleans, in a momentous decision (*Chapman v King*), ruled in his favor. On April 1, 1946, the U.S. Supreme Court upheld this decision.

33. ABRR, "America the Beautiful."

34. Herbert Shapiro, *White Violence and Black Response: From Reconstruction to Montgomery* (Amherst: University of Massachusetts Press, 1988), 378–91.

35. Martin B. Duberman, *Paul Robeson* (New York: Knopf, 1988), 19–127.

36. Ibid., 184–262, 280–95.

37. Ibid., 296–362.

38. Ibid., 342.

39. Ibid., 363–65; Shapiro, *White Violence and Black Response,* 378–79.

40. Duberman, *Paul Robeson,* 367.

41. Ibid., 368.

42. Text of report on Peekskill by New York District Attorney George M. Fanelli to Govenor Thomas E. Dewey as printed in the *New York Times,* September 8, 1949, 34.

43. Telephone conversation between the author and Paul Robeson Jr., June 19, 1997.

44. *New York Daily Mirror,* September 5, 1949, 1; *New York Amsterdam News,* September 10, 1949, 1. Pictures of Bullard being clubbed at Peekskill also appear in Susan Robeson, *The Whole World in His Hands: A Pictorial Biography of Paul Robeson* (Secaucus, N.J.: Citadel Press, 1981), 182–83, and on the dust jacket of Griffen Fariello, *Red Scare: Memories of the American Inquisition* (New York: Norton, 1995). Telephone conversation with Paul Robeson Jr., June 19, 1997.

45. "Backers Want Cops Held," *New York Amsterdam News,* September 10, 1949, 28.

46. "One Eye-Witness Account of Mob Violence in Peekskill Rioting," *New York Amsterdam News,* September 10, 1949, 1, 28.

47. Ibid.; Shapiro, *White Violence and Black Response,* 386.

48. "Stoning Victims Tell of Violence," *New York Times,* September 6, 1949, 23.

49. Fanelli Report to Dewey, *New York Times,* September 8, 1949, 43.

50. "Westchester Groups Demand Peekskill Probe," *Daily Worker,* September 12, 1949, 9.

51. Duberman, *Paul Robeson,* 381–487.

52. Ibid., 371.

53. Carisella and Ryan, *Black Swallow,* 251–53.

54. Bullard, writing in 1959, recalling his desire to prevent his cousin Jimmy from retaliating against Eugene's horsewhipping in Richland, observed, "in those

days . . . in the southern states, Negro lynchings were so common that lots of white folks went to see one like they'd go to a picnic and take the children and their lunches. The lynch mob would drag the colored man to a woods and string him up by the neck to a tree. After dark, when he had stopped kicking, his family and friends were allowed to cut his body down and bury it." ABRR, "Wild Man, Wild Horse."

55. Caroline Corner interview with Richard Reid and Jacqueline O'Garro, November 1991; "Biographical Notes on Eugene Jacques Bullard" prepared by Louise Fox Connell after his death, Box 2, Folder 34, Connell Papers.

56. Bricktop, *Bricktop*, 235–49.

57. ABRR, "Princes and Heels." A photograph of Bullard with Armstrong and his wife boarding a plane commencing the tour appears in Smith, "Incredible Life of Monsieur Bullard," *Ebony* 23 (December 1967): 128.

58. Telephone conversation between author and Richard Reid, March 9, 1997.

59. ABRR, "In the French Underground"; "Paul Damski," *New York Times,* June 20, 1965, 73.

60. Photographs of Bullard on this occasion appear in the *Ebony* December 1967 article and in Carisella and Ryan, *Black Swallow,* 253.

61. "French Air Chief Has Negro Pilot," *New York Amsterdam News,* January 7, 1956, 1, 27.

62. "Highest French Honor," *New York Amsterdam News,* October 31, 1959; Carisella and Ryan, *Black Swallow,* 9. Photographs of the occasion are in *Black Swallow,* 254–55. In ABRR, Bullard misconstrued the ceremony as occurring on his sixty-fifth birthday.

63. "Eugene Bullard, Chevalier de la Legion d'Honneur," undated clipping from an unidentifiable French newspaper carrying the story of the ceremony. The clipping is in the Bullard file of the Archives at Wright-Patterson Air Base, Dayton, Ohio.

64. Anthony Shannon, "U.S. Adventurer Wins 15th French Decoration," *New York World Telegram,* October 9, 1959.

65. Alfred Jodry's photographs of this occasion were sent to the author in October 1988 by Roger Cestac, president of the Federation of French War Veterans.

66. Milton Bracker, "French Leader Says Algeria Will Set Future," *New York Times,* April 27, 1960, 1, 20.

67. "City's French Colony Roars Salute to de Gaulle," *New York Times,* April 27, 1960, 21.

68. Carisella and Ryan, *Black Swallow,* 259–60.

69. "That Gallic Charm," *New York Amsterdam News,* April 30, 1960, 1.

70. "French Air Chief Has Negro Pilot," *New York Amsterdam News,* January 7, 1956, 1.

71. Telephone conversation between the author and Richard Reid, March 9, 1997.

72. Transcript of taped interview of Louise Fox Connell by Rosamond Hartshorn, a student at Fordham University, March 31, 1977, in Box 1, Folder 1, Connell Papers; Stephen Longstreet, *The Canvas Falcons: The Planes and Men of World War I* (New York: Barnes and Noble, 1970), 241–42.

73. Connell to Bullard, November 20, 1959; Bullard to Connell, June 20, 1961, Box 2, Folder 35, Connell Papers.

74. "A Child Runs Away from Home," Box 2, Folder 31, Connell Papers.

75. Bullard to Connell, n.d., in Bullard file in archives at Wright-Patterson Air Base, Dayton, Ohio.

76. Parsons to Bullard, April 6, 1959; Parsons to Connell, February 8, 1960, Box 2, Folder 36, Connell Papers.

77. "Adm. Edwin C. Parsons Is Dead; A Lafayette Escadrille Ace, 75," *New York Times,* May 4, 1967.

78. Roosevelt to Connell in the Bullard file of archives at the Wright-Patterson Air Base, Dayton, Ohio; list of newspapers publishing the column is in Box 2, Folder 38, Connell Papers.

79. "Some Highlights from Eugene Bullard's Adventurous Life," April 26, 1960, Box 2, Folder 38, Connell Papers.

80. Dabney Horton to Connell, May 2, 1960, Box 2, Folder 36, Connell Papers.

81. Shannon, "U.S. Adventurer Receives 15th French Decoration."

82. Photographs of Garroway on camera with Bullard and another NBC official with Bullard are in Carisella and Ryan, *Black Swallow,* 256–57. A copy of a different photograph of Garroway and Bullard on camera was sent to the author by Roger Cestac in 1988. Jack Gould, "T.V.: The Quiz Show Scandal," *New York Times,* November 4, 1959; "Garroway Upset," *New York Times,* November 5, 1959, 30.

83. Mason to Connell, May 17 and May 22, 1961, Box 2, Folder 37, Connell Papers; Herbert Molloy Mason Jr., *High Flew the Falcons* (Philadelphia: Lippincott, 1965).

84. Mason, *High Flew the Falcons,* 166.

85. Ibid.; "Foreign Service Honored," *New York Times,* March 14, 1946, 9.

86. Mason, *High Flew the Falcons,* 167; Carisella and Ryan, *Black Swallow,* 258.

87. This information appears on Bullard's certificate of death of the New York Department of Health, a copy of which was sent to the author by Roger Cestac in 1988.

88. These final handwritten manuscript pages are found in Box 2, Folder 31, of the Connell Papers. The last sheet is dated by Bullard "August 15, 1961."

89. "Biographical Notes on Eugene Jacques Bullard" in Connell Papers gives August 18 as the date he entered the hospital for treatment. Copies of letters appealing for blood and a list of donors were sent to the author by Roger Cestac.

90. Carisella and Ryan, *Black Swallow,* 260–61; "Biographical Notes on Eugene Bullard," Connell Papers.

91. Mason, *High Flew the Falcons,* 167.

92. Carisella and Ryan, *Black Swallow,* 261–62.

93. Father Maurice Carroll to author, June 24, 1997, containing information from the death registry of St. Vincent de Paul. The time of death, 10:10 P.M., appears on the certificate of death.

94. Mason, *High Flew the Falcons,* 167.

95. "Gene Bullard, French War Hero, Is Dead," *New York Amsterdam News,* October 21, 1961, 1, 13.

96. Copy of Flushing Cemetery Association Burial Record sent to the author by Roger Cestac. Coincidentally, Louis Armstrong, Bullard's longtime companion in Paris and New York, is buried in the same cemetery not far from the plots maintained by the Federation of French War Veterans.

Selected Bibliography

Acton, Thomas. *Gypsy Politics and Social Change: The Development of Ethnic Ideology and Pressure Politics among English Gypsies from Victorian Reformism to Romany Nationalism.* London: Routledge and Kegan Paul, 1974.

Adams, Barbara Eleanor. *John Henrik Clarke: The Early Years.* Hampton, Va.: United Brothers and Sisters, 1992.

Aglion, Raoul. *Roosevelt and De Gaulle.* New York: Free Press, 1988.

Aldrich, Nelson W. Jr. *Tommy Hitchcock: An American Hero.* Gaithersburg, Md.: Fleet Street, 1984.

Anderson, Jervis. *This Was Harlem: A Cultural Portrait, 1900–1950.* New York: Farrar Straus Giroux, 1982.

Aron, Robert. *Les Grandes heures de la troisième République.* Paris: Librarie Perrin, 1968.

Arroyo, Eduardo. *"Panama" Al Brown, 1902–1951.* Paris: J. C. Lattes, 1982.

Bechet, Sidney. *Treat It Gentle.* London: Twayne, 1960.

Bédarida, François. *Histoire du peuple français: Cent ans d'esprit républicain.* Paris: Nouvelle Librairie de France, 1989.

Benezit, E. "White, Gilbert." *Dictionnaire critique and documentaire des peintres.* Vol. 8, *Sculpteurs.* Paris: Librarie Grund, 1959.

Bennett, Gwendolyn. "Wedding Day, A Story." *Fire!! A Quarterly Devoted to Younger Negro Artists* 1, no. 1 (1926): 25–28.

Benoist-Mechin, Jacques. *Sixty Days that Shook the West: The Fall of France, 1940.* New York: Putnam, 1963.

Bercovici, Konrad. *Gypsies: Their Life, Lore, and Legends.* 1928. Reprint, New York: Greenwich House, 1983.

Berger, Arthur A. *The Comic Stripped American.* New York: Walker, 1973.

Berger, Mark L. "Bradley, W. C." *Dictionary of Georgia Biography.* Vol. 1. Athens: University of Georgia Press, 1983.

Blanchard, Albert, et al. *Des Années-Mémoire 1939.* Paris: Bayard Presse, Notre Temps, 1991.

Bonnet, Jacques, et al. *Histoire d'Orléans de son terroir: tome III de 1870 à nos jours.* Roanne: Horvath, 1982.

Bowen, Ezra. *Knights of the Air.* Alexandria, Va.: Time-Life Books, 1980.

Boxing's Book of Records Up to June 30, 1914. "Dixie Kid." London, 1914.

Bricktop with James Haskins. *Bricktop.* New York: Atheneum, 1983.

Brown, Alexander Crosby. *New Port News: 325 Years.* Newport News: Newport News Golden Anniversary Corp., 1946.

Brown, Walt Jr., ed. *An American for Lafayette: The Diaries of E. C. C. Genet.* Charlottesville: University of Virginia Press, 1981.

Buffetant, Yves. *Verdun: Images de l'enfer.* Paris: Tallandier, 1995.

Bullard, Eugene J. "All Blood Runs Red: My Adventurous Life in Search of Freedom." 1961. In possession of Jacqueline O'Garro and Richard Reid.

Cangioni, Pierre. *La Fableuse Histoire de la boxe.* Paris: Editions O.D.I.L., 1977.

Carco, Francis. "Promenade a Montmartre." *La Revue de Paris* (February 1922).

Carisella, P. J., and James W. Ryan. *The Black Swallow of Death.* Boston: Marlborough House, 1972.

Carswell, Kathleen Jones. "Collections of Twiggs Countians Here and There." 1973. Genealogy Room, Bradley Memorial Library, Columbus, Ga.

Castleton, Randall. "The Problem of Reconstruction in Columbus, Georgia, in Early 1866." 1990. Columbus State University Archives.

Chaplin, Charles. *My Autobiography.* New York: Simon and Schuster, 1964.

Chevalier, Louis. *Montmartre du plasir et du crime.* Paris: Editions Robert Laffont, 1980.

Chilton, John. *Sidney Bechet: The Wizard of Jazz.* New York: Macmillan, 1987.

Christienne, Charles. *L'Aviation française, 1890–1919.* Paris: Atlas, 1988.

Clarke, John Henrik, ed. *Harlem: A Community in Transition.* 1964. Reprint, New York: Freedomways, 1970.

Cockfield, Jamie H. "The Black Icarus: Eugene Bullard in the Dawn of Military Aviation." *Over the Front* 9, no. 4 (winter 1994): 362–67.

———. "All Blood Runs Red." In *Legacy: A Celebration of African-American Culture. American Heritage Magazine Special Edition* (February/March 1995): 7–15.

———. "Eugene Bullard, America's first black military aviator; flew for France during World War I." *Military History* (February 1996).

Collings, Kenneth Brown. "America Will Never Fly." *American Mercury* 38 (July 1936): 290–95.

Connell, Louise Fox. Papers. Schlesinger Library, Radcliffe College, Cambridge, Mass.

Conrad, Phillippe, and Arnaud Laspeyres. *La Grande Guerre*. Paris: Editions Presse, 1989.

Cook, Will Marion. "Clorindy, The Origin of the Cakewalk." *Theater Arts* (September 1947).

Cunard, Nancy. *Negro Anthology*. 1934. Reprint, New York: Negro Universities Press, 1969.

Dalfiume, Richard M. *The Desegregation of the U. S. Armed Forces*. Columbia: University of Missouri Press, 1969.

Damase, Jacques. *Les Folies du music hall à Paris*. Paris: Editions Spectacles, 1960.

Dartnell, Fred. *"Seconds Out!": Chats about Boxers, their Trainers and Patrons*. New York: Brentano's, 1924.

Demaison, Andre. "Jazz William's." *Jazz: L'Actualité Intellectuelle* (March 15, 1929).

Dictionnaire National des Contemporains. "Henri-Robert." Paris: Editions La Jeunesse, 1936.

Dimeglio, John E. *Vaudeville U.S.A.* Bowling Green, Ky.: Bowling Green University Popular Press, 1973.

Driggs, Frank, and Harris Lewine. *Black Beauty, White Heat: A Pictorial History of Classic Jazz, 1920–1950*. New York: William Morrow, 1982.

Duberman, Martin B. *Paul Robeson*. New York: Knopf, 1988.

Durand, Yves. *Le Loiret dans la guerre, 1939–1945*. Roanne: Horvath, 1983.

Eells, George. *The Life that He Led: A Biography of Cole Porter*. New York: Putnam, 1967.

Ellington, Edward Kennedy. *Music Is My Mistress*. New York: Doubleday, 1973.

Fabre, Michel. *From Harlem to Paris: Black American Writers in France, 1840–1980*. Urbana: University of Illinois Press, 1991.

Facon, Patrick. *La Grande Guerre et ses lendemains, 1914–1935*. Paris: Larousse, 1985.

Faligot, Roger, and Rene Kauffer. *Histoire mondiale du renseignement, tome 1: 1870–1939*. Paris: Robert Laffout, 1993.

Fariello, Griffen. *Red Scare: Memories of the American Inquisition*. New York: Norton, 1995.

Federal Writers Project. *New York City Guide*. 1939. Reprint, New York: Octagon, 1970.

Felsted, S. Theodore. *Stars Who Made the Halls*. London: T. Werner Laurie, 1946.

Fitzgerald, F. Scott. *Babylon Revisited and Other Stories*. 1931. Reprint, New York: Scribners, 1960.

Flammer, Philip M. *The Vivid Air: The Lafayette Escadrille*. Athens: University of Georgia Press, 1981.

Flamond, Albert. "Sur un Toit." *La Revue de Paris* (July-August 1924).

Flanner, Janet. *Paris Was Yesterday, 1925–1939*. New York: Viking, 1972.

Foner, Jack D. *Blacks in the Military in American History*. New York: Praeger, 1974.

Foner, Philip S., ed. *The Life and Writings of Frederick Douglass*. 5 vols. New York: International Publishers, 1975.

Ford, Hugh, ed. *The Left Bank Revisited: Selections from the Paris Tribune, 1917–1934*. University Park: Pennsylvania State University Press, 1972.

Fox, Charles. *Fats Waller*. New York: A. S. Barnes, 1960.

Gilbert, Adrian. *World War I in Photographs*. London: Orbis, 1986.

Gilbert, Douglas. *American Vaudeville: Its Life and Times*. New York: Dover, 1963.

Gilliam, Florence E. *France: A Tribute by an American Woman*. New York: Dutton, 1945.

Glubok, Shirley. *The Art of the Comic Strip*. New York: MacMillan, 1979.

Goddard, Chris. *Jazz Away from Home*. New York: Paddington Press, 1979.

Goffin, Robert. *The Story of Louis Armstrong*. New York: Allen, Towne, and Heath, 1947.

Golesworthy, Maurice. *Encyclopedia of Boxing*. London: Hale Press, 1960.

Gravigny, Jean. *Montmartre en 1925*. Paris: Editions Montaigne, 1924.

Green, Benny, ed. *The Last Empires: A Music Hall Companion*. London: Pavillon, 1986.

Green, Michael D. *The Politics of Indian Removal: Creek Government and Society in Crisis*. Lincoln: University of Nebraska Press, 1982.

Grumwald, Liliane, and Claude Cattaert. *Le Vél' D'Hiv, 1903–1959*. Paris: Ramsay "image," 1979.

Hall, James Norman. *High Adventure: A Narrative of Air Fighting in France*. Boston: Houghton-Mifflin, 1918.

Hall, James Norman, and Charles Bernard Nordhoff. *The Lafayette Flying Corps*. 2 vols. Boston: Houghton-Mifflin, 1920.

Hansen, Arlen J. *Expatriate Paris: A Cultural and Literary Guide to Paris of the 1920s*. New York: Arcade, 1990.

Hardel, Alain. *Strass: En remontant les bas résille du music hall*. Paris: Jean-Claude Simoën, 1977.

Harvey, Robert C. *The Art of the Funnies*. Jackson: University Press of Mississippi, 1994.

Hausser, Elizabeth. *Les Evénements vus par la presse, 1900–1919*. Paris: Editions de Minuit, 1968.

Histoire d'un roi: Les mémoires de son Altesse Royale Le Duc de Windsor. Paris: Amiot-Dumont, 1951.

Hughes, Langston. *The Big Sea: An Autobiography*. 1940. Reprint, New York: Hill and Wang, 1963.

Hurstfield, Julian G. *America and the French Nation, 1939–1945*. Chapel Hill: University of North Carolina Press, 1986.

Irwin, Will. "Flashes from the War Zone." *Saturday Evening Post* (July 15, 1916): 12–13.

Jablonski, Edward. *The Knighted Skies: A Pictorial History of World War I in the Air*. New York: Putnam, 1964.

Jakeman, Robert J. *The Divided Skies: Establishing Flight Training at Tuskegee, Alabama*. Tuscaloosa: University of Alabama Press, 1992.

Jakoubek, Robert. *Jack Johnson*. New York: Chelsea House, 1993.

James, Marquis. *A History of the American Foreign Legion*. New York: William Green, 1923.

Jane's All the World's Aircraft. New York: Anco, 1919.

Johnson, Jack. *In the Ring and Out*. London: Proteus, 1977.

Johnson, James Weldon. *Along this Way: The Autobiography of James Weldon Johnson*. 1933. Reprint, New York: Viking, 1968.

Johnson, John. Collection of Printed Ephemera. Bodleian Library, Oxford University.

Johnston, Alexander. *Ten—And Out! The Complete Story of the Prize Ring in America*. New York: Ives Washburn, 1928.

Jones, James Pickett. *Yankee Blitzkreig: Wilson's Raid through Alabama and Georgia*. Athens: University of Georgia Press, 1976.

Kaspi, Andre, and Antoine Mares. *Le Paris des étrangers depuis un siècle*. Paris: Imprimerie nationale, 1989.

Kimball, Robert, and William Bolcom. *Reminiscing with Sissle and Black*. New York: Viking, 1973.

Kluver, Billy, and Julie Martin. *Kiki's Paris: Artists and Lovers, 1900–1930*. New York: Abrams, 1989.

Koo, Madame Wellington, with Isabella Taves. *No Feast Lasts Forever*. New York: Quadrangle, 1975.

Laney, Al. *Paris Herald: Incredible Newspaper*. New York: Appleton-Century, 1947.

Larousse du XX siecle. "Henri-Robert." Paris: Librairie Larousse, 1928.

Laurie, Joe Jr. *Vaudeville From Honky-Tonks to the Palace.* 1953. Reprint, Port Washington, NY: Kennikat Press, 1973.

Lee County, Georgia: A History. Atlanta: W. H. Wolfe, 1983.

Lehmann, John. *Holborn: An Historical Portrait of a London Borough.* London: MacMillan, 1970.

Lewis, David Levering. *When Harlem Was in Vogue.* New York: Knopf, 1980.

———. *W. E. B. DuBois: Biography of a Race, 1868–1919.* New York: Henry Holt, 1993.

Littlefield, Daniel L. Jr. *Africans and Creeks: From the Colonial Period to the Civil War.* Westport, Conn.: Greenwood Press, 1979.

Longstreet, Stephen. *The Canvas Falcons: The Planes and Men of World War I.* New York: Barnes and Noble, 1970.

———. *We All Went to Paris: Americans in the City of Light.* New York: Macmillan, 1977.

Loos, Anita. *Gentlemen Prefer Blondes.* 1925. Reprint, New York: Liveright, 1963.

———. *A Girl Like I.* New York: Viking, 1966.

Loos, Constance, and Norma Talmadge. *The Talmadge Girls: A Memoir.* New York: Viking, 1978.

Lupold, John S. *Columbus, Georgia, 1928–1978.* Columbus: Columbus Sesquicentennial, 1978.

MacGregor, Morris J., and Bernard C. Nalty. *In the United States Armed Forces: Segregation Entrenched, 1917–1940.* Wilmington, DE: Scholarly Resources, 1977.

Macorlan, Pierre. *Montmartre Souvenirs.* Brussels: Chabassol, 1946.

Mahan, Joseph B. *Columbus: Georgia's Fall Line "Trading Town."* Northridge, Calif.: Windsor, 1986.

Mahan, Katherine Hines, and William Clyde Woodall. *A History of Public Education in Muscogee County and the City of Columbus, Georgia, 1828–1976.* Columbus: Muscogee County Board of Education, 1977.

Maiken, Peter. *Night Trains: The Pullman System in the Golden Years of Rail Travel.* Chicago: Lakme Press, 1991.

Mander, Raymond, and Joe Michinson. *British Music Halls.* Rev. ed. London: Gentry Books, 1974.

Marable, Manning. *W. E. B. DuBois: Black Democrat.* Boston: Twayne, 1986.

Marshall, S. L. A., and the editors of *American Heritage. The American Heritage History of World War I.* New York: Simon and Schuster, 1964.

Martin, Tony, ed. *Sport in Britain: A Social History.* Cambridge: Cambridge University Press, 1989.

Mason, Herbert Molloy Jr. *High Flew the Falcons: The French Aces of World War I.* Philadelphia: Lippincott, 1965.

Masson, Phillippe. *Histoire de France illustrée, 1936–1945.* Paris: Larousse, 1985.

Matthews, Becky. "The Development of Secondary Education for Black Students in Columbus, Georgia, 1920–1932." 1990. Columbus State University Archives.

Maury, A.-G. *Histoire des communes de Puy-de-Dôme.* Paris: Editions Horvath, 1987.

McConnell, James R. *Flying for France: With the American Escadrille at Verdun.* New York: Doubleday, 1917.

McKay, Claude. *A Long Way from Home.* 1937. Reprint, New York: Arno Press, 1969.

McSwain, Eleanor D. *Abstracts of Some Documents of Twiggs County, Georgia.* Macon: National Printing Company, 1972.

Melton, Ella Christie. "History of Terrell County." 1940. Terrell County Court House, Dawson, Ga.

Melton, Ella Christie, and Augusta Griggs Raines. *History of Terrell County.* Roswell, Ga.: W. H. Wolfe, 1980.

Midwinter, Eric. *Old Liverpool.* Plymouth, U. K.: David & Charles, 1971.

Mizener, Arthur. *The Far Side of Paradise: A Biography of F. Scott Fitzgerald.* Boston: Houghton-Mifflin, 1949.

Moley, Raymond Jr. *The American Legion Story.* New York: Meredith, 1966.

Moore, John Hammond. "Jim Crow in Georgia." *South Atlantic Quarterly* 66 (fall 1967): 554–65.

Morley, Sheridan. *A Talent to Amuse: A Biography of Noel Coward.* New York: Doubleday, 1969.

Norrell, Robert J. *Reaping the Whirlwind: The Civil Rights Movement in Tuskegee.* New York: Knopf, 1985.

O'Connor, Richard. *The Scandalous Mr. Bennett.* New York: Doubleday, 1965.

Ottley, Roi. *No Green Pastures.* London: John Murray, 1952.

Panassié, Huges. *Louis Armstrong.* New York: Scribners, 1971.

Parsons, Edwin C. *I Flew with the Lafayette Escadrille.* New York: Arno Press, 1972.

Patry, Andre. *Les Années folles à Paris.* Montreal: Humanitas-nouvelle optique, 1990.

Payen, Fernand, ed. *Anthologie des avocats français contemporains*. Paris: Bernard Grasset, 1913.

Penrose, Roland. *Picasso: His Life and Work*. 2d edition. New York: Schocken, 1962.

Petrie, Sir Charles. *King Alfonso XIII and His Age*. London: Chapman and Hall, 1963.

Philouenko, Alexis. *Histoire de la boxe*. Paris: Criterion, 1991.

Pilapil, Vincente R. *Alfonso XIII*. New York: Twayne, 1969.

Pinckney, Darryl. "Promissory Notes." *New York Review of Books* 42, no. 6 (April 6, 1995): 41–46.

Porch, Douglas. *La Légion Etrangère, 1831–1962*. Paris: Fayard, 1994.

Ports of America: History and Development. The American Association of Port Authorities, 1961.

Prasteau, Jean. *La Merveilleuse Aventure du Casino de Paris*. Paris: Denoël, 1975.

Prost, Antoine. Foreword to *Année de Verdun*. Paris: Charles-Lavauzelle, 1996.

Regeau, Christien. *La Drôle de guerre: Images de la France et des français, september, 1939, à mai, 1940*. Paris: Herme, 1990.

Renhard, Marcel. *Histoire de France*. 2 vols. Paris: Librairie Larousse, 1954.

Rennert, Jack. *100 Posters of Paul Colin*. New York: Images Graphiques, 1977.

Rich, Doris. *Queen Bess: Daredevil Aviator*. Washington: Smithsonian Institution Press, 1993.

Roberts, Randy. *Papa Jack: Jack Johnson and the Era of White Hopes*. New York: Free Press, 1983.

Robeson, Susan. *The Whole World in His Hands: A Pictorial Biography of Paul Robeson*. Secaucus, N.J.: Citadel Press, 1981.

Robinson, Edward G., with Leonard Spigelgass. *All My Yesterdays: An Autobiography*. New York: Hawthorn, 1973.

Robinson, Jerry. *The Comics: An Illustrated History of Comic Strip Art*. New York: Putnam, 1974.

Rockwell, Paul Ayres. *American Fighters in the Foreign Legion, 1914–1918*. Boston: Houghton-Mifflin, 1930.

Rogin, Michael. *Blackface, White Noise: Jewish Immigrants in the Hollywood Melting Pot*. Berkeley: University of California Press, 1996.

Rose, Phyllis. *Jazz Cleopatra: Josephine Baker in Her Time*. New York: Doubleday, 1989.

Rubenstein, Arthur. *My Many Years*. New York: Knopf, 1980.

Rumer, Thomas A. *The American Legion: An Official History, 1919–1989*. New York: Evans, 1990.

Sachs, Maurice. *The Decade of Illusions: Paris, 1918–1928*. New York: Knopf, 1933.

Sallaberry, Francis. *Quand Hitler bétonnait la Côte Basque*. Bayonne, France: Harriet, 1988.

Sammons, Jeffrey T. *Beyond the Ring: The Role of Boxing in American Society*. Urbana: University of Illinois Press, 1988.

Sampson, Harry T. *Blacks in Blackface: A Source Book on Early Black Musical Shows*. Metuchen, N.J.: Scarecrow Press, 1980.

———. *The Ghost Walks: A Chronological History of Blacks in Show Business*. Metuchen, N.J.: Scarecrow Press, 1988.

Schmitt, Bernadette E., and Harold C. Vedeler. *The World in Crucible, 1914–1919*. New York: Harper and Row, 1984.

Schwartz, Charles. *Cole Porter: A Biography*. New York: Dial Press, 1977.

Seigel, Jerrold. *Bohemian Paris: Culture, Politics, and the Boundaries of Bourgeois Life, 1830–1930*. New York: Viking, 1986.

Seitz, Don C. *The James Gordon Bennetts*. Indianapolis: Bobbs-Merrill, 1928.

Sexton, Patricia Cayo. *Spanish Harlem*. New York: Harper and Row, 1965.

Shapiro, Herbert. *White Violence and Black Response: From Reconstruction to Montgomery*. Amherst: University of Massachusetts Press, 1988.

Short, Ernest. *Fifty Years of Vaudeville*. Rev. ed. Westport, Conn.: Greenwood Press, 1978.

Smith, Ada Louise "Bricktop." Papers. Archives, Schomberg Center for Research on Black Culture, New York.

Smith, Mary. "The Incredible Life of Monsieur Bullard." *Ebony* 23 (December 1967): 120–28.

Smith, Willie "The Lion," with George Hoefer. *Music on My Mind*. New York: Da Capo, 1975.

Speck, Ernest B. "Henry Crowder: Nancy Cunard's 'Tree.' " *Lost Generation Journal* 6, no. 1 (summer 1979): 6–8.

Stead, Philip John. *Second Bureau*. London: Evans Brothers, n.d.

Stearns, Marshall, and Jean Stearns. *Jazz Dance: The Story of American Vernacular Dance*. New York: Macmillan, 1968.

Stoval, Tyler. *Paris Noir: African Americans in the City of Light*. New York: Houghton Mifflin, 1996.

Swanson, Gloria. *Swanson on Swanson*. New York: Random House, 1980.

Taylor, Frank C., with Gerald Cook. *Alberta Hunter: A Celebration in Blues*. New York: McGraw-Hill, 1987.

Terrell, Helen Eliza. *History of Stewart County*. 2 vols. Columbus, Ga.: Columbus Office and Supply, 1959.

"Toujours l'invasion américaine." *La Boxe & les boxeurs* (December 3, 1913): 5132.

Trevill, Ralph. *Days and Nights in Montmartre and the Latin Quarter*. London: Herbert Jenkins, 1927.

Troyat, Henri. *Kisling, 1891–1953*. Turin, Italy: Jean Kisling, 1982.

Tucker, Sophie. *Some of these Days*. New York: Doubleday, 1945.

Tung, William. *V. K. Wellington Koo and China's Wartime Diplomacy*. New York: St. John's University Press, 1977.

Wallace, Irving, David Wallechinsky, and Amy Wallace. "The Black Swallow." *Parade Magazine* (September 26, 1982): 19.

Wanderers of the World. Washington, D. C.: National Geographic Society Special Publications Division, 1970.

Warnod, Andre. *Le Vieux Montmartre*. Paris: Figuiere, 1913.

Wedeck, H. E. *Dictionary of Gipsy Life and Lore*. London: Peter Owen, 1973.

Williams, Charles H. *Sidelights on Negro Soldiers: A Special Investigation of Conditions Among Negro Soldiers in the World War*. Norwood, Mass.: Ambrose Press, 1923.

Wiser, William. *The Crazy Years: Paris in the Twenties*. New York: Atheneum, 1983.

Woodward, C. Vann. *Tom Watson: Agrarian Rebel*. 2d ed. Savannah: Beehive Press, 1973.

Woon, Basil. *The Paris That's Not in the Guide Books*. New York: Brentano's, 1926.

Yallop, David A. *The Day the Laughter Stopped: The True Story of Fatty Arbuckle*. New York: St. Martin's Press, 1976.

Index